Praise for *By Morning's Light*

"*By Morning's Light* is a touching account of spirit communication. You'll be hooked by the first chapter and inspired to the last. Ginny Brock shares a powerful personal story that will provide hope to many."

—Troy Parkinson, medium and
author of *Bridge to the Afterlife*

By Morning's Light

About the Author

Ginny Brock was born in Johannesburg, South Africa, and traveled extensively throughout her life. She and her American husband, Walter, lived and raised a family in many parts of the world, including the Seychelles Islands, Dubai, Saudi Arabia, Singapore, and the United States, where she became a naturalized citizen in 1980. She now makes her home in Virginia.

By Morning's Light is the result of a lifelong passion for writing. The author has worked in journalism for over thirty years. She is the most influenced by her maternal grandmother, whose clairvoyance she believes she has inherited.

To Write to the Author

If you wish to contact the author or would like more information about this book, please write to the author in care of Llewellyn Worldwide, and we will forward your request. Both the author and publisher appreciate hearing from you and learning of your enjoyment of this book and how it has helped you. Llewellyn Worldwide cannot guarantee that every letter written to the author can be answered, but all will be forwarded. Please write to:

Ginny Brock
℅ Llewellyn Worldwide
2143 Wooddale Drive
Woodbury, MN 55125-2989

Please enclose a self-addressed stamped envelope for reply,
or $1.00 to cover costs. If outside the USA, enclose
an international postal reply coupon.

Many of Llewellyn's authors have websites with additional information and resources. For more information, please visit our website at http://www.llewellyn.com.

The True Story

of a Mother's Reconnection

with Her Son in the Hereafter

GINNY BROCK

Foreword by Patrick Mathews

FIRST EDITION
First Printing, 2012

Book format by Bob Gaul
Cover art: Background vintage photo © iStockphoto.com/Dimitris Kolyris
       Cover photo © Ginny Brock
       Dove © iStockphoto.com/Irina Tischenko
       Aged neutral paper © iStockphoto.com/Kim Sohee
       Masking tape © iStockphoto.com/spxChrome
Cover design by Ellen Lawson
Interior Photos © Sara Bobbitt, Ginny and Walter Bock,
       Mary Katherine and James Klepek
Editing by Ed Day

Llewellyn Publications is a registered trademark of Llewellyn Worldwide Ltd.

Library of Congress Cataloging-in-Publication Data
Brock, Ginny, 1945-
  By morning's light: the true story of a mother's reconnection with her son in the hereafter/Ginny Brock; foreword by Patrick Mathews.—1st ed.
    p. cm.
  ISBN 978-0-7387-3294-7
1. Brock, Ginny, 1945- 2. Spiritualism—Biography. I. Title.
  BF1283.B685A3 2012
  133.901'3—dc23
               2011050915

Llewellyn Publications
A Division of Llewellyn Worldwide Ltd.
2143 Wooddale Drive
Woodbury, MN 55125-2989
www.llewellyn.com

Printed in the United States of America

ontents

For my Child in Heaven
And my Children on Earth

❧

"You will embark," he said, "on a fair sea,
and at times there will be fair weather,
But not always...
You will take it in turns to steer
your boat through fair weather and foul.
Never lose courage."

—*Daphne du Maurier*

Acknowledgments

*S*pecial thanks to Angela Wix, my acquisitions editor, who pulled my unsolicited manuscript out of the pile, and took a chance on me. Thank you not only for your insight but for the excellence of your editing, your professionalism, and your sensitivity.

My profound thanks go to my friend Cindy McEnry who gave me her insight, comfort, and encouragement and made me laugh out loud when I could barely smile. To Katharine Spencer McEnry who inspired me, and to Gail Meltzer who listened and spent hours reading and editing the contents of this book and filled me with confidence.

Special thanks to Drew's friend Sara Bobbitt who taught me to speak computer-eze, helped me with photographs, many of which she took, and with the final layout and submission. To Brittany Bennefield, Mark DeTournillon, Ashley Werner, and Sara, close friends of Drew's, for sharing their dreams and memories with me. To Tory Lakey who did the same, and to Clay Cowgill, Drew's childhood friend who *gets it*.

My love and my appreciation to Karen Brock Kelley, Michael and Mary Katherine Brock, Becca Kelley, Toni Le Grand, and Kellie Anne Upton who shared their dreams, their humor and their memories, and to Randy Kelley who gave us his support when we needed it.

Grateful thanks go to my readers who were kind enough to read the book with its success in mind. Their constructive criticism, thoughtful insights, advice, and recommendations were greatly appreciated, and many of them were used in the book. They are Michael Brock, Leigh Fox, Joy Goryn, Courtney Kelley, Cindy McEnry, Katharine McEnry, Gail Meltzer, and Cathy Winstead.

To Michael Fragnito, publishing veteran and friend who read an early draft, gave me valuable advice, and encouraged me to keep going; my grateful thanks.

To Patrick Mathews who understands the spirit world better than most. Author, intuitive, and talented medium, he spoke to Drew with me one afternoon: Thank you for your insightful and thoughtful foreword to this book.

To the Earth Angels: Pat Kiefer, Debbie Spencer, Toni Seidelman, Linda Wickert, and Regina Jensen who have made this journey, and walk beside me on mine. There were many angels on this trail, too many to name here, but they know who they are, and so do I.

And to Drew, who was with me every step of the way through the darkness of the deepest night and into the dawn, urging me to write it all down and share it in *By Morning's Light*. My eternal love and thanks.

Foreword

–Patrick Mathews–

*A*s a medium, I feel blessed in being able to help people by connecting them with their loved ones in spirit. My main goal in doing so is to not only prove to them that there is life after life for their loved ones who have passed, but for them to also understand that those in spirit will *always* continue to be a part of their lives.

Once a person breaks down the self-barrier they create after the passing of a loved one, another connection can be made and with that, the continuation of the relationship with a loved one in spirit will transpire.

There are many ways spirits will make their presence known, each depending on the situation of their loved ones here as well as their own abilities as spirits.

I am sure that any person in spirit would like nothing better than to be able to just appear to loved ones here and say, "Hi, here I am! I am still very much alive and well and I will always be with you." But that is just not how this classroom we call life was designed.

This is why spirits are able to only give certain specific signs to their loved ones here, as they do not want to interfere with the spiritual growth their loved ones are destined to have. And these signs and connections can come in many forms, each specific to that individual's wants and needs.

But it is always up to any individual if and when these signs and connections are noticed, all depending on how receptive someone is to receiving them. But no matter if these signs are noticed, loved ones in spirit will always continue to participate with and most of all continue to love those who are their family and friends here on earth.

Living this life, it is expected that we will eventually go through the experience of having our grandparents pass into spirit and then, somewhere down the road, our parents. These are "expected" losses that we mentally prepare for in the back of our minds knowing that one day we will have to face them. It is a part of life.

The one passing, however, that a parent is never prepared for or expecting to face is the loss of a child. Without doubt, this is one of the most challenging event any human being could ever have to go through in this life.

But even though a child's passing may not be a part of what people consider the natural circle of life that we have on this earth, it is in fact a part of a bigger circle.

Being a world traveler, the author of this book, Ginny Brock, has seen and experienced much in her life. Living abroad and learning from the many cultures she has visited, she has gained vast knowledge and insight that has cultivated her insightfulness on the world. But even with all of her experiences, nothing could have prepared her for the one journey she was not expecting ever to take: living through her son Drew's passing away.

Ginny shares with the reader her experience of the nightmare of any parent with the unexpected passing of her beloved son Drew and her remarkable journey of self-discovery in the continuing connection she has with him.

From Drew's extraordinary one-on-one conversations with his mother from beyond, Ginny is taken down the path of having to discern if the communications that she is experiencing from her son are real or just an illusion caused by her grief-stricken mind. And that path led to her learning to understand the messages she received.

Ginny's experiences of her communications with Drew are quite unique and inspiring as the reader will learn through her experiences, as she did, that the love bond we share never dies.

The last time I saw Drew alive, we said goodbye at the railway station on a midsummer afternoon in Springfield, Virginia. The next time I saw him, he was in spirit on a snowy night in Denver.

One

The Journey Begins

*U*p until quite recently, I lived a fairly normal life with a fairly normal husband named Walter. He was an explorer and liked to expand his and our horizons by moving us from one end of the globe to the other, which, I suppose, would make us not exactly "normal," but it became normal for us. Following his job we lived the lives of the expatriated American. Something like the perennial tourist if you will. For over twenty years we were guests in someone else's country. It's a wonderful sort of anonymity. You wander through your own and other people's lives, stepping in and out at will, with no pressure to stay any longer than you wish or involve yourself any deeper than is comfortable.

It's like a long cruise, sailing along the banks of a foreign country making ports of call as you get the urge.

As you might imagine, there was as much mental expansion involved as there was physical. And this was substantial when you consider the new and exotic restaurants, food plazas in the Far East, smoky roadside grilling stands, and beachside brick ovens churning out freshly baked pita in the Middle East.

This wanderlust of Walt's started in his twenties, not long after he finished school, when he left home to join the Navy and followed that four-year stint with another eight years with NASA's space program. He traveled all over the world tracking satellites and reading the signals and transmissions from the Apollo launches in the late 1960s, living in small modules with wall-to-wall radio equipment and eating out of mess halls. He went to the Seychelles Islands, deep in the Indian Ocean, and then his globetrotting took him to South Africa where his mental expansion took a giant leap when he married a girl from Johannesburg—me—much to the consternation of a few (make that most of them) Deep South relatives. One relative asked her brother to "please send us a picture..." My relatives were not unaffected by one of theirs moving to the wild, wild west, and one movie buff aunt asked, "Aren't there a lot of gangsters in Chicago, dear?" She pronounced the name with a hard "Ch..." as in "Chew." "A rather dangerous country, I think. Will they give you a gun?"

Walt and I started a family very quickly— not by design— on a rainy Sunday night in Johannesburg in the late spring of the Southern Hemisphere. It was long past five, and all the pharmacies in town were closed. Not even the corner convenience store offered anything resembling any method of birth control.

But we made love as the thunder crashed and lightning split the skies over the high veldt. The plains shook as the storm barreled through.

There's something about thunderstorms … Perhaps it's that explosion of compressed energy breaking loudly and magnificently, lighting up the world, shaking the ground, and sending ripples of itself throughout the planet and all its life forces—including us. It fills us with pent-up energy, excitement, and the very essence of life.

When I woke up the next morning, I reached out for Walt and snuggled in under his arm and said, "It's a baby girl."

"Ummm…" he mumbled, kissing the top of my head.

"I've figured it out," I said. "She'll be born in November."

"Hmmm. Okay," Walt said without opening his eyes, and we both rolled over and went back to sleep.

⤳

A baby girl named Karen was born nine months later. Somehow I knew she would be a girl, but I must have written it off as a lucky guess—after all, I had a fifty-fifty chance of being right.

She was born just thirty miles from the city of Johannesburg, the place where I was born. I vividly remembered my old home and one thing in particular that happened when I was four years old. I was standing beside my bed, dressing a doll at eleven o'clock one morning. I was completely immersed in the job at hand when, out of the blue—where else—this thought popped into my toddler head, *What am I doing here?* The question was as clear as a crystal chime, and the energy around that thought was lucid and adult. *What am I doing here? Who am I?*

How did this, the oldest question in the universe, pop into the mind of a four-year-old? It frightened me.

I'd thought about that over my life and wondered what triggered that question. Was it my spirit suddenly realizing that it had made the decision to come to this earth place to learn how to be a person? Whatever it was, the sudden realization scared us both: my spirit and me. The spark of cognitive intuition was born that morning.

❧

Michael, our first son, was born in Fayetteville, Arkansas. We planned this one perfectly. He was due to be born on my birthday—right before Walt was slated to graduate from the University of Arkansas. Well, Michael was close, but arrived four days before my birthday, which suited me fine. It was October, and the Ozark Mountains were ablaze in color. Football excitement filled the air, and in the early fall mornings, the off-key tune-up of marching band practice bounced off the surrounding hills, the flats and sharps wound their way through campus streets and mingled with the wails of my newborn son.

After that, we circled the globe at least three times to get us to wherever Walt's job took us. We picked up a little of the Zulu language in South Africa and a smattering of Arabic in Dubai—that hot city on the Arabian Gulf where Drew, the youngest of our three children, entered into this world. Walt had left NASA and was working in the oil industry on the Arabian Peninsula. It was an exotic place peopled with fishermen and pearl divers, and dhow captains who were the entrepreneurs who ferried Persian rugs from Iran and smuggled gold and silver from India to the lucrative and free markets of Dubai.

July 21, 1982, was an auspicious day to be born if you lived in an Islamic country, and that year, the moveable feast of Eid Al Fitr that officially ended the fasting month of Ramadan, was Drew's birthday. Two gateways had opened: one was for a new life to enter the world and the other for a new cycle in the Muslim world to begin. There was also a brand new moon that night.

The Holy Month of Ramadan occurs in the ninth month of the Islamic calendar. It is believed by Muslims that during this month in AD 610 the Koran was given to Mohammed as a book of guidance for Muslims. The Holy Month begins at the first sighting of the new moon on that month and ends about twenty-nine or thirty days later, depending on the lunar cycle. During that time, Muslims are required to fast from sunup to sundown when the roar of a cannon blast rumbles through the city, signaling that the fast for the day is over.

Drew was born at dawn, his birth heralded by not one but three joyous canon blasts. The cannon did not actually signal Drew's birth. We would have liked that, but its real purpose was to let the people of Islam know that Ramadan was over and the feasting of Eid Al Fitr could begin. Later that morning, completely undeterred by the real meaning of the canon's roar, Walt, the proud father, picked up his infant son, cradled him in his arms and said, "It's like Christmas day—I think he may be the Second Coming." I just smiled at Walt's comment that might be construed as egregious blasphemy in some parts of the East and the West.

The morning Call to Prayer echoed from the minarets atop mosques throughout the town and was carried out to sea on hot desert winds. *Allah O Akbar.* God is great. And as I looked at my youngest son, my soul echoed the chant. I held him closer and then suddenly and inexplicably felt the strongest urge to protect him—to shield him. An air of foreboding, like a passing cloud, momentarily dimmed the bright sunshine that flooded the morning of his birth. And then it was gone. What had it meant? Years later I would know.

I looked at my sleeping baby, smiled, and swore to him that I would protect him from all harm.

Two

The Winds Changed—
We Adjusted Our Sails

*A*fter eight years of living abroad, we returned home when Walt was sent back for a stint in his company's engineering headquarters in Houston, Texas. Even though we always knew that one day we'd return to Houston or New Orleans, where the company housed its two U. S. administrative corporate offices, repatriation was a shock. Every difference was magnified. You think you know what it will be like coming home to the USA. After all, we came back every summer to buy clothes, visit grandparents, and go to family reunions and Sunday picnics. We know what it's like here, and the smell of genuine KFC and drip coffee never failed to lure us back. Then, in the middle of a drumstick, someone will tell you that Uncle

John has lost all his money down the shaft of an emerald mine that had no emeralds and Aunt Dee's in a home for the "confused." Visiting hours are...

Now you know you're home. Real people, real life, real problems. And this is where you belong.

Not only that, when we finally came back to stay (this was no summertime pit stop), we had to re-learn a whole new culture. The American culture we thought we knew had changed dramatically.

The children, young men and women now, except for baby Drew (who came ten years behind everyone else), learned to be Americans. They picked up the slang with ease, they figured out the mall and the movies and fast-food scenes in record time, leaving their parents in the dust.

The ninth grade in a new school of over two thousand students filled Karen with trepidation and a brand-new set of fears—real and imagined. Mild panic colored the late summer holiday for her in different shades of fright, insecurity, and cautious excitement.

"What am I supposed to wear?" she wailed the night before our first school shopping trip. "I don't know anybody—I hate this place!"

So we postponed the big shop until she had time to figure out the dress code of Taylor High, and that brought its own brand of confusion for me. Through my daughter, I began to get an eyeful of who was wearing what and what was cool and what was not. Mascara at school?

"Are you kidding me!" I exploded, looking into my daughter's deep blue eyes, so like her father's, as they flashed their disdain for my objections.

"They *all* wear mascara! What's wrong with *that?* Their moms don't care—why should you?" Her hands were on her hips, her cheeks were flushed, and her dark blond hair, rolled up on impossibly fat rollers, bobbled precariously as she pushed her case. She was so young, so vulnerably lovely at fourteen, and I prayed that this mascara blowup would be the biggest problem she would ever have.

༄

In school and in the neighborhood, my children learned about prejudice and skin color and Materialism. Yes, that's a capital M. It wasn't long before we began to hear about this one's big new car, and somebody else's bigger house, and that girl's designer clothes, and how cool all of it was. Not to mention the Sex Line number that one of the neighborhood mothers said was doing the rounds at the local junior high school. This was something we never had to worry about in countries that are less free than ours. We had been spoiled in many ways.

Holy God—Where am I! I wondered. My mind lurched back to that four-year-old standing beside the bed dressing her doll and asking much the same question. Only this time, I understood the question, yet I still didn't have an answer. In fact, it seemed that the older I got, the less I knew.

It wasn't long before I began asking a bunch of transcendental questions of myself, such as: Why are we here? In fact, What are we doing? And where do we think we're going? For that matter—*Who Are We?* We used to know these people ... us and them. Who changed? What changed?

Inevitably, even though we eventually adjusted, the winds changed direction again and we had to reset our sails. Walt was reassigned to the Middle East, so we sold the house, shipped the car, and packed up our family—except for Karen, who was going to boarding school in New Hampshire because Dubai American School had no high school. We headed back to the Middle East for the next five years. After that, the wind changed again, and we sailed east to Singapore for two more years.

Dubai represented a normal life for us. We were thrilled to be back among old friends. Michael, now in seventh grade, was back at his old school with teachers he knew and the friends he'd grown up with before he had to leave them behind. Walt liked the more laid back atmosphere of an overseas office, and I picked up where I'd left off. The old fruit markets were still the same, the ancient Arab Souks, or shopping centers, were as noisy and scattered and colorful as they'd ever been.

It was like coming home.

When Drew was about four, we continued our explorations and took a long-awaited European vacation, picking up some ragged French and Spanish on a very long drive across France, the Pyrenees, and down into Spain. All three of our children (Karen came back to Dubai when school adjourned for fall, winter, and spring breaks, as well as in the summer) and a car full of maps, baguettes, cheese, and a very nice wine from the Rhone Valley were packed into a small station wagon, and we hurtled across the continent at breakneck speed. The autobahns and autopistes and all those European superhighways are built for speed, and we found out very early on in the trip that if you fail to comply, you risk being run over by vacationing caravaners and foul language.

We lived a satisfyingly hectic life. Gallivanting around the world with our young son with our older children, Karen and Michael, crossing the globe to and from school in the United States to join our excursions was a whirlwind. The deluge of sights, sounds, and adventures blurred together. I began to feel an expansion of consciousness taking shape inside me. It was incipient at first, trickling into my consciousness in the form of a much broader understanding of the strangers that peopled our lives along with their foods and customs so new to us. The smells from the market places of pomegranates, the pungent durien fruit, dates, and dried fish permeated our senses and our lives, as did the desert winds carrying the finest dust we'd ever seen. The deep and sometimes harsh grate of Arabic mingled with the singsong lilt of a variety of Asian tongues and a smattering of Mandarin filled the humid air around us, smearing all of our minds like an indelible ink, creasing our brains forever with a flurry of memories.

We absorbed it all. The colors of race fell away and the barriers of language didn't matter—in the end, hand gestures and facial acrobatics work in any language. We adjusted. And not with reluctance but with excitement and expectation of whatever new experience was hanging around the next corner.

The broadening of our horizons must have had a positive effect on us—at least that was what we told our worried parents and pursed-lipped grandparents. They weren't impressed, but we pushed on with such things as—"Listen, Papa! Karen can say good morning in French!"

A lot of the details were excluded from those conversations, as in dodging hijacked airplanes in the Middle East in the late-1970s and the cross-country vacations we took in anybody's country. It didn't matter to us. We were young and living our lives to the fullest, enjoying every new country, every path we took, every new face and language we encountered. We didn't let fear dictate to us; we knew the possible dangers, and we also knew how to be safe. Well, that's all well and good, you might say—fine to mess around with your lives, but what about the children? Here's what we felt about the children. We had lived in this part of the world long enough to know that in the Middle East and in most of the Far East, they treasure children beyond everything else. They don't willingly hurt children. We lived in countries that in spite of bad press and political struggles bore us no personal ill-will. Crime in these places is practically unheard of. We felt far safer in these countries with our children than anywhere else on earth. But try explaining that to grandparents.

There was the drive through Malaysia, a jewel of a country nestled under its canopy of lush green palm trees and rubber plantations, secure in its coral bedrock, its shores lapped by the pale green swish of the South China Sea. We were living in Singapore at the time and a trip to the islands off the Malaysian coast had been on our minds for some time, so when the opportunity arose, we grabbed it. We drove to the end of Singapore Island and crossed the Straits into Malaysia with the whole family crammed into the car. Swimsuits and towels, masks and fins, buckets and spades were crammed into the trunk of the car. We were headed for one of the outlying islands, a speck in the ocean that could only be reached by a two-hour ferry ride through choppy seas.

⸺❦⸺

The island was named Babi Bazar, and when translated this becomes "Pig Island," which elicited an intense reaction from our teenagers.

"PIG Island! You're taking us to PIG Island?" Karen's eyes were big and round. Home from college, teetering on the edge of adulthood, this family excursion wasn't something she would have chosen.

"Yes, it's a lovely little…" I started to say.

"I can't believe we're going to PIG Island!" Karen muttered. "*Oink oink…*"

"Shut up, Drew!" Michael didn't turn around but kept clicking the remote as Mario skipped mushrooms and exploded in cyberspace. "Darn! I've heard there are giant lizards roaming around on Pig Island. You know they're carnivorous and they especially like to eat *seven-year-old boys.*"

"*Mom*, Michael said…" Drew wailed.

"I want to know what we're supposed to eat on this island," Karen wailed.

"Pig," Michael said darkly.

"Food," I replied. "Regular food. Just think… fresh fish, coconut milk, cassava root stew…"

"What is *that?*" This kid, who since childhood had laboriously picked mushroom pieces out of her spaghetti sauce and placed onion bits in neat little piles around her plate all her life, was horrified.

"Okay fine. I thought you guys were more adventurous!" I said. "Someone find the peanut butter and crackers."

Pretty soon, we had filled two coolers with emergency supplies in case the food on Babi Bazar was just too weird. Cheerios, canned milk, peanut butter and honey, and crackers. Chocolate milk, Kool-Aid, and Crystal Lite. We could go.

❧

Ahhhh yes. The trip through Malaysia.

An hour out of Singapore, we found ourselves crossing the Straits into Malaysia, motoring cheerily in the wrong lane of traffic, from which we never found our way out of and wound up in the Golden Triangle with no visas, and NO permission to be there. The Golden Triangle is that part of the Far East where Burma, Thailand, and Cambodia converge to form an unholy trinity of free and easy drug trafficking. Malaysia shares its borders with all of them and wages a constant battle to protect itself against this insidious violation. To be found doing anything suspicious in this part of the world is not a good idea, which put a bit of a damper on our happy wanderer songs and excitement.

Try as we might, we could not find our way back to the border where we could re-enter as most people do—legally. We fought our way through all the back streets and side streets trying to get back to the border crossing. We skidded and shot through alleyways, through the shambles of makeshift markets, swerved in front of leaping rickshaws and narrowly missed getting slaughtered by a swarm of yellow-and-black taxicabs blasting their way through traffic, taking the curves on two wheels.

Walt was sweating. I was white-knuckled and petrified for my children's lives. Finally, he took a hard turn and swerved off the road, bumping the car over hard clay as he brought it to an abrupt stop beside a wooden shack. A flurry of backyard hens flapped out of the way of the tires, rising three feet in the air cackling and squawking.

"*Whoa! Chickens!*" Drew cried with glee, rolling down the back window.

"Put the window up!" I yelled. The idea of a chicken on my lap was not one I wanted to think about.

Walt ran the back of his hand across his forehead. "God, it's hot. Crap! I think I ran over someone's flowerpot."

"Oh crap," yelled Drew.

"*Andrew!*" I glared over the back seat.

"Dork," said Karen placidly. I heard in her voice the resignation and acceptance that this vacation was turning out exactly as she thought it would.

Dripping with sweat, Walt's face looked like something Salvador Dali had dreamed up. Any minute now it was going to melt down into a distorted caricature like warm Brie. He gripped the steering wheel. "It's no good. We can't get back—find the immigration place—and get out of here in time to catch the ferry. We have to go on. There isn't another boat for a week. Here," he motioned a brown-skinned scrawny kid with bright eyes and spiky black hair over to the car and handed him a few Singapore dollars. "Give this to your Mama. Tell her I'm sorry about the pot."

"Let's go," he said. "We've wasted over an hour." It was done. Walt backed up, swung the car around, pulled out into the traffic and headed for the northern shore of the Malay Peninsula.

"*Pig Island, here we come!*" Someone sang from the back seat.

⁂

So we entered Malaysia as illegal aliens.

This was worrying to say the least, but somehow we had a cheerfully exotic island vacation and ten days later we crawled back through the immigration line looking as guilty as the felons we were. We were herded into a small room with walls dusted with whitewash. We had no prepared statement for the border police or the customs people, but in a flash of brilliance Walt made one of his leader-of-the-pack decisions. Seven-year-old Drew would do the talking. He motioned to our youngest son, who was busy hopscotching the terrazzo tiled floor. "Drew!" No response. "DREW!"

"*What?*" He looked up from the cracks in the floor and leapt long-jump style across the room. Pink-cheeked and sweaty, his sun-bleached hair flopping over his eyes, he brushed the back of his hand across his nose.

"Over here," Walt said.

A dark-faced man of ample dimension, an immigration official with a chest full of decorations, strode purposefully toward us. From the look on his face, we had no doubt that all he wanted to do was to throw all five of us blond and asinine Americans into his jail.

"So! Where have you come from?" He roared.

I jumped.

Holding the customs official's gaze, Walt gave a brief explanation of our unintentional foray into the wrong lane of traffic at the port of entry, then put his hand on Drew's shoulder and spoke quietly. "Drew, I want you to tell this man where we've been this week."

We held our collective breath and waited. Then Drew came through as we thought he would, beginning with a long explanation of the ferry ride to the island where "some kid on the bench near me threw up..." Inviting Drew to explain what had happened was a safe bet. Drew was a people-person. He loved to engage people in conversation, even as a small child. Strangers were no different than anyone else in his mind. Once on a trip back to the United States, as we waited patiently in our seats on the plane to let a long line of passengers disembark ahead of us, Drew noticed a young man standing beside him with a knapsack slung over his shoulder. He must have seemed like a good person to talk to, so when the man looked his way, Drew pounced. "What's your dog's name?" He asked with a serious look on his face. There was no guile involved, just a desire to visit.

It was hot here in Asia, and I could feel rivulets of perspiration running down the sides of my face. After nearly half an hour and an ear-bending conversation with our son that involved the number of fish he had caught, followed by "Look at these shells I found!" as he dug into his shorts pockets, and "Have you ever seen a dragon? I think I saw one on the beach..." the man sighed, ran his braided sleeve cuff across his forehead, and let us go. But not before delivering a few final words that boomed across the room like canon blasts with a lot of eyebrow popping and wagging fingers—and included something to the effect that he thought we must be too stupid to be criminals of any kind, let alone drug dealers.

"But this one," he beamed stabbing a finger in Drew's direction, "I like! A dragon! Heh, heh!"

It wasn't exactly a dragon in the medieval sense, but it was a very large monitor lizard. And actually, we only saw its three-foot-long tail disappearing into the thick green vines and creepers that grew down onto the beach.

ஊௌ

It was a different way of life, but when we weren't white-knuckling it across Europe and stirring up border patrols, we were normal people. The day-to-day life during our two years in Singapore presented different challenges for us. We had left a small desert town in Dubai, where we had now lived a total of thirteen years, with a small friendly community and a small and very good school for our kids—not to mention a pretty white house with a red-tiled roof two blocks from the ocean and a group of old friends. To say I was dragged away from the desert Sheikdom kicking and screaming would have been an exaggeration—but only a small one. My first impression of Singapore was of a big financial center in the Far East crammed onto a tiny island off the mainland coast of Malaysia. High-rises pierced the forever smoggy skies, trapping hot and humid air in a basin of car exhaust, teeming humanity, and the smell of dried fish. I longed for the breezes of the Arabian Gulf in winter. There was no winter in our new home. The damp heat stayed the same all year round, interspersed with 3:00 p.m. downpours every day that did little more than dampen it even more. The flora loved it, but I thought we might grow mold.

We missed Karen and Michael badly. Michael was a senior in high school in New Hampshire, and Karen was off to college. The fourteen-hour time difference impeded communication and made this a difficult adjustment.

Then something strange happened. It was Thanksgiving morning. It didn't feel like Thanksgiving because for one thing, it was too darn hot. For another, our family was separated and Walt was at work just like any other day because no other country recognizes the Thanksgiving holiday. But things weren't all bad. The company Walt worked for was holding a family dinner that evening which meant seven-year-old Drew could go too, and afterward, we had promised him we would go shopping for a Christmas tree. But he was busy at his school this morning and I had to do some grocery shopping for the weekend.

The store was just a few blocks from where I lived in a brown brick sprawling villa on the edge of the city, and when I stepped out of the car into the tiny parking lot, I had the strangest feeling of dislocation. I felt as though I'd left half of me behind. It seemed as though I was completely separated from an essential part of me and I was only partially there even though I was standing outside the store with two arms, two legs, and the rest of me—but *something just wasn't there*. I couldn't even remember what time it was. And I couldn't remember what I'd come here to buy. I wandered into the cool of the air-conditioned market and stood in the middle of the aisle looking around with no idea of which way to go. I felt quite calm. Not freaking out or anything—just standing there. Then someone tapped me on the shoulder.

"Long time no see!" My Australian neighbor from two houses down was beaming over her cart of groceries. "When you're done," she said eyeing my empty cart, "come over and have a cup of coffee."

"Sure," I beamed back. She waved and headed for the checkout. I watched her go for a minute, and then I parked the empty cart, walked out to my car, and followed her home.

The next half hour was spent by a totally unfocused me listening to her chatter as she rattled cups, only half hearing her conversation and not registering any of it. Finally I said, "Mary, I have to get home."

"Why? You just got here! We haven't even had coffee—how about lemonade? I should have thought! It's too bloody hot for coffee." She smacked her hands together

"No, really—I'm feeling a bit peculiar. Don't ask me how ... I have to go!"

"Okay," she said hesitantly. "You sure you're all right?"

"Yes, fine!" I beamed and then the slash across my face, the too broad grin, turned to a frown. "I think I am. Bye!" I grabbed my purse off the kitchen table and left in a hurry.

By the time I got home, my arm was hurting. It ached like the devil when I tried to raise it. Dropping it to my side, it just hung there like a dead fish. I looked around the living room with its bamboo furniture and pale pink and green upholstery thinking how pretty it was ... There was a water-lily pond just outside the sliding glass doors and stands of green and yellow bamboo in the garden beyond the pond. And frangipane trees ... I seemed to be staring at all of this through someone else's eyes. It was almost as though I was looking through a window. I just wasn't all there. Normally I might laugh at that, but no laughter came. I was flat. And my arm was aching and as I walked across the kitchen I realized I was having difficulty breathing. That tweaked a mild response. *Am I having a heart attack?* I wondered with absolutely zero emotion. Then, Drew! Someone had to get Drew from school. I looked at the clock but it was only 11:00 in the morning. My breathing was thickening and I sat down at the telephone table, resting my throbbing arm on the chair arm and called Walt.

❧

"I feel really weird," I told him as soon as he walked in.

"Yeah? How weird?" he asked, standing there frowning with his hands on his hips.

I told him. "And I have this weird feeling of disassociation. Like I'm not all here."

His face cracked a smile and he was about to say something when he was saved by the jangling of the phone.

"What?" he said into the receiver. "Who?" There was a long silence. "When did that happen? Did you say?" He began scribbling numbers on a pad beside the phone. "Who's with them? Can I speak to them—either of them?"

He turned to me and said, "That was the hospital in Roanoke."

I jerked myself off the chair.

He put up a hand as if to slow me down. "Everything's okay—Karen and Michael have been in a car accident but they're okay," he repeated. He took a few deep breaths, visibly shaken as he continued. "Michael has a broken collar bone and Karen as some pretty bad bruising on her chest."

Strangely, my arm had stopped throbbing and I was breathing normally. My thinking had also cleared up. What was happening? Years later I would find out. But for right now I couldn't understand it. Had that part of me that had been missing all morning—like a missing limb or something—known that something had happened to two other parts of me? And had it separated from me to be with them? I'd heard of things like that. It was too weird.

ॐ

At the end of our time in Singapore, we were on our way home to America. Houston was the place old oilers are sent to die, I had heard over and over. Just like old elephants in Africa. I thought about the old bulls or mares making the long, lonely trek to some ancient graveyard that calls to them from some long buried cell memory. A place where they could lie down at last, to rest, to die in peace among the mounds of bleached bones that had been there for centuries. Houston was where corporate headquarters lived—downtown, high above the city, its hurricane strength windows peering over the city toward the Gulf of Mexico peppered with its myriad of oil wells, drilling rigs, and barges. I wondered if its blistering summer heat might bleach our bones one day.

It was 1990. Drew was going into the second grade, Karen was still in college, and Michael was entering his freshman year at Clemson University when we returned to the United States, permanently this time, as it turned out.

For the next nine years, we lived in Texas in that big rambling, love-to-hate city of Houston. It reminded me of an overgrown cowboy town: full of jealously, native Texans in big hats, bigger pickups, big money, bigger crooks, and red-hot traffic jams on a scramble of spaghetti overpasses, underpasses, and beltways that raced a hundred miles in all directions around and across the city.

We drove into town on a midsummer's day. In the distance, Houston's skyscrapers shimmered in the heat, shapeshifting in hot waves of humidity and burning sun. The acrid smell of hot asphalt wafted through the car's air conditioner, and black pools of mirages bloomed ahead of us, vanishing under our wheels as we raced through the western suburbs of the city to our new found home in Katy, Texas—and into the next phase of our lives.

❧

One afternoon in mid-August, following a school supplies shopping trip through crowded malls with Drew in the blanketing heat, I walked into the air-conditioned cool of my suburban home wondering anew why anyone with a brain would live here in the summer. Kicking my shoes off, relishing the feel of cold tile under my bare feet, I dropped the shopping bags and breathed deeply.

Drew, meanwhile, had left the scene. I could hear him yelling to his friend across the street as he pedaled off as fast as he could go, fishing pole held out in one hand, front wheel swerving dangerously, headed for the muddy bayou two streets down the road. It was the last weekend of summer, and at eight years old there were too many things to do to sit around sharpening new pencils and packing the brand-new school bag for school on Monday.

I was shopped-out and traffic weary and didn't feel like sharpening pencils either. So I filled a glass of iced water, plopped myself down in a chair in my living room, and leaned back, letting my eyes rest on a picture on the wall. It was a photograph taken the previous year, blown up and framed. It is a picture of two boys standing in silhouette beside the ocean. The older boy is seventeen, the younger is seven. Michael is bending down, hands on his knees, looking into the cupped hands of his little brother. In the picture you can see the waves frothing and swirling around their bare feet. The sea is painted in gold from the setting sun on Kuta Beach in Bali. Further out, the ocean is colored in shades of deep grays and black. And just above the horizon, mounds of raspberry clouds deepening to purple catch the sunlight, shooting it into the dark folds of an incoming storm.

It's a living picture. It's a picture of youth in all its beauty; two boys examining a tiny piece of the living universe thrown up on the gurgling shore. The eternal push and pull of powerful natural forces filled with energy, the movement of the sea and sky is alive, and there is sparkle in the light that smears and backlights a single moment in time.

What were my sons looking at I wonder? None of us can remember, but we're sure it was a shell or a starfish or a tiny crab. We know this because when the content of Drew's aromatic luggage was emptied onto the living room floor after we got home, it was filled with sand and seaweed and shells and starfish and tiny white crabs.

It's a picture of life. A snapshot of sunburned boys and their treasures. An image of preserved happiness.

I look at that picture now, and I try to take Drew out of it and I can't. How, nearly twenty years later, did it all go so wrong?

Photo courtesy Walter Brock

Michael and Drew on the beach in Bali.

Three

Home to Virginia

Walt retired in 1999. It was in midsummer of that year that we packed ourselves up, put Drew—who was now sixteen—and two Labs into the back of the car, and followed the moving van from Texas to Virginia. We were headed to the home we had bought many years ago on Smith Mountain Lake in the south-central part of the state. It is a large lake in the foothills of the Blue Ridge Mountains and the antithesis of the big city we had left behind. The closer we got to the Virginia Mountains, the more we stretched out, leaned back in our seats, and mentally left the broad hot plains of Texas, the smell of oil wells, and a chunk of our lives behind. Cool mountain air, deep rivers, and bounding streams surrounded us. We felt as though we had been holding our breath for a long time—and now we could finally breathe.

Drew felt the tug of moving more than we did. He was leaving a bigger chunk of his life behind than we were.

Moving closer to both our older children had been one of the motivations for this move. Karen was a mom now, living in Richmond with her husband, Randy, and new baby boy only three hours from the lake. Michael was in Williamsburg on the York River living with his new wife, Mary Katherine, finishing up an MBA.

Drew started school in the fall. It wasn't fun starting over at a new school in tenth grade, but he adjusted, went out for football and basketball, and began to make friends. One of the first people he met was Sara. I have a picture in my mind of him sitting beside her on the school bus, then as the bus stopped, taking the steps two at a time, running over to the car to introduce me.

She was smaller than most girls her age, and she walked and ran to keep up with him. Her dark eyes shone under a mop of chestnut hair that was scooped into a ponytail on one side of her head, silver loops swung among the strands of hair that escaped the ribbon, and a smile lit her face as she heard Drew say, "Mom! Meet Sara!"

He was going to be okay. I felt happy watching him racing headlong into his new life, with shoelaces flapping and dark brown hair sweaty and curling around his ears.

With Drew at school, Walt keeping busy with plans to re-model the lake house, and the Labs spending their days bounding through the shallow cove we lived on, I joined a meditation group.

Within the group, we learned the power of "quietitude." Is that a word? It doesn't mean silence. It means *Quiet*. It's a word of refuge. We learned how to center ourselves and maintain peace in the middle of chaos. We began to recogmize angels and guides or whoever was out there in this massive cloud of universal intelligence.

We learned about consciousness: sub and super. And life and transition or death. Within the circle, we found that we could speak to God, the universe, or any number of its beings anywhere, alive or passed on. We learned to see different colored auras or light energy around others. We played with telepathy and we delved into reincarnation, past lives, and soared into future existences. This beautiful place we lived in with its mountain air and soft waters and wild birds made it easy to understand.

Over the course of time, we studied the great thinkers of Greece, the French philosophers, and the Transcendentalists of early New England who included Walt Whitman, Henry Wadsworth Longfellow, Ralph Waldo Emerson, George Ripley, and Louisa May Alcott. We delved in to a serious study of the scriptures, Eastern and Western.

Throughout this foray into the unknown, I remained completely unaware of the real track of this part of the journey. The fact was that the incipient undertow of this exploration, this study I undertook for fun and distraction, was quietly preparing me for a number of very big adjustments.

Although nothing could ever fully prepare me for the death of my husband. Or the death of my son.

෴

Walt and I went about retirement with the same energy we had poured into the rest of our lives together. We remodeled the house where it needed to be remodeled, we added bathrooms and extended decks, and slowly turned our lake cabin into a home. I picked up my journalism again as a stringer for a couple of local newspapers. I wrote commentaries, joined a Lake Association full of people trying to keep the lake water clean and the shores free of strip malls, and Walt stayed home and mowed the grass. How things change. Mowing the grass was what he enjoyed most. He told me once, "You join whatever you want to join, Ginny. I don't ever want to see another board room. I want to ride my lawn mower, let my mind trail behind—far behind." And that's what he did. He would be gone for hours mowing everything within reach of his chugging twenty horsepower mower, puffing cigarettes, his mind, and sometimes the Labs, trailing behind. In the evenings, we sat on the deck, pleased with our home, marveling at our kid's lives and our expanding family, sipping whatever it was we sipped, and watching the sun go down in a fiery blaze behind the hills.

❧

Then it was the spring of 2005. How quickly the time had gone. "It's because I never get a day off!" Walt grumbled. "I'm going to have to go back to work so I can rest. This retirement's killing me."

I think he was only half-joking. He was a self-taught and thorough handyman, and the idea of hiring anyone to do the small jobs was not on his agenda. So he never got a day off.

Both Karen and Michael were raising families now and living in Richmond and Manhattan, respectively, Karen with three children and Michael with two. Drew had moved to Colorado in October 2004 and was working for one of the ski resorts in the mountains. It was a long way away, and whereas Walt and I were glad he was testing the waters of independence, we missed him badly. But not having to wonder where he was at three in the morning wasn't bad either.

It was Walt's idea to go and visit him. "I just want to be sure he's okay," he said. So in April 2005, we packed up the car and drove across country to see our son and gauge for ourselves how well he was doing.

It turned out that Drew was fine. He had made friends and loved his life in the mountains. When he wasn't working, he was hiking or skiing or fishing. Money was scarce, but luckily for Drew, he had a family who topped up his bank account when he got into tight spots. We spent several days with him, seeing the apartment he shared with two others, visiting his workplace and the places where he played. Then we left him and headed off to Utah and down into Arizona and New Mexico for the long drive home to Virginia.

It had been a good trip. The best part was seeing Drew happy in the Rocky Mountains, among the towering peaks and canyons of the West. A blur of purple sage covered slopes, deep shadows, and the bright green waters of the Colorado River colored my mind as I remembered our time with him. Every night of that trip, I'd gone to bed and lay there watching as miles and miles of freeway flashed across my eyes before sleep moved in. I thought of mountain roads, waterfalls, and spectacular vistas and sunsets that seared the western skies with colored light. The pictures and the postcards I sent home to the meditation group couldn't begin to capture the magnificence of this place. Then as fate would have it, someone very real and whose essence I could capture very easily, became a fellow traveler on this journey.

༄༅

Her name was Rosalind. She was a psychic medium who claimed to speak directly to spirit, and she came into my life at a time that only that invisible entity called "destiny" could have arranged. I met her for the first time in the dusty pink town of Canyon Springs, nestled high in the Red Rock Canyons of northern New Mexico. We had stopped for a few days in the small town, not much more than a village really, that looked as though it had been carved out of red rock mesa and sandstone. Surrounded by the high peaks and valleys of the southern Rockies, some miles off the beaten track, Canyon Springs slumbered among the cottonwoods and cacti in a desert oasis.

We stayed in a small hotel built with sticks and thick adobe plaster, and from the pink Saltillo tile patio, we could see the town below us. I sat on the end of the hotel bed scanning the complimentary brochures that spoke about American Indian spirits who had transited this place, vortexes, and portals to The Other Side. I had no trouble believing it. The pamphlets talked about the earth spirit Gaia, and when I walked outside onto the porch, I imagined I could hear her breathing from the cracks and crevices of the rocks. I had to explore this little town—it was as though it was calling to me to come down and walk among its ramshackle buildings.

"I'm off to town," I told Walt. "Want to come?" I knew he didn't. He was comfortable on the patio, feet up, sitting beside a small stream, deep into his crossword puzzle. Candle stores, soap, and perfume shops weren't his thing.

"Don't think so." He looked up from his puzzle book and stretched. "I'm doing fine right here." He yawned. "Bring me a pack of cigarettes when you come back?"

I frowned at him. I'd stopped nagging about his "disgusting, stinking, messy, etc …" habit years ago. All that did was turn our nest into a squabbling mess of ruffled feathers. "Please?" He smiled, peering at me over the tops of his reading glasses.

"Maybe," I said, kissed him on the cheek, swung my raffia bag-for-treasures over my shoulder, and started off down the road to town.

There was only one paved street in the village, and it wound its way up the side of a canyon, twisting and turning its way to the other side of town. A score of narrow alleyways forked off on either side of the street. Small adobe dwellings with brightly colored cotton curtains, which caught what little breeze there was, huddled beside the alleys, their low wooden doors opening onto the red dirt floors of the tracks. The fragrance of beeswax candles and incense floated out of the low doorways of the shops that lined the main street. There were no sidewalks to speak of, unless you counted the narrow strip of crumbling sandstone walks that ran along only one side of the street. Crooked signs nailed to outside walls advertised "Shaman is Here" and "Soap." That seemed like a good idea to me. I was hot and getting sweatier with every step I took, and my calves were starting to ache from the upward swing of the terrain. Dream merchants huddled in tiny shops with beaded curtains and flimsy shawls hanging about, and a tiny art gallery with rich wood floors and polished tables was squashed between a fabric warehouse and a smoky cantina. Its front door was shut and so were its windows. It looked as though it was the only air-conditioned place in town. The sign on the door said "Open," so I did and gratefully walked inside, relishing the almost refrigerated air that huffed out of an ancient gurgler of a paint-chipped window unit. Pictures of painted ponies huddled in snowy groves of white-barked sycamores decorated the walls, and a few hanging rugs draped other walls. More paintings of tall red rock canyons iced with snow graced an almost-square pillar in the middle of the tiny gallery. Behind the cashier's desk was a sign that said "Psychic on Duty." I wondered if the cashier doubled as part-time psychic or if it was the small stooped woman I saw dusting shelves full of crystals. I had never been to a psychic before. I stared at the sign for a long time. Then I realized I was blocking the narrow doorway and three people were pushing past to get into the store, so I made up my mind. The idea scared me, but I decided it was time to find out who these people are so I made an appointment to see the psychic.

But first I had to pull my thoughts together, so I wandered around the store for a while pretending to look at the paintings and a table full of stacks of handmade soap. They seemed to like their soap here. Finally, my courage as high as it was going to get, I made my way over to the desk to sign up for a reading.

The psychic wasn't in today! Wouldn't you know it. For the first time in my life I had gotten my nerve up, squared my shoulders, and was ready to walk into the unknown world of the occult and was told that the psychic was out. What was that about? What weird twist of fate?

Disappointed, I bought a few postcards instead and walked out of the shop onto the sunny sidewalk. I gazed down the street, and just as I was about to take a step forward I felt a tap on my shoulder. I jumped. Swinging around, I found myself looking into a face that was creased and as wrinkled as old, tea-colored linen.

"Come! I take you to Rosalind!" His voice rustled like wind sweeping through a dry corn patch and a broad smile creased his face, showing gums that had long since surrendered their teeth.

"Who's Rosalind?"

"She good woman ... she *Shaman* ... " The old man shook his head and rolled his eyes. "She use powerful, powerful magic. Come!" A scrawny hand shot out of a long threadbare sleeve and gripped my arm.

"Wait!" I yanked my arm back and pointed to the shop behind us. "Is she the same one who works there?"

"NO!" He looked and sounded offended. "This Missy ... " he waggled a bony finger at the doorway, "in shop for tourist ... Come! We go find Rosalind ... not far. We go!"

Against any good sense I had left, I followed him down the street to the edge of the village. There were no shops down here. No curio stands, just a grove of cottonwoods, which gave way to spiky underbrush and a path that took us over a stream and climbed around the side of a steep rock fall. We came out onto a broad ledge that overlooked a deep canyon shrouded in mist and the scent of red earth.

"Not far," the old man darted ahead, waved a hand at me without turning as he disappeared around an overhang. The path had broadened out here and I found myself looking out at a view that defied all imagery. Hills of red-stained rock striped with yellows and greens and blacks. Rocky ranges upon ranges and outcrops of tumbled stone studded with purple sage and swathes of white sand.

We rounded the next boulder and there, right in front of us, was a small round adobe dwelling. The red earth outside the home had been swept clean and a low stone bench curved around a pond that was fed by a small waterfall that trickled down from the rocks above us.

The old man beamed. "You like?" He pointed proudly at the pool of water. "Not too much water here … Rosalind like …" As he was speaking, the front door opened and a young woman appeared. She stood on the threshold shading her eyes against the sun with one hand.

"Dada!" She stepped out shaking her finger at the old man. She was older than I thought at first glance. "I'm sorry," she said to me. "He does this sometimes—just grabs people off the street … Dada what did I tell you?" She put her hands on her hips. "You're not supposed to do that! Remember what we said? Hmm?" Her voice was soft, but her eyes were fierce as he raised a hand to his forehead and muttered something I couldn't hear.

Then the old man turned his grizzled face to the canyons, cocked his head toward me and said, "You go—don' know what you hear." He leaned over and cupped his hand in the waterfall. "Don' know what story behind waterfall." He cackled and waved me off.

The young woman turned to me. "Come inside. You want to talk to me." It wasn't a question.

"What?" I took a step forward as she swirled her skirt aside and stepped over the threshold of the house.

"You wouldn't be here otherwise." She was smiling at me as I stood rooted to the swept clay, squinting into the sun.

"I don't know why I'm here..." I admitted.

"Your soul knows. Come in." Rosalind stepped into the cool shadow of her home, standing back to let me pass. I nodded. There was something compelling about this whole bizarre scene.

Fear left a faint sheen of perspiration on my face and my hands were clammy. My underarms were damp. All my sweat glands had run amok. I took a deep breath. Sister Cornelius had done a brilliant job of attempting to nail my young spirit to the path of righteousness. She had done a real number on my nervous system regarding people who dared to look beyond and into the spirit realm. I was nearly convinced that any association with the likes of these evil ones would summon the devil, and becoming more convinced by the second. What had possessed me? What was I thinking!

I was feeling faint as I stepped through the beaded doorway to begin my session.

The first thing I became aware of was a haze of incense that filled the air with the light scent of sagebrush. Looking around through the filtered light, I saw a crystal pyramid on a silver tray on a low table beside me. It was surrounded by an arrangement of pink quartz crystals. The source of the incense smoke came from a small clay-fired pot on a shelf in the corner of the room. Primitive figures were etched into its sides in black paint.

There was a low couch against a wall that was covered with embroidered hangings depicting ancient light-filled beings—a white bonneted Indian Chief, a white ruffed wolf—surreal scenes of misty pastoral beauty. On another wall there were painted pictures of beams of light, stars, and golden moons lighting up dark skies. On the floor there was a patterned rug. And a wool blanket of reds and blues, browns and yellows hung over the back of a single chair beside the couch.

My eyes roamed the room. An ancient piano stood in one corner and a diploma from the School of Music of the University of New Mexico stood in a brass stand off to one side.

She followed my eyes. "Music. One of the highest vibrations," she said quietly as she took her seat behind an old ink-stained desk. "Please sit down." She gestured to a chair opposite her.

I sat down stiffly in the chair she offered and slowly let my breath escape. Rosalind sat with her hands in her lap, saying nothing for at least a minute.

"You're not nervous, are you?" She raised her eyes to mine and smiled.

I was practically hyperventilating, but I beamed back at her and delivered a croaking lie. "No." I prayed mightily that there was no smiting angel waiting behind my chair. If there was, I was a goner.

No sign of one as far as I could see … and the lie helped. It slowly dawned on me that it was peaceful in here. The room was filled with the peace of this woman whom I'd never met before. Her eyes were closed. Her jet black hair framed her face in a pixie cut accentuating the high, wide cheekbones of her Navajo blood. There were silver rings on her fingers. Silver hoops studded with turquoise pierced her ears, and when she opened her eyes, they were inky black.

She spoke quietly, opening the session with an invocation to God and the universe to be with us in the light of the ancestral and holy spirits of her heritage and mine. She called on our spirit guides and guardians to bring only truth and clarity through the ethers into this tiny, beaded, sweet-smelling room.

When I found my voice, I had easy questions about my children, my house, and the dog. I wasn't worried about Miss Kitty, the little stray who had recently adopted us. She had settled in very well, having established her superiority over the dog and the rest of us and taken over our home as her own. But I wondered about selling the house while the market was so high. Was Drew going to be okay in his new job? There was nothing that required any "psychic" intervention here, and I was beginning to think we were wasting time with this nonsense.

Then she told me that my husband was about to die.

What! "How can you say that? What can you see … Why do you think that?"

"I can see it in his aura. What we call the 'etheric body.' It exists as a mist of energy around each one of us." She said calmly.

"Can you see it—I mean actually see it?"

"And sense it."

Great! Was my first thought. The first psychic I go to is a nut. A charlatan! Where are the smiting angels when you need one?

I thought of Walt in the gardens of our hotel high among the canyons, where I'd left him sitting beside a small stream in the shade of a grove of cottonwoods on a patio near the room. He was happy as a whippoorwill working a crossword puzzle when I left, with his cigarettes on one side of the table, his beer on the other.

Die? What a load of crap. Irritation with myself for getting caught up in this nonsense welled up, and I made a motion to leave.

"He's making a soul decision," she told me placidly. "It means that he can decide either way..."

I stopped groping for my purse under the table and sat up. A long-forgotten session came back reminding me of the day the meditation group talked about souls and free will, and I began to understand what she was saying. So I stayed and listened. "Are you hearing things...like words?" I asked.

She nodded. "Yes, from spirit. Not 'hearing' as you might hear things on the physical plane. It's more like telepathy. It's spirit speaking to spirit."

"Your spirit?"

She nodded. "His spirit is speaking to my spirit."

"Does he know...does he know his spirit is talking to yours?"

"He's barely conscious of it."

All the fear and misgivings I had felt were gone. It seemed to me that I had dislocated from the part of me that was saying, "Get out of here."

The Rosalind person was talking through my ambiguity. "It's not your decision. This is an agreement he's making with his spirit."

No one was going to give me any say in this, apparently. I took a deep breath and looked toward the door, remembering the other thing she'd said, "It may or may not happen." I could accept that, and I chose to believe that it would not happen. So I kept listening, but the skeptic Ginny kept digging sharp fingers into my psyche saying, "This is crazy! There's nothing the matter with Walt! Let's go!" But I stayed and when the reading was over, I left the hillside without a backward glance.

Four

The First Goodbye

We'd gone to bed early the evening we got back home, but Walt wasn't feeling well and he hadn't been able to sleep. In fact, he had gone into the spare room so as not to disturb me, he said.

"What do you think is wrong?" I asked when he came in our room about eight with my morning cup of tea.

"Just tired, I think. Overtired."

"That's it?" I said. I knew this man well. If he admitted to being tired, there was something wrong. "Do you hurt anywhere?"

To my surprise, he said, "Yes. Achy. It's nothing"

"You haven't had a checkup in a while; let me call and make an appointment." I knew this was a futile thing to say. Nothing could get Walt to the doctor's office.

But he surprised me again. "Okay" was all he said before disappearing down the hallway.

Something was wrong. I called the medical center and made the appointment before he could change his mind. The receptionist had a cold and her voice was muffled, as though she was talking through a wad of kleenex, but I gathered that they couldn't see him before one o'clock. I took the time slot.

My husband was puttering around in the kitchen when I walked in with an armload of vacation laundry to take downstairs. "I'm making breakfast," he said. "Want some?"

Sunlight filtered through the wide kitchen window, and outside on the patchy green grass splashes of yellow daffodils opened their petals to the morning light. The smell of baking biscuits was tempting, but I shook my head. "I've packed on at least five pounds over the last two weeks," I said and walked downstairs to the laundry room, which was directly below the kitchen.

Looking back on it, it must have taken me about five minutes to sort through the wash and load up the washer when just before I closed the lid, I heard a loud "thump" from upstairs. I stopped what I was doing. Was that Walt? Did he drop something? Was that the oven door slamming? My mind ran through the possibilities in seconds as I stood there with one hand on the washer lid, listening. Everything was quiet. Bending down, I took a load of towels out of the dryer still listening for any sounds from the kitchen. It was quiet. I should have been able to hear him moving around ... Then in a flash, I knew what that thump was. With the towels in my arms, I raced up the stairs—and when I opened the kitchen door at the top of the stairs I saw him.

I called his name. The towels dropped from my arms. My mind went into slow motion as I dropped to my knees beside him. Walt was lying on his side, and there was dark blood coming from a wound on his head. His face was the color of a deep purple plum. An indigo shadow... How long had it taken me to react and get up here? My mind raced. Seconds? A minute? Two? It didn't matter.

My mind was spinning. Call 911! No time. I lowered my head to his mouth and began to breathe into his lungs. I leaned on his chest. "Breathe, Walt!" I said. One, two, three PUSH! "Breathe dammit!" I shouted. One, two... I knew it was hopeless—all along I had known. I jumped up and grabbed the phone. And kept breathing for him. He wasn't breathing back. There was no movement in his chest—only the sound of my breath filling the lifeless caverns of his lungs. I lifted my head and ran my hand across my mouth. When it came away, the black raspberry stain of his blood streaked my face and my hair. My hand grasped the phone and my fingers began dialing 911. That's what you're supposed to do. Get help. There's no help. Dial 911. I could barely hear my voice as I spoke to the dispatcher, a total stranger who was about to get the worst news of my life. How... *oh dear God*. "Hurry!" I whispered.

The medics arrived.

"He's gone." That was all I said. Words stuck in my throat. No other sounds came out.

The men pounded into the kitchen with their equipment and began to work on Walt. I sat cross-legged on the carpet in the hallway watching in stunned disbelief. That gash on his head—where had that come from? Then I saw the oven door partially open and a streak of blood running down the white porcelain. He cut his head when he fell…

My eyes took in the scene in front of me as though I was in a trance, but my mind was moving down a dusty street, trying the side roads that trailed off to either side searching for the doorway I knew was there. My sandaled feet stumbled on, my ankle turned on a slab of crushed and crumbly pink sandstone. I climbed the hill, my calves ached, my mind raced through the red rocks above the canyons of New Mexico to a small waterfall, an adobe dwelling and from far away a soft voice was saying, *"His soul is deciding whether to stay or whether to go."*

Walt had decided to go. One minute he was there at breakfast time, standing over the stove peering through the glass panel to look inside the lighted oven. And the next minute, he was gone.

As I watched, I was aware of the warm aroma of baking biscuits. Sunshine poured mistily through the kitchen window. I remembered the details of tiny specks of dust caught in the sun's web and a gnat lying squished on the rim of the sink. These were the things I would remember.

The paramedics left nothing out of the life-saving procedures they knew. I knew he was gone. I had known that from the minute I found him. There is no stillness like the stillness of death. The absence of life is a void. I wanted them to stop; they worked exhaustively to bring him back.

And then they took him away.

Walt never knew what hit him. He never saw it coming. Nobody did. In the days that followed, I only knew that one half of me had fallen off. It felt as though half of my life was gone. Half of me had died with him. Two lives were over. An entire lifetime with him had come to an end.

Someone had removed the biscuits from the oven and put them on the countertop. They were still warm when the ambulance drove slowly out of the driveway taking Walt away. I was as cold as ice.

Neighbors came over. Friends drove me to the county hospital where they had taken Walt.

"A heart event," the doctors called it. What the heck is that? Heart attack? Stroke? Or a blood clot? "Myocardial infarction" the death certificate said. Broken heart is the best I can do with the translation.

It was time to call our children.

Walter Brock.

In the middle of the rubble of my world, I kept reading. I read everything and anything that had anything to do with soul survival. I had to know that Walt was still around me. He had to be somewhere. One morning I stood on the front steps and shouted into the woods through my tears, *"Where are you Walt—*tell me where you are ... *please tell me!"*

From the Platonist documents to Edgar Cayce to the popularized psychics that appear on television, I absorbed it all. Old lessons came back to me. Lessons that I'd learned out of curiosity and dissatisfaction with organized religion. My years of searching for clues of eternal life rushed at me from long ago. Remember, remember ... The teachers were memories, some of them clear, some not so sharp. The memory and the teacher.

⤔

My first real meeting with grief came with my parents' deaths. Then came my husband's.

He died too young at sixty-seven years old, and his absence left a giant hole in my life. I had been a cosseted wife who wanted for nothing. He was my champion, my breadwinner, lawn mower, fixer of leaky faucets and all broken things, builder of my landscaping ideas, and proofreader of my writing. And then he was gone. I grieved hard. I was scared. How would I cope without him?

I had no idea how to begin coping without Walt. But I soon discovered that I had a choice. I could rebuild myself from the foundations, or allow myself to be buried under the rubble. The foundations were hard to see at first, covered up as they were by the remnants of my life, but the alternative was not an option. So I began to dig.

❧

There have been many teachers in my life. Experience can teach, people can teach, and so can emotion. The toughest teacher I ever had was the emotion of grief. It is the roughest route to enlightenment, but in all its confusion, its unchartered depth, and shadow, it is the clearest that I have experienced.

❧

The following summer I took Walt home. He was born in the foothills of the Ouachita Mountains in a small town called De Queen in Arkansas, not far from the Oklahoma border. On a clear day high in the mountains, on the slopes of Wilhelmina Mountain, I stood in Arkansas overlooking Oklahoma in the distance and scattered my husband's ashes. The mountains were bathed in sun and haze, the air smelled of dry grass seed blowing on the breeze, and the hum of honeybees filled my senses as I gazed across the deep valley.

"You'll like this place," I told him. "You can see for miles. And there's a lake right below us." There was. I never knew its name. Its waters, sheltered by the mountain, were glassy smooth and slate colored. What a perfect place to be. The grass crunched under my shoes as I picked a bunch of wild yellow daisies, their sticky sap smeared my hands as I laid them on top of the dusting of ash. I stood for a few more minutes looking out at the magnificent view. So much beauty. "You would have liked this place…" I sniffed the air. I thought I got a whiff of cigarette smoke… Then I said goodbye and walked to the car.

My sister Toni and her friend Beth were with me. "That's odd," I said. "Is anyone smoking?" They shook their heads. "I could swear I smelled cigarette smoke… I must have been mistaken."

We started to leave the site. Then just as we were about to pull out onto the byway, I suddenly got the strangest feeling.

"*Stop!*" I almost shouted.

Toni stepped hard on the brakes and the car jolted to a stop. "What is it, Gin?" She glanced over her shoulder, eyebrows arched.

I rolled down the window. My mind was completely still. Wrapped in "quietitude," I was barely conscious of the cool air on my face as I stared in disbelief at the scene on the edge of the mountain.

Completely "centered" and clear, I became intuitively aware of three Indian Chiefs on horseback on the ridge beside the ashes. They felt vibrantly alive. They were solid. The wind on the mountain ruffled their buckskins and flicked their long black hair. There seemed to be a light mist around them. Their bonnets were made of white feathers, and their tunics were white and cream colored with wood and bone decoration. They were giants bathed in a translucent light as were their horses, also white, also huge, with long manes that stirred in the wind.

I stared at them dumbfounded, and then through some sort of thought transference or telepathy, I clearly heard them say,

Thank you.

It came very quickly and just as quickly it was gone and so were they. *Did I really hear that?* I shook my head and blinked, then looked at the ledge where they had been. There was nothing there but the bunch of yellow daisies and a smattering of white ash.

Walt's family was full of tales of their Cherokee heritage. I would listen to them for hours, sitting cross-legged on the floor while our small children slept. I pored over old pictures of long gone ancestors, hearing the stories and seeing their faces, and in them, the undeniable evidence of Native American blood.

And here they were. I had met the ancient ancestors.

"We can go now," I told Toni. She didn't ask any questions, and it was hours later, with an empty bottle of red wine between us, that I shared the vision with them.

High above the valley that separates two states, they had come to claim him. The Cherokee Elders had welcomed Walt home.

❧

Life goes on somehow. The sun comes up, the sun goes down, and everything in between just keeps rushing along the stream of our lives. Some of us laze in the sunshine, some of us bump over the rapids, and a few pull off at the exits finding shelter in the shade of dense, green oaks. And that's okay.

Others hurtle full-speed ahead with the sound of thunder rushing through their ears, toward the seductive spumes of whitewater. Sprays of sparkling light conceal the mighty drop to the jagged rocks below.

And in the scheme of things, that too is okay. This life journey we've embarked on is a bumpy ride. None of us knows for sure what's waiting around the next bend in the stream. The only thing we know for sure is that nothing stays the same. Ever.

But every morning is another chance to live and most of us don't take the exits, we seize that chance to live, because the alternative is to die, and it's not time for that.

༄

Back in Colorado, Drew focused on his job. He had been there for about six months. I worried about him most. The other two had families to keep them busy, but Drew seemed alone to me. I probably shouldn't have worried. He seemed to have been catapulted into adulthood overnight following his father's death. He was working and playing hard in the Rocky Mountains.

"This is the life," I heard. "Listen to this … I skied the Great Divide—at midnight last night. With a full moon!"

"How great was that, Drew?"

"Yeah! We camped at about 11,000 feet."

"Awesome!"

"That's it…" It always made me smile when he used this expression. It was so *Drew*. Ever since he was little, when some revelation occurred to him, he would suddenly stop in mid-sentence and say, "That's it!"

He told me that he went hiking and kayaked on the Colorado River and had learned how to fly-fish. His stories made me think of the times he and Sara went fishing off the dock at the lake when they were teens, and I pictured Sara and Drew and Ranger, his black lab, racing around the cove on his jet ski.

He loved the mountains … the rivers … the snows. He loved his job at Moonrise Mountain Lodge—a hotel built high on a pass above the villages in the valley, a lamp-lit grand lodge made of the trunks of pine and rock. It was a place for the rich and famous to feel the rush of spraying powder and listen to the swisssh of their skis through deep snow. In the summertime, they could run the rapids of the Colorado River or just stand at the top of the world and breathe.

That first October after Walt died, I went out to see Drew. He took me hiking up canyons and riding up ski lifts to take in the autumn views of yellow Aspen. It was too early to ski the Great Divide, which was fine with me. When he took me to dinner at his hotel on my sixtieth birthday, I realized how much he had grown up. He handled the wine list like someone to the cellars born, asked me if I preferred my wine to be a little fruity or a little smoky. Would I like a dry white or a sweet red? Pride filled my heart as I watched him. He was a born hotelier, someone who had found his niche very early in life.

The great stone fireplace in the hotel lounge filled the back wall, and hunting trophies of moose and elk looked down through shiny black eyes. We sat together and listened to a folk singer play guitar for a few minutes, and then he had to leave. He was meeting some of the guys at O'Malley's for drinks and karaoke—I could join them if I liked, he offered.

I declined and gave him a hug goodnight. "See you in the morning," I said and watched him go, the way I had so many times before. As I waved to him, I had a sudden flashback of my seventeen-year-old Drew charging out into the night, racing to get to somebody's party on the lake. It was raining hard that night in Virginia as he pleaded to be allowed to go out, his hands speaking the language of teenage intensity. "I'll be fine—

I'll be careful, I promise!" There's so much living to get done. And then he was gone.

❧

Back home in the east, Drew called me every day to make sure I always had someone to talk to now that his dad was gone.

He told me he'd dreamed of him. "There he was, standing in my bedroom, with Cassie!"

This made me smile. Cassie, Drew's old yellow Lab, died the year before Walt did. Walt, who never believed in any life after death, was now showing up in Drew's dreams.

He'd shown up in mine, too, and I hoped by now he knew he was wrong about the soul survival thing.

And then something different happened. Late one night, I heard Walt's footsteps on the deck outside my bedroom doors. There was no doubt it was Walt. It was his tread and the weight was right … I just knew it was him. The footsteps began about ten yards from my bedroom doors, which open onto the deck, and ended right outside them. But no footsteps turned around and walked back. When I looked, there was no one there.

I told Drew about it.

"And get this!" He exclaimed one day on the phone. "The other night Dad came into another dream. He said, 'Look at this Drew …' He wanted to show me something. He had a computer in his hands. 'You should see these computers they have here. Watch this …' and he showed me how he could bring anything up on the screen by just *THINKING* it! Man! Was that cool!"

❧

Then one day, a few weeks after I'd returned to Virginia, a package arrived. It was a care package from Drew. Inside it was the trilogy release of the *Pirates of the Caribbean*. What on earth?

"I thought you'd like these," read his note.

Pirates aren't my style. In fact pirates are definitely not my style. But there was something in these movies that must have spoken to Drew, something he thought I should see. Whatever it was escaped me for the time being.

So I watched them—all three of them.

I liked the scenery. The swashbuckling Johnny Depp's interpretation of Jack Sparrow was fun for a while, but it was exhausting watching the guy leaping off cliffs and swimming out to sea with hordes of angry people after him.

So I watched them for Drew, with a lot of breaks taken between fencing marathons so I could catch my breath. I reveled in the way all my children had rallied around me when their father died. I could feel their love reaching out and engulfing me, no matter how far away they lived. Walt couldn't be here, but his children were and they reflected him in so many ways. He must have been bursting with pride in them from wherever he was.

He was very close, actually, and sometimes he gave me signs to show just how close he really was. There was the evening during the winter following his death when I decided to host a dinner party for close friends. After dinner, as we all sat around the fireplace eating dessert, I looked over at a friend from the meditation group. She was sitting cross-legged on the living-room floor holding her dessert plate in one hand and her spoon in the other. For a moment, she looked as though she was cast in stone. She was dead still—not moving a muscle. Then she began to sniff the air. In a few seconds, she shook her head and scooped up another spoon of cake, but as she was about to put it into her mouth she stopped cold and said, "Who's smoking in here?"

"Nobody," I said.

"Then why can I smell cigarette smoke?"

Everyone began sniffing the air like redbone hounds on the hunt. "You know, it's funny," said one of the men. "When I went out on the deck earlier, I swear I could smell smoke— cigarette smoke."

Then another friend burst out laughing, "It's Walt! Walt! Is that you?"

Everyone began to smile and the chatter turned to Walt's cigarettes and his inability to quit. Then while we were talking about a recent trip to Africa, there was a sudden crash!

We all jumped.

"Look at this!" An old friend of mine from Zimbabwe bent down and picked up a book that had, without provocation, cascaded off the bookshelf and landed in front of her. "Stuart Cloete's *The African Giant!*" She held it up. "Oh my God! Walt's here."

❧

Death is a sad and difficult experience for those left standing in its wake. Every death diminishes us in some way. When Karen, Michael, Drew, and I finally came through my husband's death, bruised and shaky, I thought we'd learned everything there is to know about losing someone and grieving. That was when the teacher named grief taught me the most difficult lesson of all. It happened three years after Walt died. We lost Drew and everything changed. Again.

Five

When Heaven
and Earth Collide

On a chilly November night in 2008, the week before Thanksgiving, I was out to dinner with my old friend Jim who lived down the lake from me. Since he'd lost his wife two years after Walt died, he had become my frequent dinner partner, dance partner, and movie buddy. We were filling spaces in each other's lives. We were traveling together on a stretch of road that had become uncertain and was strewn with rocks. He helped me with my garden and I made home-cooked meals for him. He taught me how to sail, and we took dance lessons.

This Friday evening in late November, we had been having dinner at a small country music place in the foothills of the Blue Ridge, listening to the live band but not dancing because I felt sick. Stomach cramps writhed painfully through my insides and I wondered if I had eaten something bad. After about an hour with no relief, I asked Jim to take me home.

As we were leaving the building, standing in the doorway about to step outside, my cell phone rang. It rang twice before I answered it, never knowing when I did so that my world had just capsized. Never suspecting that my life was now at the mercy of a force ten gale that had begun to blow. My ship was sinking, the lights were going out, and my life was about to be changed forever.

This journey had suddenly turned into a very rough passage.

A woman on the other end of the line was telling me that Drew had been admitted to a hospital in Vail, Colorado. Brought in by friends ... unresponsive ... seizing ... My brain tried to sieve through the words spilling out of the person inside my cell phone. They tumbled through my mind like balls of quicksilver. They weren't real. They had no substance, they made no sense, and I couldn't hold on to them.

"Who are you?" I asked.

Emergency room doctor. She gave me a name.

"Unresponsive? How?" What was she saying ...

"He's unconscious. Seizing—not responding to us."

"How? Was it a car accident?"

Then, "No, ma'am. Not a car accident. He and his friends were at a party ..."

"Drinking?"

"That's what it looks like ... and drugs." The ER doctor's voice fell like cold granite through my reeling brain.

Disbelief ... then, "Oh my God. I'm on my way." Drugs? What was she talking about? What does that mean?

I remember very little about the flight to Denver at 6:00 the next morning. It was as though I was somewhere outside of myself. I felt like a disembodied entity. I could hardly feel that part of me with head and hands, fingers and toes that went through the motions unseeing, instinctively moving from the ticket counter through the baggage and security lines and on and off planes.

But right beside me, I could feel that ethereal me keeping in step, moving me forward with purpose. It was as though some unseen specter had taken control of my movements and all of my senses.

My son was in trouble. And something strange had happened last night. Something inside of me had alerted me to that, although it took me some time to grasp what it was. Then, sometime during the long flight from Virginia, an old memory of another Thanksgiving came in flashes down through the years, through the mist that clouded my mind. We were in Singapore when Drew was only six years old, and his brother and sister were both in school in the U.S. For no apparent reason, I had suddenly felt disoriented at about 10:00 a.m that Thursday so long ago. I had felt as though I was outside of myself then. My shoulder and right arm were cramping, and I had difficulty breathing. That was when we found out that Michael and Karen had been in a car accident. That wasn't a heart attack I was having. It was something inside me was letting me know that my children were hurt.

It had happened again. I thought back to the sick feeling I'd felt the night before, accompanied by severe cramps. That part of me in Drew, separated by distance, had tried to tell me that my child was in trouble. It had happened again.

My flight landed at 10:30 a.m. Colorado time. I could hear the clicking of my heels on the terrazzo as my oldest son, Michael, who had flown in from New York, led us through the Denver airport to the Hertz place. He had landed at exactly the same time as I had, two gates down. What are the odds of that happening in this day of modern air travel?

The drive into the city was short. The sun was shining on this crisp and clear morning. I cast a sideways look at Michael. He was as blond as Drew was dark. His eyes were light blue. He was only thirty-seven years old, but his face was drawn and pale. His shock was as great as mine. The sun glinted off his sunglasses as he steered the car down Highway 70 toward the city.

We had been on the phone with each other for a long time last night, so there was little news I could give him that we hadn't received the night before. This included the fact that they had moved Drew from the small village hospital in Vail to the big teaching hospital in Denver, which told us we were dealing with something very bad.

Michael's face was tense. His mouth set, his shoulders braced for whatever we were walking into. My chest tightened as I looked at him. Drew's big brother, who had played with him, fished with him, hunted squirrels and frogs with him, and cheered him on during tee-ball, baseball, and then football ... coached him and yelled at him ... teased him and loved him, was now facing something he could never have prepared for. This young son of mine, who in many ways had taken Walt's place in Drew's life, was shattered. He rested his hand on mine and said quietly, "We have to be ready for anything. For whatever we find when we see Drew. No matter what."

I could feel him mustering his strength, bringing his mental focus to bear on this terrible morning ahead of us.

"Yes, I know." My eyes were squeezed shut and I prayed silently. *Where are you, Walt? Drew's in trouble—if you can hear me, tell me.*

Michael eased the car onto the exit ramp and bumped down into the city, past small strip malls, through winding streets. An imposing hospital building emerged from Denver's skyscrapers and Michael maneuvered his way toward it. "I wish I knew what had happened," he said, shaping my thoughts with his words. "Hopefully someone will be able to tell us what's going on. I can't believe any of this."

My mind was having difficulty taking any of this in. It couldn't find its direction.

"Let's go see what's going on." Michael walked around to my side of the car to let me out.

༄

Inside the building, we walked fast down the slick wide corridor, intent only on finding Drew in this hive of specialized activity that smelled of disinfectants—and hope and fear.

"I see him! There he is," I said, as we followed the bend in the hallway, past nurse's stations and open doors. "That room— on the right."

When we entered the room, Drew looked as though he was asleep. His dark eyelashes rested motionless on his cheeks, his hands at his sides, with a mound of pillows propping him up. If not for the ventilator pumping air into his lungs, monitors, and IVs, I would never have known he wasn't asleep.

Michael drew in his breath beside me. I wasn't breathing.

My son. My boy. Lying in the grim, cold reality of an ICU bed, unable to breathe on his own, unable to speak … unable to think. Not moving, his brain not responding. What had happened? My own brain was immobilized by the sight of my child in desperate trouble and that long-ago shadow of foreboding began to invade the corners of my mind. "It's me, darling…" I leaned over the bed, picked up his hand and put my face close to his. "Mommy's here … it's okay, Drew … Mommy's here." There was no sign that he heard me. No movement. Nothing.

Later that morning, we learned what little they knew. They called it a deep brain injury. The connectors—the white matter deep inside his brain—were burned out. Gone. He couldn't speak, he was unable to think.

"Our tox report shows evidence of marijuana and alcohol," the chief of toxicology told us. "We have one of the best toxicology facilities in the nation and there is no evidence of any hard drugs in his system."

I closed my eyes. I heard Michael take a deep breath. "Then what … ?" he asked.

"We don't know yet. He wasn't brought in for about twelve hours after the event began, so the alcohol content may be inaccurate—it's showing very low at 0.10—that's barely a couple of drinks. But it was measured many hours later."

"What about those so-called invisible drugs—like roofies—the date rape stuff?" Michael asked.

The doctor looked tired. His eyes were a light gray and they showed signs of strain as he spoke. "It's possible," he nodded.

"But we ran extensive tests, not once, but twice, to make sure—and we found nothing."

We were told dehydration was a factor. "At this high altitude, you combine strenuous activity with exhaustion, little or no real fluid, and a person will dehydrate very quickly," one doctor said. "And even a little alcohol compounds the problem."

The doctor matter-of-factly rattled off the symptoms: tiredness and shortness of breath at first, then dizziness and fainting—but if not treated quickly it can lead to shock, stroke, coma, and death. *Oh my god! Is that what we're looking at?*

Then I overheard the neurologist say the lack of oxygen to Drew's brain had set off multiple small strokes. "We're also looking at the MRI and seeing that an old stroke injury has been reactivated—retraumatized—since he lost consciousness," the neurologist said. "This injury to his brain is probably about nine-months old."

My eyes opened wide. "That's from that snowboarding accident he had in March—or was it April?" I said.

Michael nodded. "He showed me the place it happened—the slope he fell on when he cracked his head. It was solid ice."

That had happened eight months ago. Compounded by alcohol, dehydration—could this be the cause of what had happened?

We would find out later that day from some of his friends that Drew had hit his head the night before.

"We were in the living room and Drew was sitting on the couch—he bent down to pick something up off the floor," Tory said. "And when he raised his head, he hit the underneath of the table. Hard."

Was that what retriggered the strokes that night? But Tory said Drew seemed fine when he went to bed. His friends had no reason to think Drew wouldn't wake up.

Nobody knew. Why not? Dammit! I wanted to yell. Why don't you know? We can orbit Jupiter but no one can tell me anything about Drew's brain ... In the twenty-first century, with all its scientific mumbo-jumbo, the art of medicine is still a guessing game.

When all the tests were in, the snow accident could have been a major factor in Drew's condition. Or one of the triggers, anyway. Was it something like the Perfect Storm? Everything coming together at once? A head injury, alcohol, dehydration? I tried to form whole sentences in my mind, but through my shock, the words that came out were stilted and disjointed.

I stroked his head the way I'd done all his life when he was sick or hurting.

Drew's friends came in late that afternoon. They stood around him in stunned silence. "He was with us all night," Tory said. "We were all partying—nothing unusual, just had a couple drinks—Drew was having a great time ..." Those words fell through the quiet hum of the respirator like stones.

Kevin stood at Drew's bedside shaking his head. Devon was silent. His eyes were filled with tears.

❧

Our phones rang all day. Shocked and helpless friends called from all over the world wanting to know what had happened. Friends from Dubai. Members of my meditation group from Virginia who had woken up to my hastily written email from the night before. My sister called from Arkansas. Walt's sisters called. Our explanations fell on stunned silence hundreds and thousands of miles away. And all our explanations were inadequate.

All of us kept trying to wrap our heads around all the words. All these words! Liver trauma—kidney failure. Diagnosis, hypo-anoxia. No oxygen to the brain...Prognosis...Oh dear God!

My thoughts kept going to Michael.

He was much too young to deal with this. First his father and now his younger brother...but as that first day wore on, he found the courage we needed. When I had none left, he supported us both. He absorbed and processed the information coming at us from teams of physicians, nurses, and specialists. We perused their notes, then Michael logged into his laptop and searched and researched everything the doctors were giving us. We looked for hope in their words, in their actions—and in all the unsaid words where we knew there was little hope.

And through it all, Drew was silent. He remained still except for mild seizures that pulled and tightened his body every so often, drawing his strong shoulders inward. And then there was the harsh sound of his breathing, mingling with the hiss of the ventilator.

Early the next morning, an old friend called from Raleigh, North Carolina. It was my skiing friend Cindy. Drew and Cindy and I had spent many hours together in the tiny village of Vail, where her condo sits beside a stream on the edge of town.

"Yesterday I went out and walked and walked around the park trying to get some sense of this," Cindy said. "I began to pray. I said, 'Drew, don't leave your mother,' and then I ran, and as

I ran I had this picture of Drew in the mountains—the mountains we've visited and skied so many times...his face filled my vision against the mountains. Bright, white clouds surrounded him. Ginny, he looked like a child at Christmas time. Full of awe—and joy! He looked like a kid on Christmas morning!"

Drew's longtime girlfriend Brittany flew in from Washington, D. C., later that day. Devastated, her eyes swollen from crying, she and Michael hooked up music—I don't know—iPods and things, and played his songs beside his head on the pillows.

There was no encouragement over the next few days. Sunday, Monday, Tuesday came and went. My child lay in a deep coma showing no signs of pulling out.

Sometime on Tuesday evening, stressed to the point of overflowing, I said, "Okay Drew, wake up, dammit! This has gone on too long...wake up, Drew—*please, please wake up*... I'll take you home, baby—wake up and we'll go home."

As I lay my cheek on his, I remembered another evening from long ago. He was days away from his eighteenth birthday, there was a party going on at the lake, and I was pleading with him. *"Please don't go, Drew..."* the words came filtering back through the years—*"... it's pouring out there—don't go out in this rain..."*

"Gotta go, mom—don't worry..."

And I remembered the song he left playing over and over on his stereo downstairs. *"I Will Always Love You."* I know you're scared for me—don't worry. I have to go! He was saying through the song...

The memory of the sound of August rain pummeling the roof—and the sound of Whitney singing wouldn't leave me.

"*Wake up, Drew…*" I whispered again. But there was no response.

No response to me, and not even to the deep-pain stimuli the neurology team was trying. Nothing. Drew wasn't there. Never would be, they were saying. I could read between the words of their carefully spoken sentences. The meaning was exact. Clear. My mind wanted to reject the words and their meaning. It didn't seem to be able to absorb it all. But the meaning was clear. With every day that passed, the likelihood of Drew ever regaining any consciousness grew more remote.

On Wednesday, his team of doctors told us that if he ever regained any degree of consciousness, it would be slight. He would have to be cared for institutionally for the rest of his life, which might mean thirty years or more. There would be no cognitive ability should he wake up. He wouldn't know us … Doctors gave us more notes, more information that Michael typed into his laptop and verified. One conference followed another. The medical team, the neurology team, the nephrology and toxicology teams … Days turned into nights. And nothing changed.

My daughter, Karen, arrived with her husband, Randy, on Wednesday night. We stayed at Drew's side through Thanksgiving Day. Late that afternoon, following a final conference with his doctors, our hopes dwindled to nothing, and we released my son from the machines that supported his broken body.

Drew survived the night with us beside him. His breathing grew labored at dawn.

I stroked his arm and his face, tracing the strong black line of his eyebrows with my fingers, my heart breaking with every breath he struggled for. And I began to sing Whitney's song

"I Will Always Love You." My voice was a rough whisper. My mouth barely moved.

"I'm sorry, darling, I can't sing very well today ..."

The echo of his voice from long ago came through my tears. "Gotta go, Mom! Don't cry."

"Gotta go ... "

∽๑

I fell asleep on the couch by the window of his hospital room in the early afternoon. His music was playing softly, and the Arkansas Razorbacks played Louisiana State University silently on the TV screen. Karen sang to him and looked for music he liked on her computer. Michael kept a vigil beside his brother, stroking his head, holding his hand, his heart breaking. He was longing for the support of his wife who was home in New York with their children. And I suspect, the support of his father.

"Let go, Drew." I heard him whisper. "You can go. *That's it Drew!* Just let go."

∽๑

Light snow was falling on the park across the street. I felt Randy, my son-in-law, cover me with a blanket, and I fell into a deep sleep. After what must have been about an hour, I awoke.

I was wide awake with my eyes closed, lying very still on the couch. My awareness was at its peak. The center of my being was still and focused. I was more alert than I had been for a week and I sensed that something was happening. Something had changed.

I could feel that there was someone new in the room … a different presence … I didn't move, didn't open my eyes, but mentally I began to count.

There was me and Drew, I could hear him breathing … and Michael and Karen and Randy. *And somebody else.* I could feel the energy of a strong, new personality. I felt its substance as solidly as I felt my own. It felt as though tiny antennae bristling all over me had picked up this presence. It was male. I felt him over by the respirator. He was a mass of energy I could feel on every level, in every layer of my being … his presence was strong, my focus was on his eyes, which were very, very blue.

I sat up quickly and opened my eyes knowing I wouldn't see anyone, and as they all turned to look at me I stood up and said, "Walter's here." I grabbed for my coat, pulling it on as fast as I could. "I have to go," I announced. My words fell harshly in the stunned silence.

"Mom!" Michael looked at me, eyes wide, not understanding. He pushed himself away from the bed, walked over to where I was struggling with my coat sleeves. "Where are you going?"

"I don't know—I've got to leave …" I felt driven, completely sure that I had to get out of there. It made no sense. "I'll go to the hotel."

He put his hands on my shoulders saying quietly, "Are you sure?"

I nodded vigorously. It had been my intent to be here until the end. If that was to be an hour or another day or … forever I would be here with Drew. *But something had changed.*

"Mom—Listen." He stared intently at me. "You know Drew may … go while you're gone …"

"Yes," I nodded, looking him straight in the eye. "It's okay. Your dad's here now." I repeated. Something was moving me out of here. I could feel the insistent pull drawing me to the door like a strong, invisible current.

He squeezed my arm gently. "Are you going to be all right with that—if Drew…leaves?"

Again, I nodded strongly. "Yes."

He let me go and stood aside as I walked to my baby's bedside. I bent down, stroked his cheek and kissed his brow for the last time, and whispered, "I'll be back in a half hour, Drew."

⁓

I raced back to the hotel not knowing why. The wind was bitter, lifting my hair, stinging my cheeks. It was snowing and sleeting and I could feel the cold sting of ice on my face. All around me, people were going about their business probably wondering who this woman was running down the sidewalk. I didn't know her either. At one point I heard somebody yell, "Careful lady! It's getting slick!" A taxi honked beside me and somebody ran to grab it, jostling me as he swept by. I hardly felt a thing.

The hotel was up ahead of me, its peaked roof was painted green. The traffic light ahead turned green as I ran toward it, catching it before it turned. I was out of breath. My chest was hurting as I crossed a small bridge that took me over the stream that ran in front of the hotel.

Then I was in front of the outside door, pulling it toward me. I stopped in the middle of the lobby looking around, but registering nothing. A bellman was staring at me. I turned and headed for the elevators.

The doors opened onto the longest hallway I'd ever seen, which seemed to disappear into the distance. Somehow I found my room. My fingers felt frozen inside my gloves as they clumsily inserted the room card into the door slot.

I should make some coffee, I thought. That's nuts! Take a shower. I'll have a shower. That's it. I'll wash my hair. Oh dear God! I held my hands to my face trying to get my breath. What was I doing? Why was I in this hotel room? Why the hell was I in Denver? I should be at the lake with Ranger and Miss Kitty getting ready to light a fire in the wood-burning fireplace. Did I have any starter logs? My mind was reeling, spinning wildly.

"Okay, breathe," I told myself. "Calm down." I inhaled deeply and placed both hands on the desk, leaning toward it. My gloves were soaked. I peeled them off and placed them neatly on the corner, then slowly I straightened up and walked across the room to the window.

It was disorienting to stand here and watch everything turning white outside. As I stood there staring down at the parking lot, it felt as though I was standing in a void … barely existing, barely conscious of the room, its furniture, the humming of the heating vent—and the snow batting against the window. There was a white emptiness all around, and in the center of it was an unfeeling, unseeing, nonentity that had been me.

After a while, when time hung in suspension, the silence around me was broken as suddenly and sharply as a sheet of cracking ice by the sound of the telephone. It was a rifle shot to my heart.

I lifted the hotel phone receiver and held it to my ear. "Mom?" It was Michael. "Drew's gone." There was silence.

Then, "Thank you, darling," I whispered. "I'm leaving now."

"Be careful," he said.

Drew died half an hour after I left his room. He died at 3:20 on November 28, 2008. The ticking of ice on the window had stopped. Snow fell gently on the city. It blanketed the asphalt, the brick walkway, and the street near the hospital. No birds sang. Nothing moved but the steady, white flutter of Rocky Mountain snow. Denver lay still beneath its crystals. Still as death, and the silence that comes with snow and dying.

I pulled on my wet gloves and walked slowly back to the hospital.

I hadn't made it back to Drew in time. What happened? My whole being had been consumed with the thought of him dying. But I wasn't there when he … what happened? My eyes were blurred, and it wasn't the misting snow. I had never planned to leave him. My sole intent was to see him through to the end—whatever that might be—to stay beside him. Not to leave him. But I had left.

When I thought about this, much later, I remembered something I'd read about death and dying, and one paragraph from that long-ago book jumped out at me. It talked about how very often, a loved one won't leave until the person or people closest to him have left the room. Sometimes all it takes is for someone to leave for a few minutes to get a cup of coffee or a newspaper. That's when they choose to go. That's what Drew did, I thought in amazement. It was just too hard to leave because the energy of my love and my grief were holding him back. It was easier for him to go after I left the room and because I had no intention of leaving … someone … Drew or Walt, had been forced to *make* me leave.

Since then I've read of that phenomena many times and learned that hospices and hospital staff see it all the time.

❦

During the following days, other people and the bureaucracy of death took over. Friends kept calling. Dorothy, Cindy's old friend and my new friend, called. Dorothy was in her eighties and she still skied the black diamond slopes, outskiing most people half her age. Drew met her only once, but he never forgot the energy of this tiny Western lady, busting with life. She gave him her card, which had inscribed on it:

"ASPIRE TO INSPIRE
BEFORE YOU EXPIRE."

I found it in his wallet when I got home.

Michael's wife, Mary Katherine, flew in from New York to be with us. They left the city the following day for Vail and the job of emptying out Drew's apartment.

Karen and I followed two days later, driving through the mountains to the slopes of Moonrise Mountain where Drew had lived and worked. Snow had been falling relentlessly for three days. A blizzard and icy conditions forced the closure of roads in and around Denver and in the mountains. Vail Pass opened briefly and we pressed through as fast or as slowly as the backed-up traffic allowed.

We were quiet. I noticed tiny lines of stress around my daughter's eyes. Driving in ice and snow wasn't something we got used to in Virginia. Her red-brown hair framed a face that hadn't had enough sleep lately. However, her eyes—that bright, light clear blue you sometimes see in dark-haired people and so like her father's—were sharp, watching every rib and skid mark in the salt-coated road. Ahead of us, Highway 70 wound through the mountains, hidden in frozen mist. The world was bright, winter white and crystal clear, the mouth of the Eisenhower Tunnel a dark void, in the wilderness. A round, black, sightless eye, embedded in the mountain. Snow banks mounded high and silently on the hillside slopes, and deep ravines plunged into the invisible depths of the valleys.

$$\approx\!\!\!\curvearrowright$$

Vail Valley was ten feet deep in snow when we got there. The plows worked ceaselessly. We drove on through the valley and up through the snowy canyons to the Moonrise Mountain Lodge where we were staying.

We went through all the motions of meeting, greeting, then saying goodbye to Drew's stunned and heartbroken friends and coworkers on the mountain. We were cared for and comforted by them, and the warmth of our visit, and their love for Drew lifted me to a place higher than ozone, which I was already breathing too much of. I think it numbed my mind, because I couldn't remember very much of those three days.

The Tuesday following Drew's passing, Michael and Mary Katherine left for New York; a day later, Karen and I drove back to Denver to await Drew's ashes before leaving Colorado.

$$\approx\!\!\!\curvearrowright$$

It was a beautiful early-winter morning. I remember that. The snowstorm had passed and we drove through the sunlit Rockies, blue sky above towering peaks, their sharp edges softened by the depth of snow that had fallen.

It was twenty-one days until Christmas. I wished I'd spent Christmas with Drew last year. I had mentioned it to Drew but he told me he'd be working over the holidays, so I decided to wait and go later. I wished I hadn't. I wished I had spent his last Christmas with him.

Karen and I drove on, sometimes in silence, sometimes finding words to say to each other, and sometimes just breathing in the beauty and strength of these mountains. Mostly, we drove on in numb disbelief, refusing to believe that Drew was gone.

We drove on, winding our way down the Front Range of the Colorado Rockies, completely unaware that ahead of us, on the Denver plain, a door had swung open. It was a doorway into another dimension. Karen and I were headed toward an invisible gateway that had cracked open while we were gone—allowing in a shaft of light.

A Shaft of Light

*T*he hotel room on the edge of town not far from the hospital was quiet, dimly lit, and cluttered after our ten-day stay. I sat in a deep chair by the window. Karen was repacking a suitcase, sitting cross-legged on the floor. The television was on with the volume low, and I stared at it blindly.

My mind was numb. My heart had sunk into some deep shadow place I couldn't find. I watched absently as Karen folded and refolded clothes, her trance-like movements in step with the slow motion of my empty mind.

And then it happened.

My senses began to bristle as I became aware of a soft light that seemed to fill the space between Karen and me. I blinked. It was bright, translucent, tinged with blue. My physical being became very still. My eyes were open and trying to focus on something they couldn't see … my sixth sense, my spirit, watched in awe as the light brightened and grew, becoming blue as Columbine skies. Right in front of me, surrounded by this light, was Drew. In spirit. All I could see were his head and shoulders. He was physically much larger than normal. His hair was dark, curly brown and his cheeks were flushed. His eyes were bright. He was alive, whole, feeling, moving inside the light.

I couldn't breathe. The hair on my neck and arms prickled, and I felt chills quivering on my legs.

"Drew's here!" I whispered. I wanted Karen to know. The calm in my voice and the certainty that filled my being startled me, but my focus remained unbroken.

"Drew?" Karen raised her head, a blank look on her face. Then before she could say anything, feeling strangely removed from my physical place, I began to tell her what I was seeing.

"He's crying. Sobbing so hard I can see his shoulders shaking. His eyes are squeezed shut, and his breath is rasping and wet with tears. I can hear him crying." His voice, when I heard him speak, was ragged, gasping. "He's so sad—for us."

I felt, rather than heard, his words. It was like thoughts in my head. The thoughts were loud and coming very quickly, almost staccato and missing in places. The communication was, *I didn't do anything to cause this! I'm so sorry.*

He was distraught, unbelieving. *Something happened inside,* I heard him say. Then I got, *It just happened. My head, something happened in my head … Don't let them say I did anything wrong—drugs didn't kill me … drinks and pot, didn't help … combination of a lot of things contributed. It was my head—something happened … no pain. I think I was asleep.*

"Oh Drew!" I spoke out loud to my son, trying to reach through the racking sobs and disbelief. "That's what we think too ..."

I felt his energy relax momentarily. Then his distress became heavier and I could see his face contorting under the stress. The atmosphere around him was saturated in sorrow, confusion. He seemed to be on the edge of hysteria and I was crying too.

I was seeing and hearing and feeling Drew in a way I would never have imagined for myself. I felt helpless, and my feelings of helplessness were magnified by the improbability that this distance between us, this unthinkable divide, could be breached. Or could it? How could I reach him? I had to reach my son. My eyes filled with tears and I felt myself craning toward him, anxiety tugging me to ... where? *Think.* I thought desperately. My fingers dug into the arms of the chair, and perspiration peppered my face. Our suite felt oppressive, closed in, and was much too warm. I could smell the apples we had bought over a week ago and left uneaten on the kitchen counter. My mind scanned a hundred half-forgotten lessons in rapid succession, the speakers I'd heard and all the areas that had dealt with confusion and fear in spirit. *Remember!* The answers were there. Then slowly they began to emerge. One by one they fell into place, lining up, pushing through the murk, reminding me of what I could do.

I breathed deeply forcing myself to be calm. I said, "Drew, where are you?"

There was quiet, and then a silent thought came through from somewhere outside of myself. From him. It felt like— AWE. He was looking all around, seeing and showing me what he was seeing. Mountains—higher than any I had ever seen— emerged from the clear, blue light around him. They were stark, high-peaked, and deeper blue than any blue I have ever seen. Electric blue mountains, infused and surrounded by clear light.

The sensation I felt in and around Drew was one of wonder and amazement. The emotion I felt in him was stronger than any emotion I have felt in my life here on earth. My mind was spinning. Pulling my rampant thoughts together, I began reaching for and pulling together the sentences out of some long-forgotten book whose authors had written about souls and crossing over to the other side. "Listen to me, Drew," I was saying, employing a shaky Mommy tone. Forcing myself to think calmly, organizing my thoughts, and drawing on a well of half-remembered knowledge, I knew I had to move him from this place of abject distress. "We have to move you. There should be a bright light somewhere. Look around you. Can you see a bright patch of light anywhere? It's probably a very bright light."

I waited in the silence. *Come on, Drew.* "Keep looking, I know it's there somewhere." And then in answer, a wide shaft of searing light emerged from the blue. I say "searing," but in truth, although it was brighter than any light I have ever seen, it was a soft light with no glare to hurt my eyes. "Can you see that, Drew?" I whispered.

As I watched in silence, the light swept a clearing in the deep blue aura emanating from the mountains. And then it began to widen, becoming softer, and as it grew it began to glow. The scene in front of me felt awash in warmth and I knew he could see it too—that I was being shown it through his eyes. I waited quietly, feeling something like love that flowed unhindered from its essence. It was gentle and powerful and at the same time, deep and strong and all encompassing. It filled the space where fear had been with peace. In the stillness, everything felt gentler, quieter, and calmer.

Drew's essence was changing. It felt to me as though he was shedding his confusion. The fear was dissipating. The medium he was in felt light now and I could tell that he was moving.

"Go toward that clearing, Drew," I whispered. "The light, Drew, walk toward it. See what's there … go inside it, go through it … beyond it." I felt his energy shift again. He seemed to hesitate. "It's okay, sweet Drew …" I breathed. "I'm with you, darling. I can see what you see. I won't leave you. It's okay."

I watched and waited, somehow knowing that things were changing. Then I saw Walt. He was walking toward us though the light. And to my amazement there was Cassie walking beside him! Drew's old Lab. Tail wagging, tongue lolling, Labrador hips sashaying toward him. She looked two years old again. Her coat shone with health and she had that funny smile on her face that wiggled her whole body when she was pleased. Then I looked at my husband. He was young, vibrant, and dark-haired as I had known him when we fell in love all those years ago. Tears were rolling down my face but I hardly felt them.

"Look Drew! Do you see Dad?" I asked out loud. I felt him move again and then I felt that movement quicken. "Go to him, darling—he's waiting for you."

Then the light faded, the blue light around the mountains retreated, and the vision was gone.

❧

"Mom!" Karen was on her feet, the blood drained from her face. She was staring at me. "Are you okay?"

"Did I tell you your dad was carrying a knapsack?" I asked. My cheeks felt flushed, my heart was pressing against my ribs. "And carrying a long walking stick?" I laughed through my tears. "When has your dad EVER owned a knapsack—or gone mountain hiking!"

"Never," she said matter-of-factly. I think she put her arms around me. Then we were both crying.

"And Cassie—and the puppies—I almost forgot the puppies!" I sniffed loudly. There were two or three Lab puppies running beside her ..."

We stared at each other. "The puppies Cassie lost!" She blurted. "One was still-born, and do you remember—I stroked and massaged another one and it began to move!"

We both began to laugh. In the strangest way, I was euphorically happy. I'd seen my boy. Through his fear and confusion, not understanding what had happened, Drew had breached the membrane of so-called death to find me. He wanted to tell me that he lived.

Propelled by the vibrant emotions of unknowable fear, confusion, and panic, my son had found me. And I began to pray to whoever was listening to help us.

"You've got to write this down, Mom ..." My daughter's voice seemed to come from a distance.

❧

We found out that they had cremated Drew's body yesterday afternoon.

Could it be that his so-recently separated spirit had been floating in some foggy realm, uncertain, confused, lost, shocked, disbelieving ... and that this act of final destruction of his earthly body suddenly hit him that he was indeed *dead?* Why do all the books you read tell of souls wandering down tunnels into the light, happy as clams, not wanting to return when given the choice—and then this? Perhaps the confusion is a part of sudden, premature death? I believe that. Drew would have been devastated for me, for us, and for him. I believe he would have tried to find me.

The words of Mohandas Gandhi came back to me, jumping from the pages of that book I read many years ago. *"The more I observe and study things, the more convinced I become that sorrow over separation and death is perhaps the greatest illusion ... there is no death, no separation of substance ... "* I had to keep reminding myself of the great man's quote, letting it soak in to my shattered mind like warm honey—soothing, healing, filling the emptiness. It was not in my makeup to accept that Drew was gone from us forever. Obliterated. That quote stayed with me through the long night and through the days that followed.

～○

My first night at home in Virginia was cold, empty, and grim.

Jim met me at the airport. He had been staying in my house looking after Cassie's only surviving puppy—my sweet old Labrador, Ranger, who was twelve years old now. And Miss Kitty, a feisty little throwaway who had found her way to our house about four years ago.

On the night that Walt died, Miss Kitty climbed up onto my bed and purred all night. She never left me. Night after night, after night, Miss Kitty lay beside me and purred. She had never done that before.

Back home again, exhausted and shattered, I sat next to Jim until the early morning hours. Sometimes in silence, sometimes in tears. Jim, Miss Kitty, Ranger, and me.

"While you were in Colorado, I saw three doves," Jim said somewhere around dawn. "Mourning doves. They were perched on the railing on the lake side of the deck. Two of them were staring into the house. And as I watched, the third rose, peeled off, and flew out across the water." He said it made him think of my three children. "It looked as though they were visiting their home together, one last time."

I've read that birds can be a vehicle of spirit. Indian lore says they can be messengers from the other side.

I pondered this as waves of exhaustion washed over me. Through the mists of near sleep, I began to relive the events of that day. The pungent smell of jet-fuel clouded my head; the seats were small and cramped. Then I felt American Airlines lift their 777 off the smoky runway of my half-awake state, and away from Denver's mile high airport. I heard music through my headphones. It was a song from way back. I don't remember who sang it, but it was called Red Rubber Ball.

Now safe at home, sleep finally came. I slept soundly following the grueling day of flying across the country with Drew's ashes by my side. Never in my wildest dreams did I think I'd be bringing my child home this way. It was a thought too dark to contemplate right now.

Pure, gentle darkness invaded my injured soul, carried me to a place of peace and quiet. Then there was nothing but sweet oblivion.

Seven

Stay with Me

*S*omething woke me very early in the morning. It had happened yesterday, too. And the day before, and the day before that. How long had I been home? About a week ... weeks?

My eyelids twitched, and I felt rather than heard the murmuring of the warm air breathing from the air-conditioning vents on the wall. No light came through the shutters of my room. If I opened my eyes, there would be no shadows. There must not be a moon tonight.

And then I heard it. Dolly Parton's song was playing on the shattered plain of my mind. The melody rising and falling with every breath, whispering through the tears that surged like the incoming tide, filling my still closed eyes.

I Will Always Love You. I knew that long before my children were born, long before they were ever conceived. Long before I understood this kind of love. Or who we really are. And now that one of them was gone ... out there ... somewhere ... it was as true now as it was meant to be, even before either of us was born. I drifted back to sleep.

I opened my eyes to the first glimmer of dawn. Where was I? This was my own bedroom. That's strange, I had the distinct impression I was somewhere else.

But ... where *was* I?

That song!

I had been dreaming. Dreaming I'd seen Drew ... Drew was there ... That wasn't a dream I'd just woken from—not a *dream* dream—*I was with Drew*. Right before the song.

This was the first dream I'd had since Drew died. I lay very still, closed my eyes, and tried to bring it back. Slowly it began to emerge, one shadow, one shape at a time blooming from the mists of that elusive place where dreams hide. It continued to reconstruct itself as I lay there with my eyes closed, arms at my sides, barely breathing. Changing shapes began taking form, shifting, solidifying, and becoming recognizable.

In the dream, I was walking through deep carpeted hallways flooded with amber-colored light that seemed to come from the walls. They were thick, cream-colored walls that looked soft to the touch.

The place I was in was a very big, strange hotel. On either side of the hallway were reception rooms and small lounges. A banquet hall ... a library.

There was a corridor that led me to a door that opened to the outside of the hotel. High walls of sand-colored adobe sheltered deep balconies with wide, rounded window boxes filled with plants. I leaned over the balcony wall, looked down and saw a tangle of waterways—moats encircled the building, wound through gardens, disappeared underground, then curled back and away through the mists ...

There was an empty patio table and chairs beside me on the balcony, and I sat down.

I was alone. Then I saw Drew ... He appeared not to notice me as he passed on my left without looking at me, without breaking his stride. He was wearing cream-colored or beige long shorts and an oversized T-shirt of the same color. He seemed to walk in that amber glow emanating from the backdrop of the dream. Or did it come from him?

Then I noticed him deliberately trailing his right hand behind him. My heart was beating hard as I reached out and grasped his fingers and they clasped mine.

It was Drew. They were his fingers. Physical. Warm and solid. I could feel the texture of his skin—I felt the heat from his body as he passed, filling me with warmth. And then he was gone.

Leaving me with that song. The way he used to.

❧

Slowly I turned my head to the light coming through the bedroom shutters. The room was warm on this cold December morning. There was frost on the French panes.

It was Drew. He touched my hand ... It had been nearly two weeks since he had left us in Denver.

Pale yellow smears of dawn streaked with silver were coloring the sky outside my bedroom. The warmth of the dream enveloped me as I lay there. The feel of his skin, the *knowingness* I feel that he was here—or was I there—filled me with hope.

Drew was here.

After a while, I lifted myself to a sitting position and gazed through the shutters at another day being born. It was another chance to live. The faint light was urging me to feel, to see again. It beckoned me ... come out and *be*.

Then the now familiar pressure began to build in my chest, tightened my throat, welled behind my eyes, surging from some depth inside me I didn't know was there. The growing brightness outside my window couldn't break through, couldn't lighten the dark where the light that is Drew went out. All it did was remind me that another day had begun. He wasn't here. He was gone.

Another horrible day, for God's sake. I didn't want it. Take it away! Flinging myself back against the pillows, grief washed over me like a giant wave. It seized my whole being, shaking my shoulders, my torso, all of me. Wrenching my heart from a place too deep for me to find, the dam burst and my tears wouldn't stop until the rims of my eyes were raw and stinging, my voice when I cried out *"Oh Godddd!"* was hoarse, and the inside of my head swelled, pushed against the smooth inner skull, trying to burst through the bone. I wished it would.

But eventually I got up as I'd done every day since Drew left. The soul quake was gone for now and I did what I'd always done. Walked to the bathroom. Brushed my hair. It was standing on end. There were dark smudges under my reddened eyes. I looked like Michael Keaton in *Beetlejuice* ... I carefully checked my eyes for any signs of wildness—madness or whatever. They were brown. So were Drew's. And sad. But they didn't look crazy. What a shame. Crazy might not be a bad place to be, I thought, pulling loose hair out of my brush. Anything would be better than this. I washed my face, scrubbing at the mascara I'd left on last night. That made my cheekbones red and flaky.

I tried to figure out what to do today. I couldn't. It would just have to unfold whichever way it did. I couldn't worry about it. Maybe I'd die, and that would be fine, too.

That was when a sliver of peace, as thin and tenuous as the pale yellow dawn, seeped in.

There was something to this stuff about going with the flow. It worked when you didn't have the will or the energy to do anything else.

Drew was with me this morning. I know it was Drew, I felt him and sensed him and felt his love. He'll come again.

‿◌

Drew's gone. We lost Drew. Even now those words are hard to comprehend, hard to think. My heart and my world broke in two when Drew left. He was gone and so were the memories we shared, the past we shared. Our family had lost our future with him. When he left, we lost his potential, we lost our hopes and dreams for him and for us. I lost a child, and it was as though some giant subterranean force had thrown my life up in the air and brought it crashing down in a million different pieces. Nothing would ever be the same. I felt robbed and the "what-ifs" were the cruelest snares. What if we'd known something was wrong. What if he had? What if, what if?... The foundations of my life were nowhere to be found. Everything had crumbled to ash. Shocked and stunned, I found myself scrambling through the miasma of his sudden death, looking for all the teaching I have ever had, from all the teachers I have ever known.

Through all of the mind-numbing horror, through the swampland of loss, through this deepest cut of all that follows the death of a child, I clung to this teacher named Death. I had to know more. Never, during all of my sessions with or without a study group, had I felt such an intense need to learn. And never did I realize that all the knowledge I had accumulated and stored as "interesting" would become so personal, so soon.

It was becoming clear that I needed help, and on that note, I acted on a thought I'd been toying with for three days, and made an appointment with Rosalind the shaman from Canyon Springs. It struck me that in my vulnerable state of mind, this might be madness. But I didn't give a damn.

I had to find out about Drew. I knew what I knew, but it wasn't enough. I needed some sort of validation from somewhere outside myself that he was safe—not lurking around like some sad ghost out of a B-movie, or wandering through the universe knocking on locked doors ...

Rosalind was busy, so I had to wait a week. On the morning of my telephone appointment, I woke up later than usual and I lay there wondering what I would say to her and what she would say back. Should I trick her by not telling her that Drew had died? See what she'd come up with when I said, "What about Drew?" That made me squirm. Maybe not. I'd just be testing her. What if she picked up nothing? What if nothing came to her at all? Nothing about Drew, that is. Or worse, what if she told me he was alive and well and having a blast snowboarding on the slopes? Well, that would settle that. It would just be a wasted call.

But that didn't make any sense. I already knew about her abilities. Maybe I'd just tell her he'd died and let her do the rest without any prompting. That felt better. She didn't need me laying out the whole scenario for her. If she knew he'd passed with none of the details, she should be able to pick up the rest. And wasn't that what I wanted? I already knew he was gone—didn't need her to tell me that. What I needed from Rosalind was to find out where he was now. So, I'd tell her that Drew died and leave it at that. That's what I'll do. No leading questions from me, no interruptions. A minimum amount of information.

Good. With that settled, it dawned on me that I had actually made a decision. Not a big one, but it was a thrust in the right direction. Through the mass of alien events and uncontrolled thoughts that had swamped my life in the last few weeks, it felt good. I was in charge! Decisive.

I climbed out of bed, put myself into the shower cubicle with the glass door and stood there letting the water cascade through my hair, down my neck, and over my shoulders. Then tears filled my eyes as sadness drifted in through the cracks, bringing with it the cold sting of grief that went straight to my heart. "Oh Walt," I cried. "I lost our child … I'm so sorry. I lost our child …" I coughed as water went up my nose and the action refocused my attention on the water. Reaching up, I twisted the shower head toward me and forced my mind to be still.

Slowly, the steam built up, filling the shower with warm vapor. The water pelted my shoulders, its sound drummed out the noise of my thoughts. My shoulders relaxed, and I allowed myself to blend into the feel of the pinpricks of hot water that tingled my cheeks, the steady stream that coursed down my back and over my legs. Lathering my hair with pale green shampoo, rubbing my scalp hard, I squeezed my eyes shut and breathed in the scent of fresh apples. My mind wandered to a summer day, an untended orchard … green apples hanging in clusters from the boughs of gnarly old trees. I could smell the ripe aroma of fermentation wafting from fallen apples rotting in the stubby grass around the trunk. Some half-eaten or pecked by jays—or crows.

The shampoo bubbles made me sneeze. Scrubbing bubbles. My imagination carried them aloft with their funny smiling faces, had them dancing in the spray, sinking into my scalp, sliding down my arms. Laughing. How silly. I smoothed my hair back and, standing ankle deep in soapy suds, I listened to the water gurgle down the drain. For the first time in days, I felt a dim glow of pleasure. So strange that this most mundane act of taking a hot shower could bring something approaching peace—warming the icy cold inside me, if only for a moment.

Standing in front of the mirror with hair dryer in hand, staring at my hair, light blond and blown to a bouncy swirl around my head, I poked at my cheeks trying hard to lift the hollows below my cheekbones. They turned pink, but the hollows didn't budge. Like the sadness in my eyes—there was no sparkle now. I penciled a dark-brown line underneath them to see if that would help. And then I turned away.

Would this be easier if Walt was here? I don't know the answer. Women grieve differently than men. I've heard that a lot of marriages break up over the death of a child. It's a crazy thing. Sorrow added to sorrow. You and I will never know, I told Walt in my heart. I just know that there's a part of me that is very glad he was spared this terrible grief.

❧

The morning morphed into midday and the shadows lengthened as the winter sun slipped lower behind the clouds that had formed in the west. And on that cold January afternoon, I sat on the couch with the phone to my ear, listening to Rosalind.

As she began to speak, I could almost picture the tiny house we sat in with its beaded curtains, brightly colored rugs, and the scent of sage. She picked Drew's Spirit up easily. "I'm getting him... he's so sad... or is that your sadness I'm picking up?"

She paused. I waited.

Then, "Did you sing to him in the hospital? He's saying that you were singing to him... He wasn't there, you know—in the bed—his spirit was—out—in the room. I know that because there's a white dove right above the bed."

My heart was barely beating. He heard us singing.

It was almost as though Rosalind was talking to herself, "No, I'm feeling your grief, but he's definitely feeling a lot of sadness... it's all around him."

Silence.

"We have to help him—he's saying he's confused... wants to be with you... wants to feel your love like he did when he was young." After a pause she said, "Okay I get it," more to herself than to me. "I've got an idea. Just stay with me Ginny and listen... go along... There's an ancient grief ritual I know of that we can use."

I waited, then together, with me listening and her talking, we traveled down the rivers, through the woodlands, and onto the windswept prairies of Native American lore. She transported me with her words through the ancient ways of the Lakota and through the rituals of grief.

Guided by Rosalind through that unique zone of consciousness that is neither here nor there, I called Drew's spirit to me, held him close, and watched as my soul fused with his in that special bond of mother and child, love and happiness. I felt his being engulfed by my soul as both of us immersed our ethereal beings in the warm liquidity of enchantment, comfort, and joy. I felt our sadness shrink as the powerful bond of love saturated our souls, immersing us in the knowledge of our eternal togetherness.

After about an hour I told Rosalind, "He feels lighter. His energy feels much lighter!" My cheeks felt flushed and damp, and the room was warm in the firelight.

"It is. He's much lighter and so are you," she answered. I could hear tears in her voice. "He's been longing for that contact. He needed to be that little boy again, loved and warmed by his mother's love. It's given him the strength he needs to move on. He wanted to just be with his mommy. To feel safe and secure and understand that it's safe to take the next step."

And I needed that little boy again. I needed to feel his closeness to give me the courage to take my next step, which was to come only a few days later.

❧

The next day, still following Rosalind's guidance, I continued the ritual. I banked some wood in the fireplace and turned off the phone. I asked close friends to leave me alone for a few days so they wouldn't be stopping by.

Rosalind had said, "You must get a white candle with a dove imprinted on it. You know, a stencil or painted, or something."

This was harder to come by than you might think. In a life turned upside down as mine had been, I was lucky if I could figure out which room I was standing in, let alone find a candle. But after a look through the linen closet, the pantry, and the drawer under the TV, I finally found it in the buffet in the dining room, where all the candles had been kept for ten years or more. There was a plain white candle and a votive glass to hold it, but no dove sketched on its side. It would have to do.

In that same buffet drawer, I found some chocolate left over from Christmas. Not a requirement, but a nice touch I thought. It tasted like crap. Musty. But I began to get used to it, and as I went about my preparations, it actually began to taste okay. Not bad at all.

"And white roses," she advised. "They are for eternal love."

Must have white roses … But it was mid-January. Undaunted, I dragged on a pair of old blue jeans and one of Drew's sweaters and drove myself into the village to the flower shop. They had a few scentless, force-fed white roses in a glass-fronted cooler, so I bought them. I had known the store owner for years, but as I stood at the counter watching her wrap the flowers and cluck around me, I realized I had no clue what her name was.

"Dear, are you all right?" She was staring at me.

No I'm not all right. I wanted to say. I'm bloody awful. Half crazy, in fact. But I managed a smile instead. "Yes. Sorry." I shook my head and handed her a fistful of ones. How much had she told me the roses were? "I was … in another world."

"I know," she said casting her eyes down sorrowfully. She patted my hand and handed me the flowers and three extra dollar bills. This was crazy. I recognized her bubbly blond hair and her pretty smile, and all I could do was stand there and stare at her while I tried to remember her name. The refrigerators full of scentless flowers blurred behind her while I racked my crippled mind. Nothing.

A bowl of chocolate drops sat on the counter and I reached inside it and picked up a handful. I saw her eyebrows pop. Are you only allowed to take one? I wondered. Then crammed them all into my mouth. That's it! *Charlene.* I remembered.

The doorbell chimed signaling the arrival of an old man into the flower shop. "Thanks, Charlene." I smiled and waved to her over the top of my bouquet. These chocolates were magic.

There was one last thing to do after I got home.

I walked down to the closet under the stairs and pulled out the old boxes of baby pictures, family pictures of old vacations, and old kindergarten report cards. I tucked a Mother's Day card he'd made me under my arm and a birthday card for me from his year in the first grade.

There was the third-grade dinosaur report I'd worked on all night while he slept. I found stories he'd written when he was ten. More stories he'd written when he was eleven. That was his "prolific author" phase.

And a letter from the teacher who threw him out of swimming class when he was four.

These things happen. I think he learned to swim the very next summer, all by himself in the lake.

Football pictures … baseball pictures. Birthday pictures of scruffy little boys, and a turreted, castle cake covered with confetti icing.

Out came the prom pictures of Drew, in a really unsuitable white sports coat. That was my idea, not his. It was probably some weird reminiscing on my part about Pat Boone's song from the 1950s. Needless to say, the former heartthrob's look didn't work quite so well in the '80s.

Then I picked up an oblong box lying in the bottom of another box and opened it. It held his Baptismal candle wrapped in tissue paper, prompting my mind to take a long backward leap.

It had been a hot and sunny Sunday afternoon in Dubai when we baptized Drew. The eucalyptus trees outside the church windows were dusty and droopy, and the portly Italian priest was sweating. So were we. We were having difficulty deciphering the prelate's English that rose and fell with melodious Italian emphasis. This was the beginning of Drew's religious upbringing, which continued through his confirmation sixteen years later because I believe in finishing what you've started.

Taking the candle out if its paper, I held it up and stared at it. I blinked to clear my eyes—"…look it this!" I whispered in awe. There was a white dove imprinted on the side of Drew's Baptismal candle. I ran my finger over the red and gold graphics underneath the dove. *"Alpha and Omega."* The beginning and the end. The engraving glittered in the shadowy light of the closet. *"I am the Alpha and the Omega,"* Jesus Christ said. This candle represented the beginning and the end for Drew. Soon it would be flaming and lighting the way through an ancient and spiritual Native American grief ritual. The candle would bring two cultures together. How very ecumenical. How very—*right.*

"Thank you," I whispered, and walked slowly up the stairs with my treasures.

With my memorabilia, the candles, and the flowers, the stage was set for the grief ritual.

I pulled on a pair of bleach-splattered warm-ups, chilled the wine, and put a bar of Hershey's chocolate on the coffee table in front of me. The roses were in a cut glass vase, a present from Walt when Drew was born, and a smiling picture of my son stood beside them.

The candles were lit. There were three of them burning. One in a jar that would burn continuously until it went out, the tall white Baptismal candle beside it, and the one I had found in the buffet drawer, also tall and white.

I settled down among the cushions on the couch and breathed deeply.

For three days (that's how long the candles lasted) I immersed myself in Drew's life and in thoughts of our life together.

As the memories flowed from some long-forgotten springs and wells, I talked to him, I laughed with him, I cried with him. My canoe followed the river that swelled with joy and tears, overflowing its banks, cascading through the years of Drew's short life. Funny how I could remember all the details.

Holding a dog-eared, dirt-smudged piece of paper in my hand, I asked him about those notes from the teacher that he had signed my name to.

"And what about the time when you and Davy and Clay decided to go mudding in an open field and used an old crane to pull your truck out of the mud? That cost us a new tailgate!" The room was still. The fire crackled in the grate. My old Lab, Ranger, was curled up beside it.

As I thought back to that afternoon of the tailgate incident, a whoosh of warm air engulfed me and I stared hard, once again, upon the spirit of my son.

He was standing in front of me surrounded by that same soft light with his hands on his hips, laughing. The striped T-shirt and khaki shorts he wore were rumpled, and the baseball cap with the Braves logo was twisted backwards.

I remember it had been raining cats and dogs all day. The mud was up to the fenders, but I just knew that pickup could do anything.

It was his voice. The words came quickly. And just as they had done in the hotel room in Denver, I sensed rather than heard them. It was that telepathic communication again. But it was Drew!

"You're here!" I breathed, not daring to take my eyes off him. I felt more of that warm surge of energy and its excitement.

You can see me, came into my head and I felt happiness filling the thought. *You know I'm here!*

"Yes!" I said faintly—or did I think it? "Yes, I can feel you."

Awesome! That's awesome. I sort of knew you could but when I've tried to reach you at other times, I couldn't ... and I can't get through to a lot of people. I was with Karen all day once—she didn't know I was there. And Michael too. But you can see me! What do I look like?

"You look just like you! Just like you!"

Yeah! I do! He paused. *Just like me! It's so cool! You can see me!* Then, *Yeah, I remember the Dodge Ram pickup! You didn't want me to have it, but Dad and I decided we would get it—for him.*

"I haven't forgotten." I was filled with questions. I dashed the tears away from my eyes that had appeared mysteriously and blew into my tissue and began to laugh. "You just knew you and that pickup were invincible," I said. "And WHO started the builder's crane to pull your truck out of the mud?"

I can't remember now—seemed like a great idea at the time! Do you know what it's like to drive a crane? He paused. *I guess not ...*

A deluge of memories poured into my mind as he spoke. "Do you remember the Spanish birthday party for your fifteen-year-old friend from the ninth grade? And the white sports coat we bought?"

We laughed. I thought you looked so handsome…

I looked like a dork. What about the music we used to listen to in the car…

"I was just thinking of that. Music was the only communication I had with you for a while…remember? I liked some of your songs. Did you like the classics I played? Or did you hate them? And Sting! Do you remember the song we used to listen to—'I'll Be Missing You?' I sang some of the lyrics to him.

They made a re-make of Sting's "I'll Be Watching You," he said. *You always had me in your sights! I couldn't get away with anything.*

"And then didn't Puff Daddy sing it? Or was that Biggie?"

Puff Daddy. Did you know his name changed to P. Diddy and now he's changed it again to Sean Combs?

"No, I didn't. But I'll try to remember that. That's what I need you for—to keep me updated on all this stuff." But you're not here anymore, I thought. You're gone…

I heard him laugh. *I'm here. I can do that.* He said.

He heard my thoughts.

"How about the time you climbed out of your bedroom window one night with me lying in wait downstairs until you dropped to the ground and scampered to the waiting car? Do you remember that?" I asked

Darn! You were standing in the doorway in dad's T-shirt yelling, "GET BACK HERE! "God, that was embarrassing!

We both felt the laughter vibrate through our souls. To me it felt like a strong rush of warm, light energy, and somehow I could feel it in him, too. I once read that laughter is one of the highest vibrations we reach on earth. It brings spirit closer and it can heal. We both felt it.

We talked about his fears in high school and my fears for him. I said, "I think I was too tough."

He said, *You were—I was pretty tough on you, too.*

I said, "I'm sorry."

Me too.

We talked about our happy times and sad times. I thanked him for calling me every day for almost a year when his Dad died. "It meant so much to me … made me feel better. You gave me something to look forward to every day. No matter how gloomy the day looked or how lonely I was, I always knew that you would call. It made all the difference."

That's it! That's what I meant to do.

Silence.

Thank you for helping me to buy my car this year. I loved that little four-wheel drive.

"You're welcome, my Angel. You took such good care of it." I paused, sadness swept over me as I remembered the day we went car shopping in Colorado. "Funny. I always thought you'd meet an icy end driving through those Rocky Mountains in the winter. Didn't happen."

Didn't happen.

"No." I worried myself sick about something that never happened.

We remembered his triumphs. The glowing letters from his managers at the resort in Colorado. Thank-you notes from guests. How proud of him I was.

"I remember the day you called me and said you'd applied for the job in the finance department. I knew how nervous you were. And when you got the job, you were so darn happy."

I was so scared—you know I got turned down for that other job I applied for. And with this one—wow! I wanted it so bad ... but accounting!! I beat out ten other people who applied ... man! That was awesome!

"Oh Drew! I remember asking you if you told Michael."

And I said, "Yes. He's stoked!"

I laughed. "You stoked all our lives. Mine, your Dad's, Karen and Michael's. We all love you so much."

And then I felt him fading.

I love you, Mom ...

Tears began to fill my eyes—"Don't go ..."

Gotta go ...

And he was gone. But he had been here—and he was happy! Oh dear God he was happy. Thank you. Thank you!

❧

I slept on the couch that night with Drew's hoody wrapped around my shoulders. I went to bed the next night with his baby blanket tucked underneath my chin. The third morning dawned and bloomed into day. There were geese honking in the cove getting ready for another long flight south. Were they still going south? I didn't know what day it was. Was it spring yet? Or was winter just beginning? It didn't matter.

The air around me felt lighter for some reason. Some of the density that had been hanging heavily suspended in its invisible cloud had dissipated. Now it felt cool and bright and clearing. I felt lighter than I had in two months. And so close to Drew.

After a while, I got up and went through the ritual of making a cup of tea. Then I handed out cat cookies to Miss Kitty and dog cookies to Ranger. I gave each of them a bowl of milk. I know—the new thinking by those people whose job it is to think for the rest of us—don't happen to think it's a good idea to give either Ranger or Miss Kitty *milk*. Well, they like it. And you know what? All three of us know that tomorrow one of us may not be around for a bowl of milk. So we've agreed to eat, drink, and be merry, for who knows if tomorrow will happen for us.

Bon appétit, my loves!

I poured a second cup of tea—loaded with tannin no doubt, and then filled the kettle again. Teacup in hand, I glanced at myself in the bathroom mirror. Not good. If we're talking about good and bad ideas, then looking in the mirror at 7:00 a.m. falls squarely into the "Very Bad Idea" column—especially if this comes at the tail end of a three-day grief ritual.

But who knows? With any luck, one day I'd wake up, look in the mirror, and the face looking back at me would have a nice "tannin" tan. A little wrinkly perhaps but … not bad.… And who gives a damn.

❧

On the last evening before the candles burned out, I asked Drew for a gift. We'd been visiting all day, he and I. It was different this time. I could feel his warmth all around me but the images were in my mind. Old memories and pictures of old times. I don't know why there wasn't that strong rush of warm energy this time. Or the vibrant sound and sight of him. All I felt was an acute awareness that if I spoke to him, he would hear me.

That morning I even turned one of the morning shows on and asked him what he thought about all the snow that was falling in Colorado. And how about the new president's speech—did he like that? I turned on his "tunes." Then watched a little MTV with him. Strange music, most of which I didn't know many or any of the words to. And the CMT channel. That was better.

Music may carry the highest vibration of all. Have you ever noticed how a song or a piece of music can lift you up instantly? Or how it will make you cry or laugh—and how a march or a marching band will give you goosebumps and courage and pride, raising your adrenalin through the roof? Or sometimes it can bring tears to your eyes.

Drew felt music deeply. You know the saying, "He had music in his soul"? That was Drew. He and music were at times one and the same entity. This is the stuff we talked about on that cold January afternoon as I ate more chocolate and watched the candles flicker and melt in their glass jars. At tea time I made another pot of tea.

It was early evening now. Outside, the sun was in that red-velvet mood, resting on the southwest horizon, its fading light somehow more brilliant at sunset than at midday. It streaked and splashed the cirrus clouds with crimson and gold. The trees' black and bare limbs stood still in stark relief against the sky, spearing and ripping the dusk apart. It looked as though some-one from the school of Van Gogh, some Oscar-bound stage decorator, had painted the backdrop, and the wings, setting the stage for the grand finale of Dante's Inferno.

The fire snapped and popped, a damp log sent up a smoky green wisp. "I've liked this time together," I told Drew. I felt comforted by his presence, felt him reaching out between dimensions lightening me and the sadness of not having him here anymore.

"Now, I'd like you to show me a sign, Drew. Please show me that this time together has helped you, too. I've felt so close to you." I stood by the paned window looking out over the ice-trimmed lake. The waters were a deep cobalt color now, reflecting the dark bruising of the sky. Silver ribbons of ice glistened on the surface and a new flock of Canada geese was nestled down on the far bank, settling in for the night. "Show me a sign, Drew. Show me that you've been with me—*you've really been with me*. Of course I know you've been here—I know that—but you know me, the doubter. Just let me know we've been together—and that you're okay."

I turned back to the coffee table, biting my fingertip, watching the candles flicker. Bumpy strings of wax coursed down the sides of the baptismal candle, swallowing the dove and the gold and red graphics and pooling around its base.

"A dove." I said out loud. "That's it! A white dove will be the sign."

I thought I heard, *Okay.*

A Sign, a Friend,
and a Butterfly

The next morning the clouds moved in early. Sullen gray clouds heavy with snow crowded the hilltop across the lake from my house. They were the same color as the great blue heron that lived in the cove. I stood on the deck in my robe with my shawl pulled tightly around my shoulders, staring out at the frozen water.

The geese that had snuggled down in the marsh last night had flown. They were probably over the state line by now, headed south. This morning there were only a couple of wood ducks bobbing about, diving and popping up again, undoubtedly irritating a resident family of mallards.

But there were no doves. No white doves, anyway. A pair of mourning doves poddled along an extended hickory limb on the big tree in front of the house, puffed up for warmth. Fluttering wrens and a few sparrows crowded the bird feeders, feathers spiky, ruffled by the wind gusting out of the north.

No white doves. Perhaps white doves was asking too much?

I shivered and went back into the warmth of the house.

The baptismal candle had gone out. The candle in the jar was burning orange, flickering and gasping for its last few breaths of air. I picked up the picture of Drew that had kept me company for three days and held it to my chest. It was a lovely picture. Pink cheeked and smiling. A picture of happiness. I felt that familiar prickle heat up behind my eyelids.

I held the picture in my lap for a long time. Oh God. What would I give to see that smile again? I held the picture against my chest and cried. When the wave of grief had passed, I held the picture and stared at it. Then I took it over to the window to get a better look. What was I seeing?

That shirt he had on . . . Had I seen him in that before? I couldn't remember. What was that on the front—across his heart? I could see it clearly now, but the image was cut off in the fold of the fabric and was hard to make out. But that shirt was here in the house somewhere! I would find it.

Putting the frame down carefully, I walked quickly to his bedroom and pulled open the drawer that held his T-shirts. There, right on top of the pile was the shirt he was wearing in the picture. It was a deep river green with a picture of a bare black tree with its branches reaching skyward, identical root pattern earthward. And there, a little to the top left, were *three white doves painted across the heart.* I'd been sitting there staring at this picture for three days without realizing that the doves were right there in front of me all the time. As was Drew.

He was here. Not only was he here but he was laughing, smiling—joking. Thank God he was out of that sad place.

In the candlelight I remembered and cried. Then I laughed with tears running down my cheeks and said out loud, "He's okay! He's happy! Oh, thank God."

❧

Later that evening I poured myself a glass of wine, took it to my perch on the couch and flicked the TV on. I stared blankly at the Oprah Winfrey show for a few minutes wondering where I'd seen her before. That's what this sort of grief does to your mind … the physicality of this grieving business is mind stopping. It bears no resemblance to the spiritual side of grief. One is worrisome—like wondering where you've seen Oprah before—the other is magic.

It looked bleak outside. There had been no sun today and the clouds were scudding ahead of a cold front that was tearing out of the western Appalachians. But it was comfortable and warm inside, and I felt uplifted by the Lakota ritual, but more than that, the lump in my chest had melted. It had been taken away by the appearance of three white doves on a T-shirt.

The late-afternoon talk show had just ended and the sponsors were lined up with their ads, ready to sell. I settled into the cushions barely seeing the screen, my mind was so full with thoughts of Drew. Then, there in front of me, a white dove filled the middle of the screen. Underneath it there were these words:

"This Message was Brought to You By Dove." It was an advertisement for soap.

Did I tell you that Drew has a sense of humor?

‍⁍⁌

The clock on the mantle chimed nine o'clock. I was tired and thinking of going to bed when the telephone rang. It made me jump. Who could it be?

A woman's voice said "I had to call you. I saw your son's obituary in the paper and I had to speak to you. I live quite close to you on the lake."

What was this…"Do I know you?" I asked. "Have we met?"

"No, no," she said quietly. "But I wanted to reach out and tell you that I feel so deeply for you. You see, I lost my son in October—the month before Drew … He was 28 years old."

The surprise I was feeling was masked in a billowing fog. This woman's kindness warmed me. She had reached out to a stranger not knowing what kind of reception she would receive.

"His name was Matt. My name is Pat."

Pat and Matt. Matt and Pat … I must remember that. Good luck, I thought.

The winter had been long and cold, but at this moment, I had been given the gift of understanding from another mother who had lost a son only a month before I lost mine. She, too, was moving in that same dark and unforgiving cloud in slow motion. Her hand reached through the shadow of grief, and I took it. It felt as though a lifeline had been thrown to me, and I seized it.

And there's another way of looking at this. Going through this process of dealing with grief, I've come to recognize that there are angels around us. I call them Earth Angels. You will feel them in a hand laid on your shoulder, or sometimes it's just a smile from someone you've never met.

Here's what happened one afternoon in Manhattan about two months after I'd come home from Denver. I was visiting Michael and his family when I began to feel one of those downturns coming on. Just when you think everything about this crappy business is looking up a little, a bolt of sadness crashes through your defenses and throws you backwards. So, I headed out onto the city streets to try and soak up enough of its energy to stop this depression.

It wasn't working. I walked into a bookstore. Bookstores were a safe haven for me and in this one I found a music disc I wanted. I handed it to the cashier, a grizzled little man with a Freudian beard who glanced up at me and said, "No matter what happens to you, never lose that smile."

Instantly, I felt the shadows recede as it brought an immediate smile to my face. "Thank you." I smiled.

That was an Earth Angel

Well that night, when I'd finished talking to my new friend Pat, I knew that an angel had come to walk beside me. Someone out there, whom I had never met, knew that I was at the bottom of a very deep well and came to help me out. She is an Earth Angel.

Angels matter.

It was the beginning of a strong friendship. Pat and I soon discovered that our sons had known each other on earth. Mutual friends confirmed that they had met out on the water and gone wakeboarding and skiing together many times.

I poured myself a glass of red wine and swirled it around. This stuff was tasting better and better. I took it over to the fireplace and sat there cross-legged with Miss Kitty in my lap staring into the embers. It had been a good fire earlier, burning away the blues, but now it had almost burned itself out.

Pictures of Drew on his wakeboard flooded my mind. The memory was clear. I watched it unfold as I saw him bearing down, riding the high wake, the board cutting through the green and silver crest as he reached its peak and raced down the center folds of the boat's wake. And then I saw him jump. His strong calves propelled him up three, four, five feet in the air—and I saw him twirl high above the wake before landing hard behind the boat.

Tears filled my eyes as in my mind's eye he raised his fist triumphantly. His eyes twinkled, creasing at the corners. His smile filled my heart and the spaces and time between then and now.

Surely Pat had those memories of Matt—he skied barefoot, I heard. And I know her heart tore as she watched the ripples in his tanned and muscled thighs and the concentration in his face that is the mark of high endeavor, she felt his heart swell with the thrill of accomplishment.

❧

William Wordsworth knew about the joy and exhilaration of youth. And also its limitations, when he wrote: *"Forget the glories he hath known ... Nothing can bring back that splendor in the Grass ... "*

Two more angels came in the days that followed. First there was Debbie. The last time she saw her daughter, she was standing on the threshold of forever. Because at seventeen, the rest of your life looks like forever. How true that was.

"She was so beautiful," Debbie said. "Her eyes flashed as she pleaded to drive to the next town thirty minutes away. And we let her because she had learned to drive and at some point those apron strings have to snap."

When the police found her car, it had gone off the road and hit a tree. Her neck snapped in the collision. How many times does that dark night on a country road play in Debbie's dreams? How often does that long dark brown hair curl around her mother's fingers, as she feels her daughter's youth, her joy, her eyes flashing through time and space...

And then Louise came into our lives. Louise lost a daughter at the age of thirty-six. Her grandson lost his mother and a husband lost a wife. The pain is great, and spread around—from a child who cannot understand, to parents and husbands who have no answers.

Louise made a memory quilt of her daughter's old T-shirts to give to her little boy.

I wish I could sew. No I don't, I hate sewing. But I love that quilt.

So we met for lunch about once a month and we remembered our kids and laughed. Sometimes we cried, but mainly we held onto each other both mentally and physically and we called in angels and they came. Earth Angels … Heavenly Angels—we took them all.

❧

There was another angel called Gail. She's a friend who also happens to be a grief counselor, and who during those gray leaden days, wielded her talent imperceptibly over cups of tea, chocolates, and long afternoon chats in my living room. Most of the chatting was done by me. She sat there mostly just looking wise—like Mrs. Freud or something—and let me rattle on. She thought I didn't know what she was doing. But I did.

So, in late January with the temperature tipping the freezing mark and a sheet of thin ice covering my lake, she asked me to do her a favor and go to Washington, D. C., with her to keep her company on the long drive. In actual fact, there was no favor required on my part. I loved The District and its surroundings. The smell of the city buoyed me, the noise of the city held its own music that drenched the Roman Greco architecture of stately historic buildings. I loved it all. But mostly, the distraction of the city lifted me out of the valley for a few days and let me feel like everyone else.

❧

Brittany, the young woman who filled a large part of Drew's life over the last few years, lived and worked in Washington so while I was there I called and asked her to meet me for lunch. Drew and Brittany had a longstanding on-again, off-again relationship. And when he died, it was off again, which had thrown Brittany into a deep hole of grief crawling with those "what-ifs," those little shovels that only dig deeper and deeper making an already deep hole even deeper. The trick is to keep the dirt from caving in on you as you sink.

They met in Colorado while working for the Moonrise Mountain Lodge on the slopes of Moonrise Mountain. From the first moment, Drew was head over heels in love with her.

"Mom, you should see this girl! She's gorgeous! She's funny. We can talk about anything and we think exactly alike. She's dynamic!"

I had to smile with him. But it wasn't very long before "dynamic" became "She's trying to control me," and from Brittany, "He's so *independent!*" So it was off for a while and then it was on again. As dynamic as ever.

The lunchtime restaurant she had chosen was churning with activity when I arrived. It was raining and the thirty-something crowd of office workers was pouring in off the wet sidewalks. As I waited for Brittany, I wondered if Drew was around. He knew I was meeting her today because I had told him. He was supposed to give me a sign if he showed up. It must be a sign we couldn't miss. A really *pertinent* sign.

It was nice in the restaurant. I liked the energy of these young men and women in the prime of their lives, living and working in one of the most dynamic cities in the world. Drew had been here just two weeks before he died, visiting Brittany and thinking about moving to Washington.

Then I saw her. She eased her way through the throng, looked up and saw me, and waved. There she was—Drew's city girl in high-fashion black and higher heels. Everything worked for her—her outfit, her makeup. Her hair was long and brown with blond streaks—more than a few heads turned as she threw her raincoat over the back of the chair and sat down.

Darn! I felt my eyes filling with tears. This was going to be harder than I thought. It was the first time I'd seen her since Denver. Pulling myself together, I listened to her talk. She hadn't been in Washington very long, so she was still looking for a permanent place to live. When Drew had been over to visit her in the summer, they had walked all over town looking at apartments. Her eyes clouded and I felt a rush of emotion threatening to envelope both of us.

"Here," I said quickly. "I brought you something." I dug into my handbag and brought out a small square box. "Sorry, no wrapping. I only found it about an hour ago—and I thought it was perfect, so I got it for you." I didn't tell her I'd spent half the day yesterday looking for a small gift that would mean something to her. I still didn't know that it would mean anything, but for some reason I was drawn to it and it seemed to fit her sophistication and the job she did for one of the biggest hotel chains in the world.

Brittany opened the box and, to my distress, her eyes began to brim with tears and she couldn't speak. We both sat there speechless. I was upset. She was struggling for control.

"Oh my God!" she wailed, as the dam broke. Her mascara was running in rivulets down her cheeks. "Oh shit! Where's my napkin?" She grabbed it off her side plate and buried her face in it and cried softly. Her shoulders were shaking and her hair tumbled over her hands. Devastated, I lay my hand on her arm.

"What is it?" I certainly hadn't expected this reaction.

After a few seconds, she raised her head, holding my gift in her hand. A silver business cardholder with a butterfly elegantly engraved into its lid. "You're not going to believe this …"

Try me, I thought. "What?"

"A few weeks ago, I went to Tiffany's and bought this exact same cardholder for Drew. I was planning to give it to him for Christmas … but then …" She swiped her napkin across her eyes, spreading makeup and mascara in streaks across her cheeks. She looked like a little girl who's had her party dress dragged through the mud. "We had this massive fight and broke up and I never had a chance to give it to him. He never knew—he never saw it …"

I sat there rigidly, looking and feeling as though a bolt of lightning had just smashed through the roof. I grabbed her wrist. If people were watching us I didn't give a damn.

"Yes he did! Don't you see? It was Drew—*this is from Drew!* He led me to this cardholder. I have never bought a cardholder in my life. I wasn't even thinking cardholder! I looked for hours before I found this … and when I did I knew it was right!" She blinked wetly at me. "Brittany … what are the odds I found this today? The exact same one you got for Drew! And something compelled me to buy it for you? *What are the odds?*" She shook her head and blotted her eyes. "He wants you to know that he knows you bought it for him. This is a gift for you, from Drew. *It's a sign we couldn't miss!*"

"Oh my God!" she said. The significance of what I had said took root. "I'm going to start asking him for signs! I want him to send butterflies," she said, sniffing loudly.

He already did. He's way ahead of you, sweet girl.

I don't believe in coincidences.

Brittany and I kept in touch over the months that followed and late one night, several weeks after our lunch in Washington she called me in tears. "I can't forget him ..." she whispered.

"We won't ever forget him," I told her. "But one day this will feel better ... you'll see."

Silence.

I could feel the weight of my years and the learned wisdom that right now seemed full of crap. There's no feeling better about this. At least not for me. But one day Brittany would get past it. She was young, and I knew it was just a matter of time.

"I think he wants us to feel better ..." That at least, I could believe. And in the course of believing I allowed in a glimmer of light in that came as quickly as it left.

"You'll see."

The line went dead.

"Brittany ... ? Are you there ..."

Nothing. The line was completely dead. I put the phone down to see if she'd call back.

She did. "What happened?" she asked.

"My line just cut off! Anyway, I didn't call you to cry .... that's so selfish ..." I could hear sniffles on the other end.

"We could cry together," I offered. "But tell me what's happening with your life."

"I'm moving to Atlanta." She coughed and sniffed once more and blew her nose.

"Oh?" Are you pleased about this?"

"Yup, I know a ton of people there. I went to school there and most of my friends never left. It's going to be soooo cool."

The phone cut off again.

She called back. "I don't know what's going on," Brittany exclaimed. "I've got a full battery! So I know it's not the phone."

"Me too—four bars." Something was going on. "Brittany," I said excitedly, "Drew's on the line! He's listening—and wants us to know he's here!" I just knew it. "You wait, it's going to happen three times."

"Really?"

"Yup. I'm starting to think because of other things that have happened that these signs from Drew come in threes. Just keep talking."

She did. The new job paid more and gave her more room to use her own initiative and the new hotel..."You should see it! It is absolutely *gorgeous!* I'm going to love it there!"

The phone cut off a few minutes later.

"He's doing it! He's here!" Brittany was shrieking when she called back. "Oh my God! It *is* him...do you think he knew about this move? Oh no! *He made it happen*...I'm sure he did...he didn't want me to be sad in Washington without him...*Oh...my...God...*"

Perhaps the reason they come in threes is that it's hard for us humans to be totally on point and "aware" all the time. So spirit will show us a sign or give us a nudge once, and if we don't pick it up, it will be shown again—and then again. Maybe the third showing is for emphasis. Maybe they're making a point. Maybe the density of this earth vibration has something to do with it.

〜

Six months later, Brittany called me to tell me there was a new guy in her life. She'd known him from college—since before Drew—and he was kind and understanding and she sounded happy. She had begun to dig herself out and I could hear the clank of tiny shovels, racing to throw off the dirt. My heart joined them, picked up a shovel, and we dug faster and faster.

That's what Drew would want.

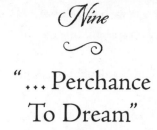

Nine

"... Perchance To Dream"

When I got home from Washington the next evening, the house phone was ringing and there was a message light blinking on my answering machine.

"Where have you been?" It was Cindy, my friend from North Carolina—the friend I would meet in Vail for skiing in late February most years. Her voice, charged with excitement, shattered the quiet of my empty house. "I've been calling since yesterday and I've left you two messages."

I said, "I've been in the capital." We hadn't seen each other since Drew passed. It was mid-winter and the weather had been a factor in the North Carolina Mountains where Cindy had been spending the last month. Neither of us had been willing to take on the snows that were making the drive to and from Raleigh treacherous, so we burned up the phone lines instead.

"*We have GOT to see you!* Spencer had this dream. We're driving up!"

Spencer was Cindy's daughter. "When?" I asked. "What dream?"

"Tomorrow. We'll tell you when we get there. It was a dream about Drew—*the night that he died!*"

❧

The next day Cindy raced up from Raleigh in her silver BMW. Spencer got to zoom in alongside her. It was the first time I'd met Cindy's daughter. She stepped out of the car and I guess I'd been expecting a bubbly, bustling shortie with bobbed wavy hair and blue eyes that crinkled with laughter most of the time. I was dead wrong. A girl in her mid-twenties stood in front of me. Her eyes were almond-shaped, rimmed with dark lashes. Her long, sleek chestnut hair gleamed in the afternoon sun. A smattering of freckles peppered her cheeks and the only thing that convinced me that this was Cindy's daughter was the way her eyes twinkled when she smiled.

I hugged her, stood back, and smiled. "She's gorgeous, Cindy!"

"Yes I know. But you have to hear this!" Cindy gave me a quick hug and thrust a potted plant bursting with orange flowers into my arms. "You're thin." She scrutinized my face for half a second then turned and pulled Spencer forward. "Just wait until you hear *this*! Spencer, tell her about the dream!"

"I will, Mom! Can we please get inside and let me get out of these boots?" Spencer said.

After settling in to their rooms, we met by the blazing fireplace in the living room for coffee. Spencer was comfortable now in a sweater and woolly socks.

"You've got to hear this!" said Cindy, who squiggled herself down into the cushions with her coffee and motioned to her daughter to start the narrative.

Spencer took a deep breath and threw her head back. "Okay." She turned to me, rolled her eyes, and said, "Mom won't let this rest until I do. And the reason I haven't said anything until now is that, well, I didn't know how. I didn't know what to think about it or whether I should say something or not."

"I'm all ears." I smiled at the girl who was sitting up as straight as a poker with her hands clenched in her lap.

"The dream happened the night that Drew lost consciousness in Colorado." She held my eyes as she spoke. "Mom's told me what's happened since then." She cleared her throat and patted her chest nervously. "In the dream, I was standing silently inside this room. It was a large room, dimly lit so I couldn't see very clearly. I knew there was a party going on. I could see a ton of people and they were all laughing and talking to one another. There was music playing. No one looked familiar to me. I didn't know a soul and I seemed to be sort of on the outside of the group. No one seemed to know me." She wrinkled her forehead. "No one seemed to notice me even. In fact, I don't think they could see me." She leaned forward, picked up her cup and took a sip.

"Did you recognize the place at all? Did you get any sense of where it might be? Was it somebody's house maybe?" I asked.

She shook her head. "No to both. It wasn't a house, and I have never seen the place before."

She went on. "The room was warm, dark, and smoky. I could catch snippets of conversation, but I couldn't make out what they were saying." She paused and raised her eyes to the ceiling, "Let me get this right. There was a boy standing in front of me. He had his back to me. I could make out the shape of his head—he had dark hair and he was wearing a black jacket." Spencer hesitated. "Somehow I knew that he was in trouble. He didn't say anything, I could just feel it." She took a deep breath. "Neither of us spoke, and then I raised my arm and placed my hand on his shoulder. When I did that, he turned around and I saw his face. There was a look of fear and deep confusion in his eyes." Spencer's eyes grew wide. "It was like he was saying, 'What's going on?'"

Then she woke up.

"I think it was a kind of a vision. Does that make sense?" she asked. "It was so real. Everyone there was real. Weird in that I didn't know a soul there, and yet it was so *intense* … "

Although Cindy and I had been friends for several years and she stayed in contact with me throughout Drew's hospital stay in Denver, Spencer and Drew had never met. And noboby knew that Drew was in trouble when Spencer had that dream— not even me—the phone call from the hospital wouldn't come until the following evening.

"And listen to this," Cindy said. "I showed Spencer a picture of Drew. I had it mixed up among several other pictures of people she knew and some she didn't know—you know my daughter, she's such a drama queen. I had to trick her. And she identified Drew right away as the boy she had seen in her dream…"

"Excuse me a moment," I said. My attention was riveted on the story I'd just heard as I walked quickly to Drew's old room and pulled a jacket out of the closet.

"Is this it?" I asked as I walked back into the living room. I pulled it on and turned around with my back to Spencer.

She didn't hesitate. "That's it," she said quietly. "That's the jacket the boy had on."

It was Drew's black ski jacket that I had brought back from Colorado when I returned home.

This is the sort of story, from someone totally unconnected to Drew, that validates this whole discussion for me. Spencer didn't know him. There was no grief to complicate the issue for her—it was just what she said it was. It was a vision or a precognitive or prophetic dream.

Had they known each other in another life? Who knows. Spencer was in New York when she had this dream and the connection between them was strong enough to bring her spirit two thousand miles across the country the night before Drew lost consciousness never to awake again in this life. So who knows?

Perhaps it was the music. Spencer is a classically trained soprano. And an actress. Drew identified himself through music. He surrounded himself with music and people who made music. Any music, he loved it all.

That same night that Cindy's daughter had this dream, Drew and his friends were in their regular Friday night spot, a pub in the ski village called O'Malley's, hanging out, drinking, and singing Karaoke. His friends told us that he was singing karaoke all evening long.

He would have given everything to have been able to sing like Spencer. How well I remembered Drew's singing. I could still hear him—alone in his bedroom with his music playing or riding in the car, singing with the radio … my music or his … his preferences spanned decades.

❧

Over breakfast the next morning, Spencer started talking about signs she's been picking up from Drew.

"When I thought about what had happened, I began asking this boy—Drew—for signs to show me I wasn't imagining the dream. I mean, I'm an actress—an *artiste*, Ginny—I can think up anything. But I know I'm not imagining him around me. I suddenly feel this *Whoosh*… And I know he's there. It's like a rush of warm air."

"And when I ask him for signs, I ask him to send me peacocks," Spencer said, her eyes twinkling. *"And they show up—like—everywhere!"*

"It's so weird. I'll be driving along and switch the radio on and as soon as I do, the start of a song I just know he loved comes on …" She tells me these songs make sense to both of them. "It's as though he's sitting in the seat beside me." She felt his presence around her constantly. "And sometimes when I'm on stage—there he is on center stage just laughing! Loving it." Spencer was sure he sent singing opportunities her way. "Do you think he can do that? I mean I went for months with no offers, no auditions—nothing. And it seems that soon after he died—after that night, that dream I had—the show offers and singing gigs started pouring in one after another."

❧

Cindy and Spencer left the next afternoon.

"Just tell me one thing," Cindy leaned out of her car window. "How come you guys can see all this stuff and I can't?"

"You have to ask for SIGNS, Mom," Spencer said patiently.

"Yeah—but what? I'm not going to ask for birds—anyone can come up with birds ... or butterflies!"

I had told them about Brittany's butterfly signs. "What about flowers?" I asked. "Don't you have a favorite flower?"

"Flowers—at least that's better than hearts." She snorted. "Flowers! Are you kidding me? There are flowers everywhere!"

"Not in winter," I pointed out.

"No! You do the hearts and flowers, I'm asking Drew for zebras." She waved her hand toward the sky and chuckled. "Drew, can you hear me? Find me a zebra."

I could still hear her chuckling when I waved them out of sight, as they drove away from the lake. The road to Raleigh did not strike me as the ideal place to hunt for zebras.

After everything that's happened to me during the last few years—I not only believe there is an afterlife, I know there is. I am more sure of that than I am of my own existence. But I still want proof. So all along the course of this forced journey I've asked for signs.

It goes something like this: I had this dream ... or, did I feel you touch my cheek? Or, as I asked Walt, "Why did the mattress on your side of our bed depress with no one there ... Were those your footsteps I heard?" And to Drew, "That song! It's playing on every channel I've switched to today."

So I say, "Okay you guys—this is weird and oh my god, I can't believe what just happened—but it did. So I ask you, Walt or Drew—show me a sign that I'm right. That I haven't lost my freaking mind."

And they always do.

"Thanks," I say. "Thanks for the sign—that was good. Could you show one more? Just one..."

And they do.

⁂

Not long after Spencer returned to New York, she called me.

"Ginny! It's so strange... there's this bluebird, *a bluebird in Manhattan... hellooo!* Sitting on my window sill! I've never heard of a bluebird in the city! In winter!"

I loved her enthusiasm. In the months since we met, I've discovered in her an acute intuitiveness. So if Spencer felt something in this bluebird—she was probably right.

And then. Here it comes. Ten months later, she was auditioning for Glenda's role in the Wizard of Oz.

"You See?" she said, "The bluebirds in the song 'Over the Rainbow'! How neat is that?"

These birds... There were Jim's mourning doves, and now Spencer's bluebirds—and peacocks.

What is it with birds? I keep hearing that they are the messengers of spirit. They form the bridge between dimensions. I actually think this is true of the animal kingdom as a whole.

I think that their vision and hearing is supernatural and that they can hear sounds we can't, so doesn't it follow that they can also see things that we can't? I think they are "Interdimensional" beings.

Spencer's dream of Drew the night he lost consciousness stayed with me for a long time after they left.

I had done a lot of thinking about dreams. For the last two months I had been trying to sort out the dreams I had and thinking about others from years ago. Old dreams, but so impressionable that they were never forgotten.

The conclusion I've come to is that there are the *dream* dreams—you know the kind. Fragmented, nonsensical, some mirror the events of the day in weird shapes and forms. Most of these you forget as soon as you open your eyes. Some are off the charts crazy where I'm running around planning a dinner party. The guests are ringing the doorbell and (Oh no!) I haven't even done the grocery shopping!

Strange people crowd these dreams. They have faces I've never seen. Why are they at my dinner party? None of them are frightening, none of them very beautiful. They're just normal faces, and I don't know any of them.

Hello … what are you guys doing here? Who *are* you?

But then there are the dreams that aren't dreams. They don't happen very often for me. When they do, they are clear and full of color, sound, movement, and emotion. They are alive, and the details are easily remembered. I think this is the sort of dream Spencer had. Some of these even have a plot or a storyline, and some of them are just one-liners, just a fleeting powerful thought that you'll spend all the next day trying to figure out. Like the dream of Drew and I walking through that strange hotel, they flash before your eyes with the same vividness—then they're gone. But they stay with you.

When someone tells me about one of these, they might say something like, "It's as though I was *there!*"

And I think, "You were there. Didn't you feel yourself fully involved, alive, breathing, thinking … and if *you* were there alive, aware and real, then why not the other people in your dream?"

The people and events that fill these alternative realities might come from across town or from ten thousand miles away or from another dimension. You'll find yourself in many places that you won't be able to identify—like the party that Spencer found herself in the middle of. You might see yourself in a garden, on a mountain, or walking city streets you've never seen before. You'll see buildings and landscapes very clearly and rooms full of detail right down to the upholstery colors, but they just don't ring a bell.

It's then you might ask yourself in the dream "What the heck am I doing here? Where on earth am I?"

Your soul knows. And it also knows that sometimes you may not even be on earth.

This is the astral travel phenomenon. Some of these places we've either been to at one time, maybe in other lives, or perhaps they are places we *have yet to visit*. Astral travel is when the soul or spirit takes a side trip outside of the body, usually while the physical you is asleep.

I had a few of those dreams right before Walt and Drew died.

Here's one that I had many years ago and have never forgotten. It happened while we were living in Dubai. The children were all young, Drew just an infant. I dreamed about a friend of mine who died back in the 1970s. He was a young man who had one of those rare heart attacks that kill people in their late twenties and early thirties. When I knew him, he was a great dancer, and whenever we were at the same party I would always pray that he would ask me to dance—and sometimes he did.

Years after he died, I had a dream that I was dancing with him on the stern deck of an ocean liner I had never seen before. I wore a long, swirling blue skirt, he wore a white tux, and we were waltzing to Strauss's "Tales of the Vienna Woods." In reality, he and I had probably never heard of this piece when we knew each other all those years ago in our early twenties, and we certainly had never danced a Viennese waltz together—or separately. But there we were, pale blue light all around us, whirling and dipping and twirling through the music on the back of the ship. That pale blue light again. I could feel the wind off the ocean in my hair, taste the salt on my lips, and I became one with him and the music.

I woke up with a silly grin on my face feeling extraordinarily happy, convinced that my friend was alive in heaven or somewhere and that he wanted us, the people he'd left behind, to know. He hadn't said a word, but I knew that was why he had come into that dream. The music stayed with me all day as I hummed and dipped and twirled through my chores, returning every so often to the glorious weightlessness I'd felt in the dream, the lightness of my partner's arm on my waist—my feet barely touching the wooden decking on the stern of the ship.

❧

I have also had a couple of these dreams about places and streets and buildings I've never seen.

After one of them I had in 1995, I woke up startled, with the dream city I'd been wandering in as clear as day in my mind.

All day it kept coming back, and I wondered where in the world I had been. Where were those tall, glass-fronted buildings of the dream? One of them had a deep sloping roof of glass panes.

In the dream, I seemed to be hovering over the top of its pointed roof, high above empty city streets. I didn't feel like a whole, fleshed out me. My body didn't seem to be there, but I know that I was. Light, hovering, seeing, and sensing. It was the spirit me.

The air was clear and the scene was filled with sunlight glinting off the glass, and as I looked around at the street below I noticed an ornate, domed cathedral with life-size statues ringed around its roof. Old-fashioned streetlamps lined the streets around it. I never forgot the streetlights.

After a day or two, the dream faded and eventually it vanished into some crevice of my subconscious where it slept, and the dream city was forgotten for a long time.

It came back in early December several years later when, walking down a street with Walt in a city we were visiting for the first time, I suddenly began to recognize my surroundings. Tall, glass-fronted buildings—one in particular with a peaked, deeply sloped glass-paned roof.

The dream didn't come back to me immediately, but as we strolled through the streets, stopping to take pictures, ducking into a café for coffee, the city began to feel familiar. Where had I seen these buildings before? On the way out, it occurred to me that I knew what was around the next corner—and how far it was back to the hotel. The feeling nagged at me until we got into the hotel room and I stood looking out of the window onto the city below. Off to my right, for the first time I became aware of that tall, glass-roofed building. I gazed hard at it, taking in all the details of the structure.

"It's so strange," I told Walt. "I've never been here before, but this whole place feels so familiar." I stared at him. "Take that building..." I pointed toward the skyscraper. "I just know I've seen that somewhere. Are you sure you've never been here before? Did you tell me about it?"

My husband lifted his head from a map he was browsing for the next day's excursion into the mountains. His glasses were lodged on the end of his nose, his heavy eyebrows were shaggy, and a thick strand of hair fell over his forehead. "Nope, I've never been here before," he said, and returned his attention to the map.

And then the realization hit me like an avalanche. That building... I *had* seen it before! In that dream... The difference was that now, and on the street, I was looking *up* at it instead of down from it and in December it definitely wasn't sunny. It was overcast and cloudy—but nevertheless, it was the same building. The dream came flooding back. The same streetlamps I'd seen in my dream were lit this time, casting their light on piled up snow along the sidewalks. When I turned my head to the corner window of the hotel room, there was the cathedral, its statues draped with snow now. Not exactly like the dream statues glinting in the sun, but there it was. I remembered it well.

❧

My spirit gets around, I can tell you. I think it scouts out places it knows I will like and gives me a preview of what we're planning for me down the road. So now when I dream of strange places I've never been to, I try to hold on to the dream because sometimes they're full of prophesy.

I walked into a hotel suite once and immediately recognized the lay-out from a dream I'd had the night before. The big windows looked down onto the street below from six stories up and the living room furniture was just as I had seen it in the dream. It was covered in a floral printed, textured fabric of red sprigs, branches, and flowers on a background of beige. And somehow I knew that if I went exploring I would find two identical bedrooms, one on either side of the suite's living room.

༄

Mostly, we don't recognize these forerunner, or prophetic, dreams for what they are at the time. But later, when some Heavenly Timekeeper decides that it's time for these events to be threaded together, we suddenly remember. Didn't I see this in a dream? Have I been here before?

Even knowing that these snapshots from the future happen, I was still unprepared for the dream about Drew almost two months before he left us.

༄

At first I had no idea what the dream was saying, but I knew it was saying something. Only after I began putting the pieces together a few months later did it dawn on me that this was one of those forerunner dreams.

The dream happened in two separate phases, almost like a play performed on a split stage. Drew and I appeared together as spirit beings and were able to slip easily from one scene to the next. We had no physical substance—not even the see-through wispiness I'd sometimes been aware of in dreams and meditations. But we were whole beings with feelings and senses. We were pure spirit with acute awareness.

The backdrops in the dream were theatrically vivid and painted in impossibly alive and shifting colors. The dream unfolded on two stages that were separated but very close together. The first act opened in an almost opalescent light. It reminded me of the sheen you sometimes see in heat vapor. The air was brilliantly clear, tinted in the pale colors of daybreak. It felt warm and dry like the air in the desert, or in the high mountains of the western states. My spirit was fully involved, although standing out of and a little apart from a dreamscape of tall, red rock canyons, falls of coppery sand, and tall magenta spires. Like an observer. There was scant vegetation and the shrubs around me looked like sagebrush. It felt like Colorado.

Drew's energy permeated the place. I didn't see him but I felt his presence, his essence. We were in the Colorado mountains where Drew lived, and it felt as though I was visiting.

Then one stage morphed into the other as the dream moved along the visual stream of my consciousness. The images changed and I was instantly transported to the veranda of a safari lodge, looking down on a valley of lush, tropical trees and vines. There was a river below me and on the riverbank, spreading acacia trees stood in groves. Huge, lacy, deep green leaves crowded around the water's edge and lilies seemed to stare at their reflections in the running stream.

The air here was warm and moist and heavy with the scent of raw earth and chlorophyll. Scarlet wings fluttered through the trees, and I was suddenly aware of birds in full foliage of blue and yellow and deep turquoise perching on low-slung branches. Others swooped and dived from the treetops. Green parrots and cockatiels filled the air with the sound of their cries. And warm breezes ruffled the subtropical landscape.

I stood there entranced, with that same feeling of Drew's presence all around me. It was as though we were both being shown this place and looking at the scene together. We were both observers.

Then, without warning, a tiny brown monkey swung out of the trees and landed in the palm of my hand. It's black, boot-button eyes gleamed as it chattered, rolled on its back, then jumped up and danced. It grinned and performed for me. It was so happy, so full of joy in this beautiful place and totally unafraid.

Then I woke up.

"What was *that* about?" I spoke the words aloud in the darkness, startling Miss Kitty who was stretched out on the end of the bed. I thought of Drew, still sound asleep in Colorado that early in the morning. Here on the East Coast, the sun would be rising soon.

It was a pretty dream. The red rock canyons are awesome in any season, but in summer they shimmer. Then dense greenery and tropical birds ... talk about flip-flopping around. I lay there reliving the images, struck by their vibrancy. And that tiny monkey with black shiny eyes and the pure joy that emanated from its tiny being! It occurred to me that a dream that clear had to be one of those dreams that's trying to communicate something. But I wasn't hearing it. Not yet. So, as I do with all these things, I put it away and waited. Clarity usually comes sooner rather than later, and I knew that when it did, there would be no doubt.

Ten

Looking for Drew

Not long after Drew died, that dream flashed before me one morning, trying to pierce the fog of sadness that surrounded me. But with my thoughts running rampant through my shattered mind, its meaning stayed hidden. It couldn't come through. I tried hard to piece it together, but I was still stumbling blindly through the nightmare of my son's death and nothing made any sense.

But it kept coming back to me and I kept probing.

Then one day it burst through like sunshine from behind the night. The darkness parted, the clouds broke up and let me see what was hidden beyond the swirl of deep blue dawn. The dream was a warning of things to come. It was one of those nudges from the universe, one of those heads up events, that *we want you to know this ... now! Hey! Ginny, listen up!*

Its meaning was suddenly and completely clear. I was being told that *"This Place"* (act one,) these high red rock canyons, *"Is Drew's home now,"* and (act two)*"Here's where he's going…"*

The brightly colored birds, lilies, and a happy little brown monkey playing in the palm of my hand sounded like paradise to me. It felt like Africa. It would be Drew's paradise, I felt sure.

That's it, Mom!

Drew traveled with Walt and me to South Africa, my birthplace, twice. And like millions before him, the place captivated him and never left him. Africa will do that. I'm convinced it's a spell of some kind, and after the last trip to Africa, Drew made no secret of the fact to his friends and coworkers that he planned to go back one day to run his own hotel there.

⁂

The house was empty after Cindy's visit, and with my mind locked on dreams, I couldn't stay in it. I needed to get out and breathe in some real earth smells and feel the ground under my feet. I wanted to see the water of the lake and feel the cold damp air on my skin. I wanted the watery breeze to blow the ephemeral wisps of these dreams out of my mind—away from me. Leaving the lunchtime sandwich plates and half-eaten bowls of chips on the counter, I climbed into the car and drove into the village.

The road wound its way past the Dairy Queen, the old grocery store where Drew held his first job bagging groceries, and toward the church where he had been confirmed all those years ago. "You're everywhere I go…" My chest felt full of gathering clouds again as I drove into the parking lot at the bridge. There was Jack's Pizza where Drew worked for a summer chopping peppers and onions. There was the marina with all its boats and shops where he met Sara when she worked in the gift and tackle shop.

There were only a few cars in the parking lot today. How different from the Friday nights when Drew and his buddies would spend all evening on stage singing karaoke, drinking, and shelling shrimp at the Coconut Grove restaurant by the water.

Pulling into a parking space I got out, locked the doors, and then climbed the stairs to the top deck of the marina. Its old wooden floors creaked under my feet. I walked through one of the gift shops and out the back door onto the lakeside deck. I leaned on the railing. Down below at water level, I could see the stage where the band played and Drew sang. It was empty now. The Coconut Grove must be shut down for the winter. The smell of pizza baking—a mixture of warm bread, garlic, and cheese—drifted through the damp air. The lake waters here were deep green. A hundred boats bobbed at anchor, and mallards paddled among them racing for the tidbits a few children threw into the water.

There weren't many tourists in winter. Only the pizza place stayed open. By April this place would be opening all its storefronts, the art galleries would be signing up guest artists, and the fishing crowd would be filling the restaurants. By May and June the place would be swarming with holiday makers.

As I gazed at the lake, I could see Drew in my mind's eye racing into the marina, kicking up spray behind his jet ski, roaring across the water, and then swirling one last doughnut as he slid into one of the parking bays. I watched him take the wooden steps two at a time, hastily stuffing his T-shirt into brightly colored shorts, which were damp from the ride over from the house as he whooshed by me. My eyes filled with tears.

He wasn't here.

It was hard to see as I pulled out of the parking lot and back onto Route 122. It occurred to me that driving while crying my eyes out could kill me. What does it feel like to be killed? I wondered and then decided that it wouldn't matter—I would see Drew … I kept going. And then I caught myself short. A mother and two small children were crossing the road in front of me. "*What th'!*" I had to brake hard. What were they thinking crossing a highway like this one? I dashed the tears out of my eyes with the back of one hand and saw a car on the side of the road with a flat tire. They were looking for help and I could have killed them. Shaken, I realized that I was also going the wrong way. So sitting straight up and concentrating hard, hauling in all the attention faculties I could find, I got the car turned around and headed home.

After a few minutes, I switched the radio on and cried some more. Then, through my sobs, something on the radio caught my attention. I leaned over, sniffed loudly, turned the volume up, and listened.

It was one of Sting's songs, "I'll Be Watching You." Are you watching me, Drew? Somebody was. Somebody had just rapped me between the eyes to get my attention. I drove in silence, listening to the harmony of the group and the compelling melody of the music, remembering a day in October, one late autumn afternoon, when Drew was in the tenth grade. We were driving home from football practice. My young son sitting in the passenger seat beside me leaned his head against the headrest and said, "You know, I don't think I'll live to be very old."

What was that supposed to mean?

A brisk wind whirled through a pile of dried leaves on the roadside as we passed, throwing papery pieces of leaf and bark into the air and under the tires. In the rearview mirror I could see his football pads and bulging backpack crowding the back seat. His helmet was lying loosely between his feet, and the car smelled faintly of sweaty teenager.

Drew's CD was playing a song I'd never heard before. It turned out to be a poignant rendition of Sean Combs' "I'll Be Missing You." It was an a cappella remake of Sting's old song, a sad song eulogizing another rapster who had been murdered. They lived pretty rough lives, some of these guys, I'd heard, and the old saying, "Live by the sword," came to mind. However, when I removed that judgment, I found myself listening to the message and feeling the emotion of the song. Truth be told, I had never pictured myself listening to Puff Daddy's music, let alone being moved by it. Puff Daddy, who later became more commonly known as Sean Combs.

I looked at Drew's dirt-smudged arm lying on the console between us, his handsome face was serious. "Why do you say that?" I asked.

"I just can't see myself getting old."

"Nobody can see themselves getting old," I countered.

Silence. Then, "*That's it!*" A revelation. "I just can't see myself at forty or fifty … or old. When I try to see myself in that picture, I'm just not there."

The music with its sweet male and female voices filled the silence. It was a sad melody full of heartbreak. Drew seemed to find some connection to this song, so we listened to it together, bridging the stream of his disturbing remarks. Crazy teenage thinking!

I forced myself back to the present. "Oh Drew." I smiled through my tears. This wasn't the first time this song had played when I switched on my car radio. It seemed to come on whenever I was anxious about something, stressed, or missing Drew. A pattern was forming. The radio deejay must be as retro-minded as I was. I was glad. He was someone that Drew could work with to play the right music for me.

"Are you here, Drew?"

Retracing my tracks, I drove home dreading the long winter evening ahead of me. I turned onto Lakewood Forest Drive, and as I did I noticed a small red car in front of me.

It belonged to Mark—Drew's friend whose family had lived on the lake as long as mine. He had called me every day Drew was in the Denver hospital and had helped us get in touch with all of Drew's friends when we came home for the memorial service.

He must be going to his job, I thought. On the spur of the moment I followed him, yearning for the contact with one of Drew's young friends. I had discovered this is important. I like their energy, their scruffy shorts and tees, and their tousled hair. They reminded me of other times, and I could see Drew in their grins, in the crinkles around their eyes, and the light stubble on their chins. It's funny how I found myself longing for the company of young people. I wanted to be around them, to listen to their slang, to hear them laugh and to listen to their off-key singing.

Or was it that I just wanted Drew back?

It was a little crazy for sure, but I pulled up beside his car and climbed out. "Hi, Mark! I thought that was you."

"Hi, Mrs. Brock! How're things?" He ambled over and we gave each other a hug and stepped back. I asked him how his jet-ski fixing business was going. He said it was fine, and we spoke about nothing for a few minutes.

After a while he said, "I'm really having a hard time with Drew's … passing … Is that what we're calling it?" He wrinkled his forehead, drawing his dark brows together.

I understood.

He said, "You know, I had a dream of him one night. I saw him standing in front of me—just as real as you and me. I mean, *solid*." He shook his head and gazed into the distance where the Blue Ridge Mountains stood high and misty.

"I said, 'Hey, Drew! I thought you were dead!' and he replied, *Look at me, Man, I'm fine!*

I understood that too.

"It was weird! But it felt good at the same time."

Boy, did I understand that! "Not weird, Mark—it was Drew."

When I get really sad and down, Drew finds a way to break the mood. The rest of the ride home was lighter.

∽

Drew and Ranger on the jet ski.

At this time of year you can see pairs of Canada geese sailing down the creek through the cove, one on either end of a line of babies. They mate for life. I know from watching them all these years that not all their goslings will survive. By early summer a brood of six may have shrunk to two—or there may be only one left in their birdie family. There's always danger out there. A snake or a snapping turtle … or something flies at you out of the blue and you can't protect against it and next minute … they're gone. Nobody escapes this stuff.

Occasionally I see a single mother goose who has lost all her young. She paddles endlessly up and down the creek for a few days searching. Searching for her babies. Or a replacement baby? Sometimes, she'll tag along with another goose family. Maybe she just wants to be around someone else's babies. I can relate.

Then I think about Karen and Michael. I have other babies and what's more, THEY have babies of their own. Six of them. And that's very, very good.

But talking to Mark for a few moments, hearing him remembering his friend, my son, was very good, too, and the evening didn't loom monstrously long in front of me anymore.

When I got home it was getting dark and I turned all the lamps on and started a fire. The fireplace was looking scruffy from overuse this winter. I should have had it swept in November, but I'd forgotten about it. As a result of that mess-up, the minute I turned away from the newly lit fire, there was a sudden and awful *whooomp*, and flames went roaring up the flue, sounding like an express train in a tunnel.

I stood there frozen and then came unglued and went hurtling through the kitchen to find the fire extinguisher. There was no time to think, to call 911, and as I came charging back ready to fight the inferno, I heard footsteps walking through the living room and saw a shadow pass down the hallway.

The sudden fire went out as quickly as it had sprung up. By the time I got there it had died down and was no more than a single flame greedily consuming one of the three remaining logs. It was over.

"But who just walked through the house?" I asked out loud. No one answered. There was no one there—but I recognized those footsteps. They were Walt's. Walt was here.

❧

I'd kept in touch with many of Drew's friends, but after visiting with Mark, I wondered about Sara—Drew's childhood sweetheart. I called her his "forever love." They met when she was in the eighth grade and Drew was in the tenth. I think they met casually at parties and in groups, but I don't recall many "dates." I knew that they sat together on the school bus every day because she told me that.

When Drew went to Colorado, Sara flew out from Roanoke to see him once or twice over the years. They also spent many hours on the phone cheering each other on or commiserating over some injustice in one or the other's lives. She was one of the last people he called the week he died. I'm glad she made time for me now.

The last time I'd seen her was at Drew's memorial service. She was distraught and beside herself. We all were, so conversation was scant. However, on this beautiful spring afternoon she bounced into my living room all smiles that broke into tears as we hugged each other and sniffled and cried. Finally, we separated and I led her over to a couch by the fire.

My heart broke as I watched her tuck her small body into one corner, mop her eyes with the tissue I handed her, and cross her legs. She looked so young. She looked so defenseless in the wake of this tragedy.

After a while, Sara tossed her head, flipping her chestnut hair over one shoulder and said, "There! I'm okay now."

I smiled. The lamp light in the late winter afternoon bounced off the red highlights in her hair, and glinted off the silver hoops in her ears. When she opened her mouth, a flash of silver gave away the tiny silver stud on her tongue.

"Did you know that I talked to Drew for hours two nights before … before this happened?"

I shook my head.

"We talked about everything. We always talk—talked—about everything, but that night he was trying to tell me about a dream he'd had of Walt."

She had my attention.

"Oh damn! I wish I could remember it all!" She wrinkled her brow in concentration and framed her faced with both hands. "It's not coming back."

My heart sank.

"Anyway," Sara continued, tossing her hair back again and rubbed her index finger with its satiny black nail across her eyebrow. "He told me that he had had this dream where he and Walt were together inside this small room—it seemed to be bare—I think he said they were sitting down ... they must have been because Drew said the dream went on for what seemed like a long time while Walt was talking to him. He said it seemed as though they talked for *hours*. But you know what dreams are like. I mean, I'm sure it wasn't hours."

She took a deep breath. "He said they seemed to be in a very deep conversation—a serious conversation ... intense." Her head flopped down and she stared at her hands in her lap. "Darn! I *wish* I could remember more!"

Me too, I thought. "Well, don't worry. Maybe it'll come back later," I said. "Here, look at these." I pulled out the photo albums his friends at work had put together for us and put them in front of her.

Sara went through all the pictures in all the albums, pointing and commenting on those she recognized, many of which she had taken herself, and laughing at others. "Oh my God! Look at my hair in this one!" she said tearing up a little. "I looked like a poodle—but Drew said he liked it." She choked back a

sob and pointed to another picture, "I love this one of Drew …"
Silver rings shone on her fingers as she turned the pages and
circles of silver bangles jangled softly as she moved her hands
and shifted position.

It had gotten dark outside when we looked up from the albums. I left her on the couch and moved around the room turning on lamps, then went into the kitchen and poured us each a
glass of red wine.

Drew's forever love took a long sip, closed her eyes, and declared, "My favorite! Cabernet, isn't it?" She picked up the bottle
and looked at the label. When had this child become so grown up?
We talked for a long, long time. Once again, I wondered why
the relationship with Drew hadn't moved into something permanent as they got older.

Hours later when she got up to leave, I suddenly remembered something for her. I had wanted to give her something
of Drew's to keep, and I couldn't make up my mind what that
would be until now. Sara straightened her silky black top, flicked
the strands of silver chains into place, and ran her hands over
her black denim jeans, smoothing them out over her knees. A
thin black belt showed along the line of the hipster pants, and I
knew exactly what I was going to give her.

She caught me looking at her. "What?" she said.

"Hang on a minute!" I grinned. "I've got something for you."

Hurrying down the hallway and into the bedroom, I
opened the drawer that held Drew's belts and ties and other
miscellaneous items and grabbed one of the belts.

Uncoiling it, I watched the lamp light glinting off the
metal as I handed it to her. "Here, Sara … what do you think?" I
frowned. "It might need shortening."

The belt was black leather with silver diamond studs that went all around it to the chunky silver buckle.

"Oh …" she whispered taking the belt in both hands and running her fingers over the studs. "It's Drew's … for me?" She raised her eyes to mine and they glinted with fresh tears in the lamplight.

I nodded.

"I *love* it."

We hugged.

She whispered, "Thank you. I love you."

"I love you, Pretty Girl." Sara may not have been able to remember the dream, but just hearing part of it was gift enough for me.

Eleven

Let Me Eat Cake

hree days before Valentine's Day, I began thinking that this would be the first time that there wouldn't be a call from Drew on February 14. These milestones were hell. At first I found myself keeping track of how many days it had been since he passed away. And then I was counting the months. Birthdays—his and mine. First Christmas without Drew … The list of milestones was long.

Valentine's Day was a toughie because it was supposed to be a day of love. A day of light. The love would be there as it was every day, but that year there was no light in the place in my heart where Drew used to live. There was nothing there but a deep, dark shadow where he used to be. Occasionally I managed to keep that darkness at bay, but there were days when nothing could hold it off. I knew this would be one of them.

So I had a piece of chocolate cake in anticipation. I've heard that chocolate does something with the serotonin input to our brains. It stirs up the endorphins or something. "I'll have some more on the fourteenth. And maybe I'll eat a piece or two tomorrow ... and the next day too." I promised myself.

That night as I lay curled up under my comforter almost asleep, I watched a purple orchid drop lazily in front of my closed eyes. It somersaulted slowly, once, twice ... and then I slept.

It must have been very, very early the next morning because it was pitch dark outside when the bedside phone rang. It felt as though I had only just fallen asleep, but that couldn't have been. I had been sleeping on my right side when I heard it, so I rolled over halfway and reached out with my left hand to grasp the receiver. Bringing it to my left ear, I turned back on my side, curled around it, and said "Hello?"

It sounded as though there were not one, but two open lines.

On the one line I could hear a man's voice. He spoke faintly, with a Southern accent, but I couldn't understand the words and I didn't recognize the voice. He wasn't speaking to me and I couldn't hear the person at the other end of his conversation. For some reason, I had the distinct impression that it was a police line. It made no sense.

Then I became aware of the second open line. It struck me that it was like the old-fashioned phones we used to have out in the country during the era of "party lines." Quite often these lines would get crossed and you could hear whole conversations between two other people.

I lay there alert and listening. The second line sounded like a long, hollow tunnel.

And then I heard, *Hi!*

My breath caught in my throat. A flash of light lit the corners of my eyes the way it does with the onset of a migraine aura. I lay there stunned.

How often had I picked up the phone and heard that same "Hi!"?

Then I heard, *Hey Mom!*

Oh my God. I let out my breath very slowly. It was Drew. It was without any doubt, my son's voice. I heard him as clearly as if he was on the other end of a very good connection.

Listen to this... he was saying.

I listened. The line was filled with the sounds of birds... I could hear birds crying, cawing, squawking, and shrieking. They sounded like big birds. Like parrots, cockatiels, toucans, and parakeets... loud birds. Slashes of bright color lit up my brain. They came in flashes of reds and blues and yellows and images of birds in flight.

Did you hear that? I heard him as clearly as I ever have on the other end of the phone line.

"Oh Drew!" I breathed. "Birds."

I felt myself begin to cry. "Where are you?"

Almost immediately, his energy seemed to fade. Did my tears cause that?

You can be with me.

"Where? You mean like this? I can't be where you are..."

Very faintly, *Yes you can—you are now.*

And then he was gone. Both lines were silent. I put the phone back on its stand and as I did so, I distinctly heard him say, *Birds of Paradise.*

My mind shot back to that dream I had a few weeks before he died when I dreamed of this tropical place with the big colored birds in a place that felt and looked like paradise.

❧

Aside from the sound of my breathing, the room was silent. My eyes were wet, and while dragging myself up against the pillows, I could feel the impression of the earpiece against my left ear. I put my hand to my ear and held it there as if to recapture his words. Then I switched the bedside light on and stumbled toward the kitchen.

It was just beginning to get light outside as I poured myself a cup of tea and took it back to bed. Dawn was breaking over the Blue Ridge

Sitting there in silence, I replayed every word of what had just happened. In spite of everything I thought I knew about this ethereal world—the Other Side—the enormity of how much I didn't know had just walloped me like a baseball bat.

That was *him* on the phone. In spite of my dazed mind I have never been so sure of anything in my life. He called me. Valentine's Day is the day after tomorrow ... *you can be with me ...* I was with Drew! He was with me.

I stared at the now-silent telephone on my nightstand. If only it could talk. I had to know more about what had just happened.

With the sound of my son's voice ringing in my ears all morning, I went over and over every word, every sound of that phone call—from the long empty line to the stranger's voice and bird cries. I had heard many times that spirit will use electronics to bring themselves into our dimension. Radios apparently come on all by themselves, stereos begin to play, songs come on the car radio, and lights blink on and off.

I felt so happy. That place in my heart where Drew lives was light again. This was pure *elation!* Jump for Joy Happy! I felt as though I was bursting with boundless energy.

I jumped off my bed, startling the cat who was not amused by this amount of activity this early. Then, throwing on a pair of shorts and one of Drew's tees, I grabbed a broom from the closet and strode into the kitchen. My house was a mess. All my energy had been flowing through my survival pipes and there had been none left for anything else—including dustballs, fur, bread crumbs, and coffee-stained countertops.

Staring at the smudgy floors and then the windows where winter had left its murky fingerprints, it suddenly hit me that something had to be done. Things had to change. "Or, Miss Kitty," I told the cat who had retreated to the window seat in the living room, "this place is going to be condemned." She sat there bolt upright giving me the evil eye, a cobweb hanging off her right ear, and then arched her back and stalked off to her next favorite place under the dining room table.

The carpets got vacuumed, loosening dust and fur and fluff. Bathroom corners got swept, churning up two months of accumulated hair and dust. I pulled out chairs and tables, then went for the vacuum cleaner to finish the floor job. This was finally too much for Miss Kitty, who regarded the machine as a malignant, back-firing, and racket-making instrument from hell and disappeared through the cat door onto the deck for the rest of the day.

For the first time in months, I had the will to take charge—to make things better, to clean house. Something close to joy crept through the doors I'd kept closed, the eyelids I didn't want to open, the mind I'd kept locked behind my heart, and a voice box that had been hushed.

The feeling followed me from the bedrooms to bathrooms, scouring brush in hand, to the living room where I dusted and polished wood furiously, and then to the pantry, which should have been on the burn pile months ago. It had become an eyesore and a verifiable health hazard with all the accumulated foods and junk that filled its shelves.

Food had been pouring in steadily from helpful people just trying to be kind in the wake of Drew's sudden death—people who didn't know what else to do or say. It was going to take months to get through it all.

As if seeing all this for the first time, I began to take stock. Five cans of peaches ... nice. The can of corned beef ... never. Tins of cookies, and then a jar of caviar from an old friend who remembered the "Break-Up" party she and I had when her boyfriend walked out. Oh God! That seemed like eons ago ... but it wasn't even six months. I turned the can over in my hand and a sort of smile-snort came through my nose. That was a good evening. We lit some goodbye candles, broke out the caviar and capers and sour cream, and drank more than one bottle of wine. After that, we burned the love-notes. Maybe I should call her, I thought.

It would have to wait until later. This place had to be cleaned up.

Sorting out the pantry and straightening things up took a good part of the afternoon. I had no memory of having stacked any of this stuff, so it must have been the stuff that friends had brought over. By the time I got all the cans and boxes right-side up in the cabinet so they could at least be identified without having to stand on my head, things were starting to look up. Halfway through the chore, I stopped for a break and a gulped back a can of Diet Coke.

My hair smelled dusty and my hands felt sticky. I had been working furiously all day, buoyed by this morning's phone call. I hadn't been this energized in weeks.

A flood of thoughts kept running through my head. I rubbed the back of my hand across my forehead, leaving a sticky mess of honey or syrup or something at the hairline, and took another swallow from the can in my hand, thinking about the phone call.

"Okay, Drew," I said out loud. "Although you know I know it was you on the phone—would you give me a sign so I can be sure I'm not hallucinating? Which isn't impossible lately. I mean, you have to admit, darling—this is way more than I've ever experienced, and I'm questioning everything. I think it's entirely reasonable to ask you for a sign. I need a sign from you."

I put the cup on the kitchen table and flicked at a small pile of rice that had oozed out of a new bag. This was not a good sign. Picking up the bag, I noticed a couple of mouse droppings underneath it. That's what I thought! This is the time of year, mid-winter, when small, gray field mice find their way into houses looking for food and warmth. This small ragged hole in the bottom of the bag sent the rice into the trash can. By now, I had a trash bag full of expired cereals, stale crackers, some dried apricots that were now green, and a box of pasta with a gaping hole in one corner. That made sense now. Varmints!

"Yes. Show me a sign, Drew, and I will know that what I know in my heart—is real. That it was you on the phone."

No reply. "Okay. We should probably agree on a sign … You seem to be surrounded by tropical birds, monkeys … plants and things … but what."

Then I remembered the orchid that drifted though my almost sleep last night. "How about an orchid … Will you show me an orchid, please?"

How about that unexplained orchid just falling through my near sleep state? It was another preview, of course, another forerunner of something that was on its way down the pipes.

I turned back toward the kitchen table where a pile of cereal boxes and tea boxes and other boxes were waiting, and started to load them onto the shelves. Shelves that were dust free, honey drips wiped up, and not a mouse dropping in sight. Somewhere, there was a box of small mousetraps—but where … It wasn't a nice thought, but neither is the hantavirus.

Distracted momentarily by the thought of mousetraps, I picked up the last box left standing on the kitchen island, raised it, and just as I was about to shelve it, I took another look, grabbed it back and stared.

❧

It was a box of chocolates from Hawaii, and its lid was painted with sprays of purple and white orchids. I had no idea this was in here. I didn't buy this—I'd never seen it before! This was the sign I had asked for.

I hugged it to my chest smiling. "I *knew* it. Thank you, baby." My heart swelled and happiness swept over me. "Thanks for the orchids..."

There it was. The Sign.

Lying in bed late that night I had no idea what the next day might bring. My eyes were heavy, exhaustion had seeped into the void left by sadness and hyperactivity, and I fell asleep.

⁂

The following day the sun was shining and it was warm for so early in the year. My old friend Jim was turning hamburgers on the new fire pit he'd built. He wore a bush hat and a wind-breaker, and his sneakers were dusted with ash. He looked up shading his eyes against the glare.

"Is someone coming?" he asked. A wrought iron café table held the plates and salads and drinks while my dog Ranger lay beside Jim with his nose against the stones, not missing a thing. If one of those burgers dropped, it was his. "A car just turned into the top of the driveway," Jim said.

We could hear its tires crackling over the gravel road, hidden by the garage as it came down the hill. Then a small red Chevy emerged and ground to a stop at the wooden bridge half-way down the drive.

"Who is it?" He flipped a burger and Ranger looked up hopefully as the patty thwapped and spat on the grill.

Three young people climbed out and walked down the hill, across the winter grass.

"It's Mark! And JD! And there's a girl with them. It must be Mark's girlfriend." My heart jumped as I recognized Drew's two best friends walking toward us. I hadn't seen JD since the memorial in December. "Mark! JD!" I walked toward them.

"Hi, Mrs. Brock!" Mark reached the place where I was standing and thrust a bunch of red roses into my hand. "Happy Valentine's Day." He grinned, his dark good looks lighting up my day. Mark ran his dad's marina and faint smudges of grease showed on the backs of his hands. They were hands that had spent weeks winterizing boats and jet skis.

"Oh Mark—thank you." I hugged him, and held him for a long moment. This youngster had been Drew's sweetest and most reliable friend over the years.

"JD!" I stepped away from Mark and held out my hands. "How are you, guy?" Big boned, dark hair falling over his forehead making him look as though he'd just come off a football field, he hugged me quickly and thrust a single spray of orchids into my hand.

Purple, white, and yellow orchids. His eyes were watery as he stepped back.

I could hardly speak. All I could hear was the wind rustling through the leaves on the forest floor behind us and feel the presence of this young friend of Drew's beside me. When the words came they were more like a whispery croak. "JD ... you cannot imagine what this means," I told him, and reached out and hugged him again, feeling my own eyes well up.

JD was a good friend, one who allowed Drew to crash on his couch after late night parties and one who gave him a ride home if he needed one. He was also one of the friends who gave me heartburn. I worried about JD and Drew when they were together—two free spirits. JD had a lot of independence and a lot of living to get done. Like Drew, he was galloping into the rest of his life faster than I could keep up with. It worried me to death thinking of all the things they could get into. Were they driving too fast? There were more than enough poor choices to be made out there, and it was a given that if one didn't make them, the other would. Booze was one of them and for sure too much of it.

Yes, this lifestyle of high living and kicking it up, crashing here and there, driving country roads in the early morning hours scared the daylights out of me. Drew argued with me—"We're not bad, Mom! JD's a good guy! I like him!"

Well, I liked him too, but he and Drew together scared me to death.

Yet Drew chose JD to be his messenger that Valentine's day…I get it, Drew. One, two, three orchids.

Twelve

Where Angels Fly
above the Clouds

Late that February afternoon, when the boys had left, the pit fire had been doused and Jim had gone home, it started to rain. It was still raining when I went to bed that night, and I lay there quietly listening to the steady patter on the roof, my eyes closed waiting for sleep. A ghostly Hamlet drifted in. "To sleep, to sleep—perchance to dream ..." or at least wipe out my life for a while so I could stop thinking.

A great weariness, born of sorrow that was just too deep, enfolded me as I lay there in the dark and relaxed into its softness, closing out the night, the sound of rain on the roof and the gentle chime of the wall clock in the living room. The night felt like a giant cloud, billowy and black, but welcoming and warm. I slept.

And as I slept, I dreamed.

I heard, *Hey Mom—watch this!*

"Was this a dream? Or am I really there?" I asked as I gazed around in wonder. The space around me was filled with mounds of puffy clouds. Some were white, some tinged with blue and gray, some streaked with dark shadows. Then there were birds ... There were seagulls swooping around me, as big as dolphins. *As big as dolphins!* Get outta here! Gray and blue and white seagulls, and there was Drew clinging to one of them, astride the bird's back, holding the top of its wings, veering, racing, and flying through the sky.

Joy radiated from him. His eyes shone and his teeth were whiter than white as he smiled. His energy sparked the sky like lightning. It was contagious and I began to laugh. My laughter carried me upward and when I looked down I saw that my feet were swathed in clouds. "I want to fly like that!" I yelled. And when I jumped for joy, I found I could hover. Like a bird! A dragonfly!

Drew swooped low beside me. *You can! Watch me—there's a knack to it.*

His cheeks were flushed, and his eyes were bright with excitement. Exhilaration like none I'd ever felt filled the air. There were the two rosy smudges on his cheeks I knew so well. Then he waved and flew up and over a bank of clouds and let go of the bird.

He was standing in the clouds, hands on his hips saying, *Now watch this!*

As I watched, one of those giant birds came swooping out of the sky, flying close to him. As it did so he leapt from the cloud onto its back. *Try that!* he shouted.

So I did.

Choosing a cloud to stand on wasn't as easy as it sounded. The first one I picked caved in like a soufflé. It had no bounce. The next one moved out from under my feet. But finally I found the perfect cloud. It was puffy, firm, and springy.

Doing what he did, I waited for a bird to fly close enough to me so that I could grab it. One did and I sprang! Slipping sideways on its back, I could hear Drew's laughter from far away. This was going to take some practice. I felt as though I was hanging on for dear life as the bird flew through the clouds with me straddled across its torso, one leg barely dangling over the other side. But as it turned and dove and soared, I suddenly shifted and landed right in the middle of its blue-gray feathered back.

It all felt so normal, so real. I felt as though I was one with the bird and I felt great love for it. I wondered, "Am I in heaven?"

Up ahead of me, Drew was flying fast—racing hard, jumping clouds and diving, turning on invisible currents. I followed, almost expecting to see a tall plume of vapor spraying out behind him. Racing in the wake of his elation felt like flying through warm, brightly colored bubbles, effervescent and alive. The air was electric, sharp, and ecstatic and shot through with silver and bright light.

Don't be scared—you'll get the knack ... His words came to me, flying on the wind ... *WhooooHAAAA!* I heard him yell as he bounded higher, skimming the tops of cumulus, diving the valleys, skating on the edge of cirrus.

I wasn't scared. I wanted to whoop for joy! So I did. "Woweeeeeeee!!" I flew with him, and we flew like the wind.

༺ঔ

My eyelids fluttered open briefly. Everything was quiet. The clock on the wall was chiming. Miss Kitty lay stretched out alongside my leg, purring. She always began to purr when I awoke in the middle of the night, like a mother crooning her baby back to sleep. My comforter felt soft and as warm as seagull feathers. I pulled it up around my neck and slept for the rest of the night more soundly than I had in weeks.

When I awoke again, my life felt as light as those billowing clouds. My soul was still vibrating to the joy of flying with Drew. "Drew, that was *awesome!*" I whispered. "That and the phone call. Speaking of which, I know this is asking a lot, you know I know that call was real! Look at the orchids! But could you come up with one more sign? Will you show me a pirate? You know, parrots, orchids—I just think that a pirate would round things off."

The sound of his laughter and his happiness stayed with me all day. Standing on the deck early that morning with my coffee cup in my hand, hugging my robe around my chest, I watched the sky as pink as new dawn unfold like a rose to present the day. Thin wisps of cloud tinged with bright winter light, hung like Belgium lace above the hills that stood dark blue and silent waiting for the sun to light the indigo to mauve. Wild geese had landed in the cove during the night and I could hear their chuckles and sleepy honking as they gathered for the long flight ahead. Where were they headed today? Were they leaving ahead of the storm I'd heard was making its way toward us? Would they fly east? Propelled by the storm's strong head winds, they would reach the shore early. Do they like seagulls, I wondered?

Seagulls. I felt a rush of pleasure as I recalled my wild ride with Drew through the billowing clouds. Lifting my face to the sky I felt again the softness of cloud on my cheeks as we raced through the sky, holding on for everything I was worth. Maybe that was the message in the dream. *It's a wild ride. Hold on for all you're worth. I'm riding with you.*

I went back inside and made a hot cup of coffee to sip while I got dressed for the day. Like the geese, I had things to do and places to go. After my energetic cleanup, the pantry was bare, and common sense told me that you can survive just so long on canned peas, the sole survivors of the mouse invasion. After Walt died, I learned that it was a good thing to have a plan for the day. It didn't have to be a major plan, maybe just a trip to the grocery store. But I forced myself to get out every day. On some really down days, all I could manage was a hike to the mail box half a mile up the road. But that was okay, too.

By late morning, with a car full of grocery bags, I pulled into the parking lot at the library and headed inside. A thought had popped into my head as I was starting the car and about to head home, so turning around, I'd headed the other way. The librarian at the front desk recognized me and waved as I walked quickly by on my way to the fiction aisle. My eyes scanned the alphabetized shelves, and among the B's I found what I was looking for.

"Jonathan Livingston Seagull." The check out lady intoned. "I just luuuv this book." She sighed and pushed her glasses higher up her nose as she stared into the computer. Her knuckles were gnarled with arthritis and decorated with large rings from another time. Gold bangles clanked loosely on her thin wrists. "Here you go, dear." She handed me the book and her hand touched mine. "Are you doing all right?" she asked gently.

I nodded and blinked rapidly. Darn. Every time someone showed me concern these days, I teared up. "I'm okay," I smiled at her and picked up the book. "Thanks for asking." This was a small town and everyone knew about Drew.

❧

Later that day, Cindy called me. "I'm on my way to the beach!" she said. "It's such a gorgeous day that Spencer and I decided to run down and check on the condo."

I wished I was there, driving down the road, flying down the freeway in Cindy's BMW with the smell of salt air wafting through the car.

"There's almost no traffic," she was saying, "but there are birds all over the utility wires. Huge seagulls or something!"

They're gathering ahead of the storm that was plunging south and east from the Great Lakes, I thought.

This must be the day for seagulls. One, two, three acts starring seagulls. The dream, the book, and the birds on the wire.

❧

Vegetable soup was simmering on the stove. It was a dandy. I'd spent most of the afternoon chopping the fresh veggies I'd bought that morning and thrown in a ham hock for good measure. My taste buds must be waking up again because my mouth was watering. Black dog was salivating beside my feet, and Miss Kitty was curled up on the loveseat by the window not caring much but purring loudly. There was no fish in the pot so she wasn't interested.

Outside the window, the storm was moving in from the northwest, just as the weather people had said it would. Hulking masses of dark gray clouds made their way toward the lake, mounding high against the back drop of yellow sky. I turned the living room lamps on and heard a far away rumble of thunder echoing through the hills.

Much later these clouds would invade the seashore hundreds of miles to the east. Would there be seagulls there? Would they dive and swoop and skim the wave tops as they raced ahead of the approaching storm. I was smiling as I sat down with a bowl of warm soup and a packet of chips. I picked up my library book and with the rain beating against the windows, blowing through the evergreens and misting the lake, I began to read Richard Bach's book for about the fourth time.

Flying with Drew, remembering Jonathan Livingston. Life was okay for now.

⌇

The next morning wasn't so good because at about 10:00 a.m. I remembered a fund-raising meeting for a new Civic Center that I was supposed to attend. I had forgotten all about it. I hadn't even written it down anywhere. At least, nowhere that I could remember. That's the trouble with this sort of grieving. It absorbs and takes over life, and because it has its own timetable, you can't move it out of the way. This wasn't the first time I had forgotten something. It took real concentration to keep my life together, which is harder than it used to be because concentration itself is a casualty of grief. So is short-term memory.

I called one of the Earth Angels. "I'm going crazy," I said. "Losing my mind..."

"No, you're not," she said cheerfully. "A few months after my daughter died I forgot a dentist appointment, a school conference, and a music lesson all in one day. And last week, Friday was one of those anniversary days and I was so distracted that I put the newspaper into the oven instead of the pan of biscuits."

I've heard this kind of grief equated with Post Traumatic Stress Syndrome. Is this what I was experiencing?

What really bugged me was that there were people I've met over the previous two years that I had no conscious recollection of meeting. I didn't know their names or where I met them. But they definitely knew me and they always said, "How nice to see you again!" Yes, well... I wanted to say, "I have no clue who you are, but you seem very nice..."

It was one of those days. While I was worrying about the meeting I'd missed, I almost missed a lunch date with a friend that I remembered just in time, and then left all the bills I was supposed to mail on the kitchen counter making one of them at least two days late.

Finally, I just gave up and went out for a walk with Ranger. Miss Kitty came, too. She liked these hikes. Either that or she didn't want the breadwinner getting lost in the woods. Ranger and I hadn't decided which it was.

The woods in spring were lovely. There were no orchids here, but the Joshua trees were in full purple bloom. Long spiky branches coated with blossom trembled in the early evening breeze, scattering their petals, carpeting the woodland floor. Pale green and curly fiddlehead ferns broke through the deep loam beneath the trees and star white dogwood blossom lit the gloaming.

I walked down to the spring that ran through the deep gulley on the edge of my woods and watched the water seep and tumble over white and yellow quartz, bouncing between moss-covered banks. Tiny fish darted among the bubbles, and my eye was drawn to a pure white heart-shaped petal. I reached into the stream and held my hand under the flow to capture it as it bobbled by. The water was icy, coming as it did from the mountains that surround this valley, and my fingers turned pink as I raised the petal and held it up to the sun.

Droplets of water-speckled white satin and twilight added its sparkle in the shadow of the woods.

Raising my head, I noticed a dogwood limb overhanging the water, and in the crook of its branches there was a second heart-shaped petal. I reached above my head and brought it down to join the other in my palm.

There would be three of these, I knew.

It was early for the dogwood to lose its petals, so there were only a few of them on the pathway out of the forest—and those petals were brown and crushed. I gave up the search for that third one, and would have stepped on it if I hadn't looked down at the exact moment my foot was poised to crush it. There it was! As perfectly shaped and white and creamy as its two sisters I held loosely in my hand.

Three perfect heart-shaped petals. When I got home I placed them between the back pages of my journal, and as I did so I could feel my spirit reaching for Drew and Drew's responding. We're two spirits joined in a dance I've never seen before, I thought. Or more accurately, it was a dance I couldn't remember.

But the birds in flight, soft clouds, and flowers were good things to have in any dance, I thought. So, play on. Give me excess of it … as Shakespeare once wrote about music in his play *Twelfth Night*. My mind fished that out of some long-forgotten recess in the gray matter as my mind went back to my junior year in high school. I think it was the Duke speaking to Malvolio.

Well, the dance and the music were fine, I thought as I drifted off to sleep that night. A sad song, but beautiful music often is. Then a flash dream streaked like a shadowy phantom across the stage of my fading consciousness, stopping the music. It was smeared with images of high waves, heavy seas ,and a sailboat rocking … and then it was gone. A bright light on a far horizon shone … and sleep moved in.

༄

About a week after Valentine's Day, I had asked Drew to send me a pirate. A pirate would go well with the orchids and the tropical birds. It didn't come that day or the next, and I forgot about it for a while as I went about the tasks of daily life on this planet. Then it was March and a cold wind was blowing off the mountains as I stepped out of my car and hurried toward the library to return Richard Bach's book. I had to pass a small gift shop on the way and as I did, the display in the window stopped me in my tracks.

Five o'clock Somewhere was the theme the decorator had chosen, and the window was filled with strips of lighted sand and big macaws painted in reds and blues and yellows, perched on stands among paper palm trees and martini glasses. Colored glass jugs and brightly patterned napkins, light-catching glassy pebble-filled trays full of tiny beach umbrellas, and multihued strings of beads that had been strewn on a painted floor were also set out. The scene was bright and happy and sunshiny and tropical. It drew me inside on this cold and windy day.

It was midmorning and inside the store a few early tourists mingled with the locals. I picked my way through tumbling arrangements of silk flowers and baskets of stuffed animals and trays of seashells and candles, toward the outside window near the back of the store. The whole place made you feel as though you were on a tropical island. Any minute now, someone was going to hand me a pina colada and a straw hat.

A noisy nine- or ten-year-old boy was darting around in front of me. He picked up and shook everything in his path and he was beginning to get on my nerves. Locals around here are easily irritated by crowds of tourists. We know we shouldn't be, but that doesn't stop us.

So I took a deep breath and with pursed lips I kept walking toward a giant parrot in the window display. Then the boy stopped short, right in front of me, and I almost collided with the brat as he reached toward the display to grab a teddy bear that was sitting beside a bunch of parrots and fake bananas.

I choked back a "Watch Out!"

He pressed the teddy bear's paw and the toy bear began to sing, "Ole Ole!!" And as I looked at it, I realized I was staring at a teddy bear pirate with an eye patch, a red striped shirt, and a broad-brimmed black hat. It had a parrot on its shoulder that squawked in harmony with the bear.

The boy lost interest after a minute and shoved the toy bear back on its shelf where it sat cockeyed and slumped over with its black patch shoved down to his nose.

There was the pirate I'd asked for. I might have missed it completely if it hadn't been for the child.

And a little child will lead the way... a quote straight out of the Christian bible.

Of course I bought the bear.

It felt a little crazy to be carrying the toy out of the store. My toy. Not a present for one of the kids. But you know, crazy isn't a bad place to hang out until things get better.

When I got home, I lifted the little furry guy out of his bag and sat him on the window seat overlooking the lake. Then I pressed his paw and he began to sing. Miss Kitty was appalled. She opened one eye and sat there growling quietly for as long as it took for her to figure out that he wasn't going to be a problem.

A singing pirate—with a parrot... I named him Jack Sparrow after Johnny Depp's Pirate of the Caribbean.

Drew had done this perfectly. "Shall we dance?" I offered Jack Sparrow my hand, but he didn't move. So I danced alone. Here, months later, was the meaning of the DVDs Drew had sent me before he left us.

A pirate that came with a parrot. It occurred to me sometime on the day I brought the bear home that it's funny that the pirate's name is Jack... and *Sparrow*... *those birds*...

Karen called me the following day. I told her about Jack Sparrow the bear and made her laugh. It was a good sound. Karen hadn't had a lot to laugh about. Her father's dying had opened a gaping hole in her life that even a young and boisterous family couldn't fill.

"It's because with them, I'm the grown-up. I can't be daddy's little girl ever again... so I have to act like a mommy. Even when I don't feel old enough or smart enough to be anybody's mommy," She told me. "I just want Dad to be here. I want to hear him say, *'Tell me what's wrong—we'll fix it…'* No matter how down I got when things went wrong, I always knew Dad would be there. Now he's gone."

There was a broken bond there that I couldn't fix. That's the way it sometimes is between fathers and daughters. And sometimes there are no right words either.

"Did I tell you that once after he died I thought I heard dad laugh?" She added. "I know it was him. No one laughs like him."

She paused for a moment and I could hear the frustration in her voice. "I haven't been getting *anything* from Drew!" she said. "I don't know why he doesn't come to me! I'm the one who *always* understood him and talked to him, and it's as though he's completely forgotten who I am!"

"You're going through a rough spell—he can't find room in your head," I suggested.

"But what about you? He comes to you all the time."

I shook my head. I couldn't explain that. Maybe it's the bond between a mother and a child.

"But there was one thing," she said. "It's probably nothing, but there were strange birds around yesterday. I was sitting out on the porch with my computer and I saw a pair of red-tailed hawks—I've always only seen one. It struck me as strange that there were two together. And then a bald eagle landed on the tree by the river a couple of hours later!"

American Indian lore says that hawks are powerful messengers of insight, vision, and courage. They embody strong feminine energy. Bald eagles are said to capture the light of the sun to illuminate our way. They light up the past, present, and future. The meditation group had spent a lot of time learning about animal spirits. It helped that we had an animal communicator in the group and he guided us to the right reading materials and articles.

"It sounds to me as though you got some powerful messages from Drew. He sends birds…"

"And early this morning, there were six cardinals on the front lawn," she said. "Two's the most I've ever seen." High esteem, the Native Americans say, is the gift of cardinals.

"Three powerful messengers." I noted.

⚬⊃

Two weeks later, Cindy's daughter Spencer called me. Her voice was breathy and excited. "The strangest thing has happened!" She took a deep breath. "Do you remember us telling you that we were going to Memphis for auditions? And that there would be company reps from all over the country watching and looking for people to cast in upcoming shows?"

"I do!" I replied. "What happened?"

"Just listen to *this*, Ginny… you know how I believe that Drew is all around me since he died? That in some ways I think he's guiding my music—leading me to the right places, and I really and truly think he's my soul mate." She gasped for air, "And that when I'm faced with a decision, I ask 'What should I do, Drew?' and I get an answer, and if I act on it—*it's right…?*"

"Yes, I remember." She was going to hyperventilate.

"Well! Right before this big do, with all these producers there, *I lost my voice! Can you believe it!* I did everything I could think of the night before to make it better, and when I got up this morning it was *terrible! I could barely croak!*"

"Oh no. What did you do?"

"Well I went to the audition, and I went out on stage thinking that if I opened my mouth and no sound came out, no sound would come out, and that would be that! And I also said, *Drew! If you can do anything about this—something big—this would be the time!*"

Silence. Spencer paused for dramatic effect. "Are you ready for this?"

I said, "I can't wait."

"Well ... standing backstage, waiting for my call, I was soooo scared. Then, when it came, I walked out onto the stage and all of a sudden ... I was absolutely, totally calm."

"No way!"

"Yes way! I opened my mouth and hit every note. *Perfectly!*"

"*NO!*" She was so funny. I felt a laugh bubbling up and threatening to break the surface. I coughed to cover it up.

"*YES!* And here's the rest of it ... When I finished the song, one of the producers walked up to the stage *clapping*, and handed me his business card. *And guess what!* Guess where he was from?"

I got an eerie feeling. "No idea. Where?"

"*The Rocky Mountain Repertory Theater!* The guy had come all the way to Memphis! He said he was *very impressed* and told me I would be hearing from him!" she squealed. "Oh my God I'm so excited!"

The end result of this audition was that Spencer was given the female lead role of Mable, in *Pirates of Penzance.* Those pirates again. Three "sightings." The DVDs, the teddy bear pirate, and Spencer's show.

Those darn coincidences.

Thirteen

Walk Through
the Storm with Me

The winds of March blew strong that year of 2009. I could hear dead limbs cracking and falling to the forest floor in the woods beside the house. Since it was also colder than usual, I spent a lot of time indoors wishing for summer and warm sunny days.

Sometimes on this tough journey, when the road just seems too long, I have just had to drift through the fog and try not to think.

This year had been a roller coaster ride. There were oases of calm and some peace, and even a few happy times. There were distractions that appeared in the form of my children and their children, candy bars and good wine, and better friends. When they showed up, life was doable for short spells.

Then sometimes the pain washed over me from out of the blue, the loss became too big, and I thought it might be easier to die than to live in this world without Walt and Drew. It was not a good place to be. These jet black thoughts came from a well so deep that I couldn't find the bottom. Going down, down ... down, I didn't know if I was coming back. Perhaps, if I could ever reach the bottom I would find peace in its unfathomable depths ... If I could only find the bottom ...

And then there was a day when sobs wrenched what remained of reason and all meaning from my life, and I lay face down on the carpet and cried out loud and long until my head hurt. My heart hurt. My body hurt. I put my hand to my chest, turned over and faced the ceiling unseeing, my mind unable to cope. I couldn't feel the hard floor beneath me and my tears coursed down the sides of my face to roll off and bury themselves in the short fibers of the carpet.

"Help me. Somebody help me," I screamed silently at first, and then out loud. *"Pleeeease ... help me! Where are you, Walt"* My hands clawed at my cheeks, pulled my hair and clutched at air. Then I saw Karen's face, Michael's—and the phone was ringing.

It's jangling "Rrrrrrring ..." ripped through me, startling me out of this dark, hideous place called grief. I stood up unsteadily and walked slowly to my bedroom ignoring the phone. I climbed under the covers and stared out through the shades. It was dark outside.

As dark as my soul.

The phone stopped ringing. I slept.

It was a worried, fettered sleep. I felt myself tossing from one side of the bed to the other. My head found no comfort. Pillows that seemed fine yesterday had for some reason become lumpy and misshapen, and raising the back of my hand to my closed eyes I found that my cheeks were wet with tears. Pieces of carpet fuzz stuck to my face.

Once again I called out to God, to anyone. *Help Me.*

Then I slept again and in my sleep, I dreamed.

❧

It's as though I'm being thrown around in a storm like a help-less butterfly. One minute I'm flying high on some hair-raising current and the next, I'm flung with demonic force upon the ground. I can taste the dirt inside my mouth and feel the grit on my knees.

My voice calls out, "Drew! Drew! Walt! Where are you? … Remember the sandstorms in the desert?" The Arabs call them *shammal.*

I raise my head and look skyward, but there is no sky. Massive sand clouds fill the air, blanketing the land and everything on it. Trees become ghostly pale forms, dunes mound higher and higher as the desert is swept clean of everything but sand—beautiful sweeping shapes and ridges of high mountainous sand. Blowing dust covers the road, wiping out visibility. Sand mats my hair and coats my skin.

Is there anyone here? Where is the road? I don't know where to go or which way to turn. Everything is covered with sand. I'm alone … blowing in the wind—my eyes are caked with sand and water—they are filled with fine dust, blinded and stinging.

There is silence. The wind is muffled by the shammal. If there's any life out here, it is buried deep, deep down.

I find myself looking down at the ground. My feet are bare and clean. How can that be? And I see footprints … there are footsteps. There are clear footsteps in the sand leading away from me.

In the silence, I hear Drew speak, *I'm here. Walking with you. I'll always be here.*

Oh Drew…

I feel calm. A gentle fog drops in and folds around me. Soft hands bathe my face in cool moisture. My eyes no longer sting, there is no dust in my hair or on my skin. The air is clear and I can see beyond the earth.

When I woke up, the Dolly/Whitney song was playing in my mind. It was okay. I would walk this path taking only my bittersweet memories. With Drew beside me, I could survive this.

❧

I had been making plans for a trip to New York to see Michael and his family. Michael, as it turned out, was feeling the same neglect that Karen was. "I want to *see* Drew or Dad," he said. Pushing his skepticism aside, he had been trying hard to make sense out of the "other worldly" parts of my life that I talked about, but he never fully grasped or believed any of it.

"It's not that I *disbelieve* it," he said. "I'm not dead set against it, but I really want to feel these things you talk about. I want to see them for myself."

He was feeling the weight of his younger brother's death deeply. He had always been there to help when Drew asked for it, and even when he didn't. He took the responsibility of being the "big brother" seriously.

"I just feel so shaken. So helpless…" he said. "Anything from Drew would help. HEY DREW!" He yelled once, looking skyward and cupping his hands around his mouth. "Can you hear me, buddy?"

I prayed for just one little "pat" from Drew.

∽◌

In the second week of March I flew up to New York for my grandson James's ninth birthday, as I had done the previous two years. We had a ritual, James and I. When I got there, we would make a special trip to Times Square where the worlds' largest Toys 'R' Us stands. Together we would brave the crowds both inside and outside the massive toy shop so that he could pick out a birthday present.

This year was no different. In fact, this year was especially important for me to be with my children and grandchildren. The sounds of children playing, shouting, squabbling, laughing—the sounds of a young family LIVING—lifted me out of the depths for an hour or two, a day or two, at a time and gave me the push to keep going.

Then there was Manhattan. Have you ever felt the city's energy? It's alive and young and exciting and it won't be ignored.

Ahhh…to lose myself in the sounds of the traffic, the smells, and the millions of people on its sidewalks…to breathe in the scent of sweet roasting nuts and exhaust fumes. Right in front of the toy store was a pile of steaming, fresh manure from one of the daisy-bonneted Central Park ponies. I didn't care. I wrinkled my nose. It was life. Everything here was alive and kicking up stink and sugar and dust and noise. It was alive and real.

My children, their children, the life of the city, and all of that combined energy were confirmation of life continuing, no matter how bad things got.

❧

Mary Katherine, mother of my three red-headed grandchildren, met me at La Guardia. "Did Michael tell you about his dream?" she asked as we drove through the city, across Central Park to the West Side where they lived.

"No." I shook my head.

"It was all about Drew and Walt. He woke me up at about five o'clock in the morning to tell me about it—he was so excited!"

I felt my spirit soar. This was what I'd been hoping for.

"But I'm going to let Michael tell you himself," she said.

I couldn't wait to hear it. I could see she was excited about his dream but I didn't push her.

It was early afternoon as she drove through the traffic that crowded the streets and bridges from La Guardia to the city. Taxis missed us by inches as they sped past us, horns honked as they ferried passengers from Long Island to wherever they were going. It took about fifteen minutes to get to Manhattan. Hurtling down the streets, the garish signs hanging from Harlem's storefronts and diners flashed past us; the streets were full of people on bicycles and delivery men wheeling across the intersections with their wares. Mary Katherine swung her car down a side street, taking the shortcut through Central Park to the

West Side. The park was an oasis of calm with its massive shade trees, trails, and stone bridges.

The children were home from school when we got to their apartment. The baby had just woken up from his nap and as soon as the sitter had left, we took everyone into the park, accompanied by a bike, a scooter, and a stroller, as well as a bag full of snacks, drinks, and balls.

"I don't know how you do this," I told my daughter-in-law as I watched in awe as she herded everyone through the door, helmeted and strapped in, shod and knee-padded, and veered them all to the right, down the block, and to the park entrance.

We stayed about an hour, and by five o'clock we were home. Michael called to say he was on his way and the first thing he did when he walked through the door was to hug me and say, "I dreamed of Drew and Dad." He stood in front of me smiling, his hands on his hips. "How about a glass of wine?"

"Okay," I nodded.

"So, here's the thing." He walked to the kitchen and opened the fridge. "I was at the lake house—in the dream that is. The lake looked beautiful!" He paused and looked over his shoulder at me, the bottle of red wine in his hand. "I had the distinct feeling that it was our lake but so much more beautiful. It was broad, with deep, sparkling blue water—clear and warm."

Michael found three wine glasses. "I was with Drew and Dad. Everyone was happy. You could just feel it in the air. We were all happy, calm, and enjoying the beauty of the place. The house looked the same in a way but bigger, and much better than ours."

He handed Mary Katherine and me each a glass of red wine. It was that warm, deep red, almost black color, and was slightly chilled. Outside, the sounds of the city climbed high up to the seventh floor of the apartment building, providing a muffled rendition of background music. A cacophony of taxicabs, screeching tires, and horns.

"Dad was on his riding lawn mower—just like he always was, only this machine was a BMW! I didn't know they made those!" He laughed. "And this was when I began to doubt the dream, thinking to myself that this is the kind of thing I would buy—not Dad."

"Well, I think if they make BMW lawn mowers on the other side, he'd get one," I smiled. "He owned at least two of their cars—remember?"

"Yes—now that you mention it!" He stood there, hands on his hips, remembering. "The dark green one and that terrible yellow one he bought secondhand for Karen. Anyway, while I was standing there watching Dad, Drew came tearing across the bridge on a motorbike." Michael grinned wryly. "It was so Drew. And as I watched, he drove it right off the bridge and into the lake." Michael smacked his palms together in a sliding motion as he spoke.

"I can just see it," I said. Drew had put two cars into the lake when he was sixteen and again at seventeen when during a dry spell—a drought, to be exact—he thought he could drive his Toyota truck along a newly risen sandbar beside the house. He sank the truck up to its axles in mud.

"Typical!" Michael placed one hand behind his head and pursed his lips remembering. "How many times did Max's garage have to come and tow Drew out of the mud on the edge of the lake?"

Mary Katherine giggled.

Michael shook his head. "Anyway, the thing that struck me was that—no one was upset!"

"That's weird. Dad didn't yell?" I asked.

"No! Then suddenly," Michael went on, "Drew and the bike were back on the bridge. I don't know how they got there, they were just there all of a sudden. He was grinning that big, goofy grin as he walked up to me, and he said, *I'm fine. Look! Nothing happened to me.* He pointed to the bike and said, *Just a little scratch on the fender!* I remember him showing me the mark. The bike should have been smashed! And he wasn't even wet ... I don't get it!"

He brought the wine bottle over and topped up our glasses. "Just a dream though—right?"

I smiled. "Think so?" A siren wafted up from the street, echoing around the canyons of tall buildings.

Michael took a sip out of his glass. His eyes were serious. "It was so real—I was *there*—in a place that I recognized but much, much better ... *I was there!* Then I woke up. It was very early in the morning—still dark outside, but I had to wake Mary Katherine and tell her about it."

"He did!" Mary Katherine said. "He was shaking me, saying 'Wake up, listen to this!'"

"I didn't want to forget any details—and it was very detailed—so clear! The colors were brighter than anything I've ever seen. But the thing that impressed me most was the feeling around the place. Especially the *warmth*. Everything was good. It was all okay. We were happy." He paused. "The place was just full of love. You could feel it everywhere. Like a glow."

My handsome son was reliving the peace and warmth of the dream. I could see it in his face, in his eyes ... eyes that had been given a glimpse of another dimension.

"He showed you a piece of heaven ..." I said.

"That's exactly what it was."

～⌒〇

Lying in my bed that night facing the window seven floors up from the street, I looked out at the skyscraper lights of Manhattan. I was surrounded by lights. Down below I could hear the sounds of the city, and up above I could see the lights twinkling on and off as late-nighters came home and early-nighters turned out their lights. I knew that if I woke up at 3 a.m. there would still be lights on.

I thought about Michael. What a dream! He seemed more peaceful than I'd seen him since Drew died. That dream was exactly what he needed to pull him through the sadness.

"Thank you Dream Boys." I said silently to Walt and Drew. "Your visit and its timing were perfect." Even I could feel something close to happiness when Michael was telling me about the dream. That big goofy grin ... How clearly I saw it. My mind traveled backwards through the years at breakneck speed as I remembered Drew at two years old. Even then he had a taste for speed.

Walt and I had gone into town leaving him in Michael's hands for an hour. We came home and as we rounded the corner and thumped over the packed sand of the access road into our driveway, we caught sight of our one-day old three-wheeler, tearing across the dunes with Michael at the helm and Drew bouncing a foot in the air every time the machine hit a trough or a mound in the sand.

Walt and I leapt out of the car, and cupped our hands over our mouths yelling, "MICHAEL!!"

How he heard us, I'll never know. But he turned the machine around and jogged it over the stretch of desert to where we stood exploding with a multitude of recommendations about NOT putting two-year-olds on the back of three-wheelers.

"Goddammit!" That was Walt.

They were both spattered with sand, and though sweaty, they both sported big goofy grins. The three-wheeler was sold before lunch the next day.

❧

There was an email from Cindy waiting for me when I got back to Virginia a week later.

"You know that, of course, because I've told you a dozen times, Spencer has been offered, and has accepted, the female lead in Gilbert and Sullivan's *Pirates of Penzance* put on by the Rocky Mountain Theater Group. But get this! The male lead, *the lead Pirate is named Jack in real life!*"

Drew was doing everything he could to get me through this. I felt him at work. He was the same, sensitive being that he had always been. Loving, empathetic, always there to help someone who needed help. His personality was unchanged. He was finding myriad ways to show us that he still lived, he loved, and he was still here. Somehow I knew that his shock and sorrow was as deep as mine at this parting. But he was reaching out to me in the same way he did when his father died.

Fourteen

No Tears Will
Fall in Heaven

*I*t was a bright April morning as I drove to the gym. My girlie circuit gym had non-scary pale pink machines for girls. I started going there when Walt died and discovered that it helped to reshape me on many different levels. It was a place to trim the excess, firm up the rest of you, and chat as your skin popped with sweat. The music was good. They played all that retro stuff like "La Bamba," "Blue Suede Shoes," "Johnny B. Goode," and a bunch of songs I actually knew the words to.

Some of us girls were in our thirties, most of us were forty to fifty, and some of us were sixty and seventy plus. These were the "girls" who wore their dangling earrings, full makeup, and suede booties to gym class. Jocks we were not. But we were all therapists and "Chicken Soupers."

Then there was the hard core section who crammed dimpled cellulose and expanded veins into spandex, and were willing to dole out psychology and medicinal fixes at the drop of a hat. Nobody in this group had a license to practice medicine, but who needed one? And then there were the timid ones who never had any cellulite to begin with, but were here for "strength training." They were all ears, tuned into the repartee among the more outgoing crew and spent the afternoons drinking tisanes of acai berries and cinnamon, of chamomile and blackberry brandy, and God knows what else.

The girlie gym was a good place to get my endorphins zinging. And listening to the stories and dramas of their lives, so tame compared to mine, lifted me up like a candy bar full of nuts. They gave me the urge to try this life for one more lousy day. They kept the shadows at bay and the sounds of emptiness that filled the airwaves around me.

Then on the way home when the endorphins were wearing off and just when I was thinking how pointless all this living was without Drew, I got stuck in traffic. It must have been a Friday. This is the day when all the weekenders came into town, and I was stalled in a line of cars waiting for a break in the stream of traffic so I could cross the road.

How many times did Drew travel this road on his way home? Home from school, home from town, home from a friend's house ... Not for the first time, I wondered, "Is he okay wherever he is?"

I leaned forward and turned on the radio. A girl country singer was singing the last stanza of a sad song about someone who had died young. But she could see him smiling from heaven and he wanted her to know that he was fine and she shouldn't be sad.

The song ended so I switched channels. Close to tears myself, I landed on a station where Eric Clapton was finishing with the last line of "Tears in Heaven." The very next song that came on opened with words that my heart had been repeating over and over since Drew's passing saying that one day, he and I would be together again.

Now try stringing those concepts together.

He was fine and she shouldn't be sad … in heaven no one sheds tears … and we'll be together again.

How coincidental is that?

One, two, three songs all saying one thing. Message received, Drew Boy.

As if to give substance to the music in the car on my way home from the gym, I had another dream that night.

The clearest dreams, the most lucid dreams, the dreams that are not dreams but spirit visits, often occur in those few minutes before waking as we hover between the realms of alpha and beta consciousness. They burst through the night easily, unhampered by the busy conscious mind and the heavy walls of emotion holding back the ever constant flood.

Meeting no resistance, spirit is able to filter through the veil that separates dimensions as easily as mist.

It struck me in those wee small, lightly sleeping hours, that this is what was happening on the front porch of my home that night.

I was standing there at the top of the front steps. The air felt still. The light was dusklike, filtering through translucent grays and pale cobalt morphing into darker shades of grays and pinks. My body felt weightless in a dress of flimsy cotton, which fell in soft folds below my knees.

My hand was almost transparent on the railing of the steps, and when I looked up toward the garage on the hill, I noticed someone on the walkway. There were actually two, maybe three young male beings, and Drew stood out in front. He was smiling. He didn't seem to be completely solid, but he was whole and there was a faint glow around him. Although I could see the others, I could barely make them out. One was clearer than the other, but I didn't recognize either of them.

Aware that my heart was pounding, I put my hand on my chest, and as I did so I heard my son say,

Hey Mom! Dad was wrong. I didn't expire! He grinned at me, his hands on his hips and the dimming light flared for just a moment.

"Drew!" *Expire?* That wasn't a word Drew would use.

Then before I could think about that, instantly it seemed, Drew was beside me on the porch. I don't know how he got there. He didn't walk down the walkway, I know he didn't fly— he was just there.

We embraced. We held each other, my face buried in his shoulder. I was crying, but strangely, they were tears of happiness. My son was here. I felt the physical warmth of his young body, the smell of his skin, and the feel of his cheek on my forehead. There was gentleness all around us; we were wrapped in a strange softness that was softer than anything I'd ever known.

When I awoke from the dream I could still feel his skin, his warmth and the intensity of our meeting. There was no doubt in my mind that he was here. And then, as if to confirm that he was here, he had used a word I had never heard him use before —*expire*. But it was a word I heard him read one night when an old friend Dorothy had given him one of her cards.

Cindy and I were with Drew in Vail the year before he died. Cindy was there to ski and I was there to visit Drew. We were all out to dinner with Dorothy, who had a place in Vail. At the end of the evening, I saw her hand Drew one of her cards. He looked at it then read it out loud: *"ASPIRE TO INSPIRE BEFORE YOU EXPIRE!"* He said, "I like that." And put the card in his wallet.

∽◌

I drove into town the next day, still buoyed by the dream. The city of Roanoke surrounded by mountains was misty and cool in late spring. As I climbed to the top of the mountain, I could look down and see it nestled in the shadows of the Blue Ridge that deepened the valleys, coloring them in deep purple haze.

The landmark Hotel Roanoke, nestled in the city center, with its Tudor exterior and high turrets, brought back memories of Drew's first hotel job.

He was everywhere I went inside the big Valley Mall. I saw him walking toward me, I saw him in the doorway of Abercrombie's. I saw him in the food court and in Barnes and Noble. And when I looked at the backs of young men walking away from me, I sometimes saw him in them—in the cut of dark-brown hair at the nape of a neck—in the way they walked...I wanted to follow them.

When I left the shops, I passed the turnoff to Plantation Road where he once lived. Then I was on Windy Gap

Mountain; the main road wound up and then down again toward the lake valley, taking me home. I felt Drew here, too.

There was a red Toyota pickup ahead of me that looked like his. But that's where the resemblance ended. This one was driven by Methuselah. He had a thick, springy beard and long gray hair, one of the mountain men that lived in these here hills. He had deep creases in the back of his neck and cigarette smoke wafted out of the driver's window. He also drove like Methuselah. It took me an hour to get to get off the mountain and cruise into the tiny hamlet of Burnt Chimney.

"You're everywhere I go, Drew." I told him.

Drew had friends. The philosophy he lived by was simple. He loved people and people loved him. All kinds of people. There were no labels in Drew's thoughts. If you were a good person—a "mountain man" or a hippy-dippy guy, a mosaic of walking tattoos, or the general manager of one of the most exclusive clubs in the world—if he thought you were a good person, young or old, he loved you. And even if you weren't such a great person, he would find something in you that he could like.

In a world where we are so harshly judged by others (and often by ourselves), it feels very good to be with someone who thinks you're okay—you're the way you are supposed to be, and that's the way you should be. And as such, you are valuable. That's the way Drew thought. He thought we were all okay.

This attitude of Drew's was responsible for a lot of my gray hairs and many sleepless nights. We never knew, for instance, who was going to be sleeping downstairs on any given night. But we could be sure that Drew would bring home anyone who didn't have a place to go, someone who'd had too much to drink or someone he thought would like us. "You gotta meet my mom and dad …" Or maybe it would be someone who just didn't feel like going home.

Meeting the owner of the body that was lying wrapped up in comforters on the downstairs living room couch or floor was always a surprise. One night there was a soldier on leave from the war. Another night it was a youngster who'd been kicked out of his own home, and another night it was two girls who didn't want to go home because no one would be there.

Half of Drew's guests were totally unknown to us. But he thought they were all fine, even if there were times when we couldn't agree. Then again, neither Walt nor I were half as evolved as our young son.

I'm working on it.

Hotel guests that Drew looked after at the resort were stunned and heartbroken when they went back to find he wasn't there. He touched people from all over this country and all over the world. He went ten extra miles to make them feel as valued as the most important guests that the hotel had ever hosted. Even now, so many people who worked with Drew in the resort have told me that whenever a sensitive situation arises with a guest they ask themselves, "How would Drew have handled this?"

His friends keep in touch. They keep our connection going. It's good to hear about their lives, about the hotel. It lets me imagine what he might be doing if he were still there.

It's difficult to have a child living thousands of miles away from home, and he was in my thoughts every day of his life. I used to think of him at all hours. I would think of him in Colorado in the morning, two hours behind my time zone in the East, wondering if he was just getting to work to open the club floor for the early risers.

I pictured him at lunchtime doing whatever it was he did—and I pictured him in the evening, getting off work, riding down the mountain either by bus or in his car to get on with the rest of his life.

His friends at the hotel kept those memories alive. And none more so than Ashley, Drew's friend and mentor. She told me there were many nights when she and Drew worked late on the club floor, and when all the guests had gone to bed and the floor was quiet, they would sit together and talk.

"We talked about everything," she said. "He was so easy to talk to. It was like being … at home. I felt so comfortable with him."

Since Drew's passing, Ashley had told me about lights being turned on and off in the club lounge when she was the only person there. One night she heard a crash of dishes in the pantry—and nobody was there.

"Are you messing with me, Drew?" she asked.

She told me about a dream she'd had one night. It came nearly two years after his death.

"It was strange," she said, "because in the dream it seemed as though it wasn't long since it all happened. I seemed to know that Drew had passed away, and I felt all those initial emotions all over again. But then we got a phone call that he was still alive and would be coming home."

"I think we were at your house," she told me. "Everyone was at the house. All our family and friends were here. And it felt as though we were all waiting for Drew. And just then, a car drove up. I could see him sitting in the back seat, being driven by a woman with dark hair," Ashley went on. "I ran out to the car as quickly as I could, yanked the door open, and wrapped myself around him, not believing he was alive. I held him so tight. I held his head in my hands, I kissed his face, and I cried tears all over him. I helped him out of the car and held onto him as we walked up to the house where everyone was waiting for him."

Ashley said that the dream was so real that she woke up with a momentary feeling of relief that he was alive, but when reality set in, she realized he was gone and then sat on her porch and sobbed. While she sat there, the song "Let It Be" was playing on her radio.

"Now, let me tell you," she said. "Shortly after Drew passed, this song would come on the XM radio on the club floor at least once, and sometimes twice a day … It had huge significance to me, because it always came on when I was thinking of him, and I truly believe he was playing that song for me—letting me know that everything would be okay. It happened so often that it got to be a joke on the floor!"

"It was absolutely surreal that that song came on as I cried on the porch … I know Drew was there." After Ashley told her story about the dream, I began receiving more and more messages from Drew.

Other people told me they felt that same warm rush of air, or a surge of energy, just before Drew popped into their minds. Tory, one of Drew's closest friends said, "I *know* that Drew is here when that happens—and he encourages me when I'm contemplating something—like I can almost hear him saying *Go for it, man!*"

Clay, his lifelong buddy from Texas, could hear his voice, and feel his presence. "I was just sittin' and starin' in my apartment" he told me one day, "and suddenly I hear, "*Hey!*" What was that? It was exactly his voice! Scared the shit out of me! I jumped up and I heard Drew laugh. I know Drew's laugh. Loud and hard."

"We had this thing," Clay said. "When he and I shared the apartment at River Rapids in Colorado, whoever got home first would hide and then jump out and scare the crap out of the other. I got Drew every time! I always knew where he was hiding." He laughed, remembering. "Well, he got me good this time!"

"And then we talked," Clay went on. "I didn't ask him any questions—he just seemed to want to talk about me. He asked me a bunch of questions—like how was I doing—that kind of thing."

"I've wanted to tell you," Clay said to me. "He and I always wanted to learn about this paranormal stuff. He told me that you could do a bunch of stuff—and we made a pact." Clay was quiet for a minute. I knew this was hard on him. "We always said, that whoever learned to do any of this stuff first—would teach the other."

"Well, listen to what he's saying, Clay," I said quietly. "That's Drew, teaching." I have these images of Drew and Clay, Kevin and Jeb—bunches of little Texans paddling through the bayous, scrambling over rocks.

There was that hot day one summer when I heard Clay's voice yelling at the back door, "Miss Ginny! Miss Ginny—you gotta see what Drew's got!"

I went tearing out onto the driveway to see my ten-year-old holding up a snake as long as he was tall.

His face and arms were mud covered, scratched up, and bleeding. That big goofy grin was ecstatic. "We caught him in the bayou! Look at it, Mom!"

I think I screamed. I must have screamed. The only way I wouldn't have would have been if I'd been lying passed out on the driveway. Which I wasn't—but I could easily have been. Snakes are not high on my list of best friends.

"Don't worry, I'll put him back," he assured me.

That was the least of my worries. I wanted the thing *dead*!

❧

Drew's been one of the strongest teachers in my life. It's supposed to be the other way around, isn't it?

I tried awfully hard to shape him into the good man that he became, but I wonder how much I really had to do with that. I could never teach him tolerance—the way he taught me tolerance. I could never teach him to be nonjudgmental—the way he taught me to be nonjudgmental. I could teach him how a mother loves a child, and a family and friends, but I could never teach him how to love everyone else out there—not the way he did, anyway.

❧

One night in early May I was standing in the kitchen all alone, tidying the counter before I went to bed. It had been a long and emotional day with off and on phone calls to lawyers in Colorado, sorting through the details of probate and insurance and all of that stuff that just keeps coming at you.

The clock chimed ten just as I brushed off the breadboard and put the trash under the sink until morning. Then just as I was about to turn off the lights, bone tired and longing for a bath, that whooosh of energy came suddenly, I knew it was Drew and instantly I was alert. I had no doubt that he was with me. I felt him all around me. It was like that afternoon in the hospital when I felt Walt in the room. Only this was stronger.

His smile melted into me somehow, releasing the tension in my shoulders. It seemed to bathe my being in soft light. It felt to me as though he was thinking about something As though he was preoccupied with something. I stood dead still with my hand on the light switch, listening.

"Drew?" I walked back to the island in the kitchen.

He acknowledged me. It was nothing tangible—but I felt him there beside me. So I began to talk to him.

I had questions about his death, and I wanted to hear from him what happened the night he lost consciousness and was taken to the hospital. "I have so many questions, Drew. What happened that night? What happened to you?"

Then I heard him speak. It was that thought-transference again. Telepathic, but clear.

It was a buildup of things, he said. *A combination of things, taking risks—no helmet on the slopes, general stress ... not enough water ... something happened inside my head ... it almost felt electrical ... like something snapped.*

"Wait!" I pulled open the catch-all drawer and grabbed a piece of paper and a pencil that was lying by the phone. His thoughts were transferring to my mind faster than I could keep up with them. The words were like dashes—quick and fleeting—and I had to listen hard. The speech was clear, but quick. Not many full sentences, but his meaning was clear.

"Okay." I was ready.

He was saying that he was tired, drinking too much, already dehydrated—no fluids —no water—headache? No answer. He banged his head on the table at the house.

His friends had said the same thing and I had forgotten that.

Then he fell asleep. Sometime during the night the seizures started. *Kidneys and liver crashed. There was pain, no air … brain crashed—it was over. But you must know this.* He continued. *It was my time to leave. There was nothing anyone could have done to stop it … you have to believe that. I had things to do that couldn't be done here on earth.*

I waited in silence for a few moments, absorbing what he was saying. The air around me felt dense and filled with his energy. My mental focus was sharp, picking up his thoughts, and even though they came and went like quicksilver, I was able to get them and store them.

Then I asked out loud. "What about now, are you okay, Drew?"

I'm fine. I'm with Dad and Mamaw—we're waiting for Papaw. There are lots of friends here, I'm happy. I will see you again. Yesss! For sure.

I love you, he said — *Oh man! All of you. I'm here with you.* I could feel his closeness, his arms around me. I could feel great compassion coming from him.

Then he said, *Love is everywhere—can't describe. You don't have the right words on earth. But love is everything here! We are love …*

Then he described the place he was in. *Just like earth but all colors are alive here. The air is alive. So clear it shines, has a sort of tinkling sound …*

I had the impression of tones, sweet and clear—alive. I saw the color green flowing like jade-colored water. The ancient words of Saint Paul echoed in my mind as Drew spoke. "Eye hath not seen, nor hath ear heard the glories that God hath prepared for those who love him."

Animals everywhere—It's like, you know, that song—The Lion King. It's like that! I knew somehow he was grinning.

… there's so many things happening here, so many things to see and learn about—it's awesome. Some things the earth reality has never seen or heard of. I can't explain it all. I love it. Soil is alive… Made up of all nurturing and loving cells. Cell love. Then he said he was *getting acquainted—meeting people,* then I felt him smile that big smile again and I heard him laugh.

Our animals are here—Cassie's here. Zu's here. And lions, tigers… and elephants in an African sort of place… Tell Cindy there are zebras, too.

I heard the sound of his laughter. *So many animals… none of them aggressive—no fights.*

Then like lightning he switched thoughts.

Clay can do this stuff… he's good at it—always has been. He does it better all the time. He can hear me when I talk to him. He knows when I'm there… talk to him about it.

His energy was fading. The words filtering through my mind were becoming intermittent and faint.

Love you. I love you all. Gotta go now.

"I love you, Drew…"

On the morning after this conversation with Drew, I was sitting at my desk trying to read the scratchy notes I'd been taking while he was talking. To make sure I wouldn't lose a single word or sign I got from Drew that year, I was transcribing it all in a journal that Cindy had given me about a week after he left. Miss Kitty was snoozing on the rug at my feet, Ranger was already outside scaring up squirrels in the woods, and I was thinking about a second cup of tea when a text message dinged my phone. It read:

"Something really weird happened this morning!" It was Sara, Drew's young friend from the school bus.

I don't like this text messaging stuff. It takes me half an hour to send a two line message. The kids click them off in seconds.

"My cell phone rang and guess what," she said. "There was nobody there when I answered. The line was just empty. *But it was Drew's old number!*"

What were the odds? The odds are slim to none with all the numbers in Sara's list of contacts—and you can imagine how many that was—that this number accidently dialed her phone. A number that must by then have been assigned to someone else. His phone was dead, lying in the bottom of a drawer, long-since disconnected.

"*And!*" She went on. "Shortly after that, there was an email sent to my phone—nothing in it—from the same number. Said 'Unknown Sender'... What's *that* about?"

You tell me, Pretty Girl.

The same thing happened months later when Sara was spending the day with me at my house helping me with the formatting of a book I was writing. We had spent all day reliving old times while she showed me all the tricks this computer has up its sleeve. She left at about five, and at about six she phoned me to say "Drew called again! It was the same thing as before. I'd just left your house and my phone rang. It was his old number, an unknown sender and no message. What is going on?"

I told her what I knew and that was that I had learned that spirit can get through to us through electronics. "Somehow, it's easier for them to cross dimensions via electricity or some other medium like it. The telephone...remember the call I told you about?" I asked her "That's another way they can come in."

Drew's thing seems to be phones, I thought. I remembered that call to me in those hours before dawn when he talked about Birds of Paradise.

"I bet he heard us talking about him all day," Sara was saying, interrupting my thought.

❧

I wrote that message from Sara down in my journal and pulled myself out of the recliner, dislodging Miss Kitty, who wasn't pleased. It was exercise day, so I dragged my workout pants on without enthusiasm and ate half of a Mounds candy bar to give the endorphins a head start.

Two hours later, as I was driving home from the girlie gym, my car radio was playing a song I hadn't heard before. That in itself didn't surprise me. I don't know a lot of songs my car radio plays, but my ears perked up because I thought it might be Taylor Swift.

It was.

I've caught the occasional glimpse of Taylor Swift—on posters in my granddaughter's bedrooms, in music shops, on

TV. She is cute and blond and sunny, and her music makes me want to sing and smile and be like her. Oh to be young and untouched by sorrow. I wanted to be like her for all of those reasons, and the fact that my granddaughters loved her and played her music all the time. I loved that.

But this particular song had sadness woven through the lyrics. Not quite so young, not quite so perky, touched with longing for something that's just out of reach—or appears to be ... and when I listened, I heard her singing about a boy named "Drew." She yearns for him to turn around and talk to her. He just keeps walking ... so she sings about him, tears falling on her guitar.

What a coincidence.

∽⌒

Cindy called me early one morning in late May—or was it June already—the days aren't all that clear; they run into each other. Sometimes, before I open the shutters, I wake up thinking it's early fall again—or is it springtime. Then I look outside and see the daffodils in bloom and I decide it must be spring.

She had called last week, I think, telling me she was going blind looking for zebras. "You should know, Ginny, that there are *NO* zebras in Raleigh." Her voice was somber.

But this morning, before my second cup of tea, Cindy was bubbling like a brook. "The zebras have appeared! *They are Everywhere! I can't cope.*" She was practically spluttering. And I was beginning to feel as though we'd stumbled into Noah's Ark—only hers were arriving not in twos but in herds.

"Listen to this! I'm driving to the gym and there, right in front of me is a U-Haul—big sucker—and on its sides there are *painted zebras.* I'm in the parking lot at the gym, and this woman with wild blond hair walks out wearing *zebra tights!*"

"Are you sure you were at the gym?"

"Yes! In my sweats—but there I was, zoning out on the treadmill, flipping channels on the TV control, sweating like a horse, and there, right in front of me on the screen, are zebras! Three of them. And you're not going to believe this! *They're fornicating!*"

"*All three of them?*" The Serengeti plains must be heating up.

"What? No, I don't know. There were *zebras making zebras!* These guys are everywhere!"

"Or they will be." I was laughing hard.

For the next several weeks, my computer was choking on pictures of zebras. Everywhere Cindy went with cell phone in hand, I got zebra reports and pictures.

Then there were the peacocks. Spencer's peacocks that blazed onto my screen. Cell phone pictures of peacocks in cafes in Manhattan, peacocks on billboards, peacocks in the zoo. Peacocks in art shops and painted on vases. A peacock in a top hat and an eye glass—well, this is New York…

I can't cope! But at least they're colorful—feathery eyes all over the place. *I'll be Watching you…* Flocks of the darn things.

And don't start with the monkey…

Why am I surprised that all these creatures are showing up? Drew loved animals. When he was small, his best friend was Cassie, a blond Lab who joined our family at four months old. Drew was six, and they were joined if not at the hip, in spirit. They were of one mind. Whether the plan was to cruise the creek in Drew's paddleboat or chase squirrels, they were two for one and one for two. He didn't know where he ended and became a puppy, and neither did Cassie. They were puppy boys, and it didn't matter one bit that Cassie was a girl.

Cassie died when she was fourteen and Drew was twenty. She had been suffering from congestive heart failure and one day, when her breathing became too hard for her to handle, Drew scooped her old body up in his arms and took her in to the vet.

He stayed with her and held her and soothed her as she was put to sleep.

His heart must have been heavy with Cassie's passing, but it was much braver than mine.

Fifteen

Show Me
Heaven, Drew

I knew it was June because I had just looked at my calendar to double-check an appointment. Virginia was
warming up steadily, and as soon as I woke up, I opened the
French doors to my bedroom to hear the birds waking up and
smell the dew on the grass beside the lake. At least that's what I
was thinking when suddenly, my senses were flooded with the
warm scent of tall dry grasslands—the bright gold savannah. I
could hear the rustling of small animals and a rush of sunlit air
engulfed me.

Drew was here. Dropping in from the place he's in now.
There was no mistaking the African bush for the soft green lake
land of Virginia.

"This is early for you, baby." I smiled. I was getting used to that whooosh of warm air that signaled Drew's arrival. "You seem a little sleepy..."

He said, *It's early—I like the early mornings now.* A little laugh. *I like to be with the animals, lying here in the grass waking up with them. They wake up gently—with soft snorting noises, sleepy growls, and yawns...*

I waited. The air felt hazy to me. It seemed to be dusted with tiny flecks of glitter. My senses told me that Drew was leaning with his back against the mottled bark of a baobab tree. It's massive, misshapen trunk blossomed into stunted, thick branches giving it a grotesque, almost prehistoric look. The tall grass around it rippled on an invisible breeze.

Drew's hair was tousled. He wore a pair of shorts and no shirt. His feet were bare.

They're extra loving in the early mornings. This would be Drew's Heaven. Waking up in the African bush, warm and sleepy, surrounded by extra loving, sleepy animals.

I got the image of a full-grown, male African lion. His muzzle was flecked with small scars and the thick black mane was tangled. His tufted tail flicked the air.

He's special, Drew said.

Several years ago on a trip back to South Africa, we had stopped at a lion sanctuary where orphaned lion cubs were fed and cared for by park rangers who had found them abandoned in the bush. There were three very small ten-week old cubs, their eyes barely opened, and Drew was given one to hold.

"Why do I get the feeling that he's connected somehow to the lion cub you held in South Africa," I asked.

Because he is—it was his cub. He watches him from here. The cub is full grown now—in fact he's quite old in earth time. My lion (laugh) has been with him all his life. And the young lion knows that. I can see him listening when his dad speaks to him…

"Does your lion purr?" I asked.

He's purring now. Listen…

I heard a deep even rumbling coming from somewhere inside the lion. Then I saw him raise his giant paw and place it on Drew's leg.

He says he wants me to be his cub. He'll teach me to run the way he can. He never had a chance to teach his cub on earth how to run, how to spring…

Your happiness reaches out to me. It fills my being like an incoming tide, then dimly, and from a long way away I hear, "… he wants to learn to fly…"

Do lions fly in heaven?

⁘

Drew and the African Lion Cub.

While I was the happiest when I was talking to Drew or with him in some other way, there were times when doubts assailed me. There were times when I trudged along, minute by minute, mile by mile, and then a shower of rocks would scramble down the mountain, blocking the way, making this road, so filled with twists and turns, more difficult.

These doubts came in the form of questions about how good a mother I was … Yup—that old boogey bear. Was I the best mother I could have been? This one's full of potholes and I don't recommend taking that fork in the road. But I did.

Sometimes the answer has to be No.

And then there's this one. Did I always try to be the best mother for Drew? Or Karen or Michael? And the answer is always Yes. I didn't always get it right, but sometimes I did. You too?

These thoughts weighed on me one day when I was with Karen and Michael: "I should have been more understanding—I shouldn't have yelled at him that time…" And my grown-up children both said, "You're a mom. That's your job."

But I should have listened to him more carefully, I should have been more understanding. I was too tough on him.

Then I heard Drew say again, *I was pretty darn tough on you…*

It goes both ways.

He came back about a week after our talk about the lion. His energy seemed worried to me and I had the feeling he'd been wondering if I always knew he loved me.

"I never doubted it" I told him. "Even in our worst battles, with my fear for you making me yell, and once, your teenage frustration with me making you yell back, I always knew you loved me," I said. Please tell me you never doubted mine. It was always unconditional. It was always there.

I remember a long time ago going to Drew's elementary school in Memorial Parkway. Second grade, I think. When he saw me, he came flying down the hallway, arms outstretched. "You took my breath away with your love, Sweet Drew. You loved me so much. I always knew that. As a child, as a boy, and as a man. And now that you're no longer here, it feels as though a light has gone out of my life. I wish I'd known how to keep you here. Maybe guided you better."

He replied, *Can't you see I had to do things for myself—my way. I know I pushed the envelope sometimes—a lot of times—I always loved you—my love for you… huge—always will be.*

I could see his energy like bright clouds of mist, growing as he spoke.

... love for everyone. Loved all the places we lived, love Karen, Michael and Dad ... so much ... all my friends too. You most of all ...

Then he said, *Don't cry for me. Can't you see, I'm here? I'm as real as I was before. I want you to go on ... you'll be with me someday ... be sad sometimes, but be happy for me. Those sad memories are forgotten here.*

"Are you really happy?" I asked, although I knew the answer.

He said nothing but a feeling of intense euphoria swept over me. I felt love all around me. *This is what it feels like here,* he said. *Warm. Complete.*

Then I felt him move toward my dresser and pick up a jade heart I had placed beside his picture. I could feel him handing it to me and I felt rather than heard him say, *Your love for me, and mine for you.*

He seemed to understand so much more than we did here. But those earthly scars flared up from time to time and when they did, these chats were good for the soul.

❧

Brittany, Drew's longtime girlfriend, called me one evening from the capital. It was summertime. The cherry blossoms had dropped, turned pale brown, and faded in the Washington heat. It was warming up early this year and she was tired, working two jobs to make ends meet.

"I want to tell you about this dream I had a couple of nights ago," she said.

It sounded as though she had been crying. "It made me so sad—but also soooo happy! It was so ... *Drew*. You know, it was always *something* with us. We were either crazy mad for each other or fighting like roosters. He could really push my buttons. Anyway, the dream was happening in a very dark restaurant. I was wearing black and I seemed to be working there. When I looked around, I noticed that everyone there was wearing black. Maybe it was some kind of weird dress code or something. Then Drew arrived. He was wearing black, too—a black suit, and it looked like he was carrying a white towel or something—it was so strange. But he was real ... he was so real, and sooo close!"

Brittany paused. "He was smiling. So sweetly—all I could feel was *kindness* coming from him. It was like he was trying to make me feel better ... and then he said, *I'm sorry I couldn't tell you I had to leave.*"

Her voice rose. "He apologized for leaving! He said, *I'm sorry I couldn't tell you I had to go* ... And then he said that he wanted to be sure I was okay ... and I began to cry and I said, "'GO AWAY! I can't do this! GO!'"

She started backing away from him.

"I was crying and I yelled, 'You're GONE! *You're freaking dead!*' I got very emotional and I backed into another room ... and he followed. Still kind, still sweet."

She sat down on a chair, she said, "I kept crying and he sat down in another chair—smiling—just watching me with such compassion ... then he waved, and I woke up."

Every time I hear something like this from one of Drew's friends, I'm so happy I could burst. So many people have felt him. Not just me.

Not long after Brittany's call, Drew's youngest cousin Kellie Anne phoned me. Kellie is, among other things, mother to three little boys, and sister to two big brothers. She has a head on her shoulders that is as down to earth as brown bread. She has a special wit and she's as smart as a whip. She was telling me about a dream she had of Drew.

The first words out of Kellie's mouth were, "Aunt Ginny, it was so real! I KNOW Drew was with me. It's not like it was a huge dream, or a long dream," she said. "But he was looking at me smiling, and he had his hand over his heart. I felt so warm, so happy!"

Her smile could be felt from a thousand miles away at the other end of the line and her voice was full of love. "It wasn't a long visit, but I know he'd come to see me. There's no way I'm wrong. Could be crazy, I suppose, but somehow, I just *know* … have I gone round the bend?"

I was laughing, "If you have, you're in good company, my love."

"The dream left a feeling of happiness that stayed with me all day. I was with Drew! Incredible. *That is so incredible!*"

Sixteen

Fly—So High

*I*t was almost July. The trees were in full leafy green splendor, day lilies bloomed on the banks of the lake and last
year's zinnias were opening their scarlet and yellow, orange,
and pink faces to the sun. My flower gardens received no help
from me this year. Any energy I could muster in 2009 was being
streamed into my survival—it took every ounce of strength
to survive Drew's dying. But the trees and the flowers around
my house had energy enough for all of us, and it seemed that
in some way I was drawing on that natural energy, the beauty
of nature, to replenish my own. The weeds, their energy more
vigorous than the rest of us combined, were doing their part,
too. Dandelion fluff floated on the warm breezes and thistles
bloomed shamelessly among last year's tomato beds. The ivy was
climbing unhindered and ecstatically up the twin oaks in the

back garden. At times, I would stare at the sprawling ivy, wondering what to do, and it would give me a headache. So I closed the blinds and stepped away from the windows. It would all just have to wait until next year.

Drew came again one day toward the end of June. He arrived in those early hours just before waking when images are sharp, sounds are clear, and there's no interference from conscious thought. I call it The Place Where Souls Meet.

From my perch in that dream state, I saw five fighter jets, painted in camouflage, streaking across the sky. This is not something I would normally dream about—not many of us in the girlie gym dwell on war machines. But there they were, sun glinting off the tips of their wings, sleek, pencil thin, almost rocket-like. I rubbed my bare shoulders in the cool morning air and as I watched the scene unfold, one plane peeled off. I knew it was Drew. He was flying. *Really flying!* I caught my breath as I watched him. It was as though he and the plane were one. It veered and straightened out and dipped and soared as if it were an extension of him and he had complete control. I think Drew was guiding it with thought.

While I stood enthralled, I watched him circle the formation, leaving a trail of white vapor that morphed into the shape of a heart. Then he sped away. Far, far away, I saw him diving for the earth, and then he vanished. My earthly being felt fear for him, but my spirit, flying with him, felt peace.

I sent the thought up to him, "Better than skydiving, sweetheart."

In July of the year Drew passed, he went skydiving with a couple of his old high school friends to celebrate his twenty-sixth birthday. He didn't call me to tell me about it until after he landed, which was a good thing. If he had, it might have turned into one of those scenes where I was less than supportive and not inclined to listen well … I mean, why flirt with death?

"*Oh my God, Mom!* It was *awesome!*" He called me laughing, exhilarated, and talking ninety miles an hour with excitement.

"Weren't you scared?" I asked.

"Yeah, I was some. The most scared I got was when the 'chute opened. I just wasn't expecting the huge jolt and drag. It sent me spinning. *Oh man!* But when that stopped the gliding was awesome!"

When I thought back on that conversation, I was glad he got to go skydiving. Glad he'd lived his life so fully for the short time he was here.

༄

The mystical Miss Boo, whose real name is Becca, had a dream one night. My granddaughter is the youngest of Karen's children and has a corner of my heart that is all hers because she is so sensitive, spiritual, and entertaining.

At two years old, Boo talked to angels. That's about the same time she saw my father on the stairs in her house. Her vocabulary was sparse, and she certainly didn't have terrific language skills yet, but she called him by name, "Papa," although she had never known him. He died long before she was born, and we're not even sure that she had ever heard his name.

When Karen got over her freak-out she said, "What is Papa doing, Boo?"

Becca moved her fingertips along her lips from side to side, making Karen shriek.

"He's playing his harmonica! Oh my God! *She can see Papa!*"

My father was a multitalented individual. He played the piano and he sang, but most of all, he loved his harmonica. Whenever friends and family gathered at our house, someone would drag up a stool to the piano, my father would reach for his harmonica, and one of us kids would bang on a saucepan with a wooden spoon.

Miss Boo can tell you things about other dimensions that'll stop you in your tracks. In June, she told me about a dream she'd had. She was eleven now and still pretty tuned in to this spirit stuff. Children do grow out of "invisible" friends and "see-ing" things and phantom one-sided conversations, though that's mostly because we adults call it nonsense. But we hadn't done that, so Boo was still very comfortable with her sixth sense.

"Uncle Drew and I were *everywhere!*" The tiny freckles on her nose all crinkled together and with a dramatic sigh she leant her chin on her hands. "But I was so mad! I was the only one who could see him!" she said. "I kept saying to everyone, '*Can't you see him? It's Uncle Drew! He's right here!*' And nobody could." Her eyes were big and blue and sad.

"Tell me some more," I said.

"It was so real. We were traveling all over the place—here at my house, then we went to the lake, and then we were all in Uncle Michael's apartment in New York. We were everywhere!" Becca shrugged. "But nobody could see him but me. I think they just weren't looking hard enough, don't you, Mimi?" She looked right at me and said, "You've seen him, haven't you?"

"Yes, Boo, I have."

There are continual reminders that life goes on. Right on time, the Fourth of July came to my lake house, as did Michael and Karen and my niece Kellie Anne, and their families.

There were lots of happy times this Independence Day, lots of memories and nine kids that seemed to fill every crevice of my house for a week—a jam-packed bundle of high energy that kept everything moving at full speed.

Michael rented a fast boat so that anyone who wanted to could ski or wakeboard, or simply ride along and take in the sun. Karen and my oldest granddaughter, two honey-blondes who could be sisters, were the bathing beauties; Mary Katherine, blond hair flying behind her, the champion skier; and my youngest granddaughter, the champion fisherwoman.

My male grandchildren kept themselves busy. Brock is the oldest. He was fifteen that year and bored when he wasn't out on the boat, skiing or tubing, so he decided to rearrange the waterfall that curves around the big maple tree on the side of my house. He dislodged a few sleeping toads, while the nine-year-old, took the fountain apart to see how it worked and the two-year-old ate the dog food.

Everything was as it should be.

Jim, my old friend, a landscape architect and builder of the waterfall, lost sleep wondering how he was going to keep his masterpiece from being demolished. Every morning he could be seen standing on the edge of the pond counting his rocks and the goldfish that all four little boys were hell-bent on catching. One of them asked if he could take one home.

Jim had one little boy of his own, but never before had he dealt with a mass of kids at his house—all of them on destruction missions. It gets pretty darn nerve-racking sometimes, even if you're used to it. So he was a wreck. But Jim likes food, and on this holiday the girls kept it coming. Great food piled up on picnic tables and on kitchen counters. It helped calm his nerves.

That is, until my youngest granddaughter fell off the dock, taking a loose piling with her. We don't think she was pulled in by a baby bass, as she suggested. She may have been reaching for Jim's broken rod, which her cousin had been fishing with before it got snagged in a hideous brush pile beside the dock and snapped in two.

Luckily, Jim wasn't there when one of the kids got carried away at the marina while feeding the carp—huge, ugly creatures with fat pink lips—and fell into the swarming mass of gaping jaws and slime. But his mother, in one of those inexplicable, superhuman feats, snatched him from the jaws of carp with one hand while hanging on to the dog food taster with the other, and dumped her nine year old unceremoniously on the deck, covered in fish spit. And duck poop and gasoline. Stuff you don't want to think about.

We picnicked in far-away coves, kayaked in the cove by the house, and fished off the boat dock. We cooked out on the fire pit and we swam and we put away plenty of wine and beer, and ate S'mores.

We pretended for each other that we were fine without Drew, but we never were. Reminders of other Fourth of Julys with him were all around us. Snapshots popped into our minds of Drew being chased by a swarm of yellow jackets and heading full tilt for the lake before they nailed him. Drew tearing into the cove on his jet ski, circling the dock, kicking up water and mud in the shallows, with Sara shrieking with laughter on the back.

That was the weekend that Brittany came to spend the fourth with Drew at the lake. I had a picture in my mind of her standing on shore at Bumpy Landing patio, hands on her hips demanding to know why he'd been gone so damn long, and, "Where the hell have you been?" When she saw Sara on the back of the jet ski, all hell broke loose. She let him have it in a litany of colorful language they don't hear often even on the South Side of Chicago.

"Brittany! Would you get my blue T-shirt?" he yelled. *What was he thinking?*

I'm pretty sure I heard her yell back. "*It will be my f------ pleasure, you a------!*"

Drew loved Brittany, his grown-up sweetheart; and he loved Sara, his childhood sweetheart, too. It probably never occurred to him that they might not be on the same page he was.

I caught glimpses of Drew as a little fellow, catching fire flies on hot summer nights. And more pictures of Michael and Drew, the Firework Kings, lighting explosives and racing for the trees, to the delight of my grandchildren.

♌

Sometime during that week of the Fourth, after the children were asleep, my daughter-in-law, Mary Katherine, reminded us of a dream she had years ago. She had shared this dream with us once before, in Denver, the day after we lost Drew. At the time, it struck us as strange. But as she re-told it that night, it was uncanny.

"I remember seeing us all together in a house I didn't recognize. It had high ceilings and tall windows. There was a lot of light inside and it was painted—like—a pale yellow it seems."

She told us. "Our whole family was there," she said. "We had gathered for an occasion, and the occasion had something to do with Drew." She knew it wasn't a wedding but wasn't sure why we were all there.

"I noticed there were three children with Michael and me. James, Caroline, and a toddler I didn't recognize. But I knew he was part of our family."

A year before Drew died, Tucker was born into their family, and Mary Katherine recognized him as the toddler she had seen in her dream.

In Denver the day after Drew died, we had sat together as a family and briefly discussed the idea of a memorial for Drew and where we might hold it. I thought Jim's house might be a possibilty. No one else in the family had seen it, so Mary Katherine asked me to describe it. When I did, she told us about the dream and wondered if it was the same house.

Then one day when we were all over at Jim's during that weekend, I noticed Mary Katherine staring up at the loft over the living room, and watched as she turned around to scan the tall windows on the lakeside of the house. "This is it," she said. "This is the house I saw in that dream."

Just then Tucker, her youngest child came charging through the room. "And there's the toddler I saw," she said.

This was one of those previews we're given now and again. One of those scouting trips when the spirit goes ahead of us to pave the way. But apparently we were not supposed to know any more at the time.

And what about that snapshot of Tucker in her dream— years before he was born? To me, it was a real case for the idea of "pre-existence," which gives credence to "post-existence" or Soul Survival.

⁂

We also planted a weeping plum tree that July Fourth, 2009, and scattered some of Drew's and Walt's ashes around the base of its trunk. Everyone laid a blue, white, or pink hydrangea on top of them and we sprinkled fresh earth over the flowers.

Jack Sparrow, the bear, was there and one of the kids got to press his paw for the "Ole, Ole" chorus. The mood could change like quicksilver around these guys. James, my nine-year-old grandson, wanted to trickle the ashes through his fingers and so did the others and we let them.

Brock was quiet, remembering. His Uncle Drew was closer to Brock's age than any other uncle, and it showed. It showed in the joyrides in the mud with Uncle Drew and the racing around the house at midnight when Uncle Drew was supposed to be babysitting. Drew, Brock, and Courtney, Brock's younger sister, shared music and connected on Facebook and MySpace. He was just a bigger kid than they were, and they all loved Uncle Drew. Courtney had tears in her eyes.

Children grieve, too, and they need closure just like the rest of us. My little people were actually quite fascinated with the whole ceremony. We read a poem that I wrote when Drew was four. We played Alan Jackson's song about dying young and a song that Karen liked.

And then the week was over and everyone went home.

I sat outside on the deck the evening they all left, watching the sun go down and staring at the unruffled water and the tidy dock. The kayaks had been pulled up neatly and secured, the fishing rods were stashed in the boat shed, and the only evidence of any one having been here at all was a tiny pink bikini top dangling from one of the Adirondack chairs on Bumpy Landing.

I took a long sip of wine and reached for a Hershey bar, but I didn't cry.

It was one of those golden evenings. Soft yellow light warmed the rocks by the water. The trees in full-summer leaf were dappled gold and the sun's dying rays dabbed each blade of grass with a gold-tipped brush. I could hear the children's voices coming from the amber shade and from somewhere down the molten, glowing lake, I heard Drew laugh.

Mary Katherine, Karen, and Ginny.

Seventeen

The View Through
Heaven's Window

*I*t felt very good to lie down at about ten that night in the cool of the air conditioning and breathe deeply. I was happy. Tired but feeling good. I had almost forgotten how good that feels.

Leaning over, I switched off the bedside lamp and lay there on my back, relaxed and comfortable, waiting for sleep. My eyes had barely been closed when suddenly, I felt that whoosh—in the doorway to the bedroom. The energy was almost palpable. Warm and light.

Here he was again. "Hi, Drew. You're here?" I asked.

I'm here. I felt him smile.

"Wait, I've got to find my pen!" I switched the bedside lamp on. I knew he wanted to talk, and I climbed out of bed and padded into the darkened living room, returning to bed with my journal and a pen.

"Okay. I'm ready!" I was wide awake now, propped up on my pillows, pen in hand. I knew he'd been with us all week so I didn't ask him about that. Instead, I said, "Please tell me what it's like over there."

His thoughts came fast and light. I wrote quickly as they came into my mind, trying not to miss anything…

There's everything here we have on earth. Houses—beautiful houses! Some of them are like ours but more beautiful. All of them are more beautiful than anything we have on earth. The tiniest cottage is … like a picture!

There are so many people here. I feel as though I know everyone around me. We're all like family. And then there are others that come and go. Not sure where they're going, but I think some of them leave for another life somewhere. I'm meeting people all the time. Some are just back from earth like me, and there are some people who've never left here.

"Tell me about your close friends over there…"

So many. People I know from here, and people I've known on earth … and some people who have come back from long journeys away.

"Away?"

They've been on other worlds.

"Other worlds?"

Yeah … other galaxies, other worlds, planets like ours, but very far away…

"Astral worlds?"

That's it!

"Do you think you'll ever go to one of these worlds?"

I think I could if I wanted to ... too much to see here for now.

"Where do you live?"

In a house like ours. With a view—like off our deck at the lake—looking at the water.

"Who's with you in the house?"

Sometimes Dad ... sometimes Nan (my mother). Papa (my father) comes over. He likes building things. He smiles. I can feel the smile in his energy. When I'm speaking to him it's as if his aura engulfs me. Our two energies are in complete alignment and I can read his perfectly.

I see Mamaw (Walt's mother)—like her a lot. I never got to know her on earth. She likes to cook. Been showing me how to make things.

"Is there food like ours?"

Great food! We cook it or it just appears. We can think it and it's here! Same with clothes, everything is like that here ... Want to watch movies? Just think it. Whatever you feel like.

I can feel his lightness, his happiness. "You sound happy."

I am. I miss you. But we'll be together again—you'll see. It'll be soon to me. Things happen quickly here because we have no time like you do on earth.

"Were you scared at first, Drew?" I was remembering the very first time I saw him and he was crying.

Yes. But fine now ... everything is "love" here—and kindness. Just didn't know where I was at first ... or what had happened ... Very scared.

Then I saw Dad. He took me with him. Up a hill. High mountain. Light everywhere—all around us. Soft light, bright but soothing, behind the mountains. Then ... people! Lots of people I knew. So loving ... pleased to see me. So caring. They welcomed me back—warm—wonderful. I had to take in. Dad helped. Dogs were there ...

"And then?" I asked.

Dad took me home to my bed, my room—just like my room at the lake. He cooked dinner—beans I think, then I slept. He woke me up and we talked and he told me what happened. He said I died. Then he said, "But you can see there's no such thing. I was wrong about that.

"Something's puzzling me. I know I saw Dad in the hospital room the afternoon you passed over. I thought you were going to be all right because he was there with you, but then when I saw you in the hotel you were crying and alone. You didn't go with Dad right away?"

I saw Dad in the hospital room and I started to leave with him ... but then something happened—I got confused I think ... something seemed to be pulling me back ... I didn't want to leave.

"Okay."

I actually did—leave—in a way—don't know how long I was by myself—just hanging—or something it seems ... a lot of confusion ... everything swirling around ... But then, I remember—Dad came in later when you showed me that light ...

"I remember."

That's when I left.

Silence. Then,

I came to find you. I love you.

"I know."

Thanks.

"Can I kiss you?" I asked him.

I imagined that he kissed my cheek. "Thank you. I love you, Drew."

He waved and touched his lips. *Going now. Gotta Go.* I heard it echo from years ago.

❧

My daughter, Karen, had been getting more and more despondent and despairing of ever being able to feel Drew the way some of us could.

Then he finally made contact. It was around the end of July when she called me. She was bubbling over. She couldn't get the words out fast enough, and I could hear her breathless and excited on the other end of the line, "*I spoke to Drew! On the phone.*"

"Oh wow! Calm down, I'm listening. Tell me what happened." I said. My cheeks were flushed; I was as excited as she was.

"Okay," she paused to get her breath. "In the dream, I heard the phone ring," she told me. "We were all at your house and I was standing in the kitchen, by myself, doing something, I can't remember what. I lifted the kitchen phone up and immediately realized that Michael had already picked it up in the bedroom. Your bedroom."

"It was sooo weird. I realized that although I was in the kitchen holding the phone, I could 'see' Michael talking on the bedroom extension."

"You can't see into the bedroom from the kitchen ..." I said.

"Course not," she said. "It was the strangest thing. In the dream I could see down the hallway, around the corner and through the walls. It was as though there was nothing separating us!"

"What was he saying?" I asked.

"He was having a normal sounding conversation with someone on the other end. I was picking up the tail end of it and couldn't figure out what they were saying to each other. Then I realized—without any doubt—that it was Drew's voice on the other end of the line." She went on, "I said, 'Drew! Drew!' And he said, *Hi!* Just like that! Just the way he used to. Then just as quickly, he said he had to go. That he had something to do ..." Karen paused. "And then he said, *I'll call you. Talk to you later.* And he was gone."

Another call from Drew. It doesn't surprise any of us. Drew had more phones during his short time on earth than most of us own in a lifetime. His phones were his lifeline to the world. Apparently that hasn't changed.

Eighteen

Milestone

Drew would have been twenty-seven on July 21. I didn't want to wake up on that day in 2009. It was just too hard. My mind kept going back to "This time last year." Oh God! I wanted to die.

Friends called, but I didn't want to talk to anyone. There was nothing to say. There were no words I wanted to listen to or to share. I just wanted to die in peace. But the universe isn't always that kind. It wanted me to live so I did.

I fed the dog and the cat and the birds and the fish, and I mopped up hairballs in the kitchen. "I know how you feel, Miss Kitty," I told her as I stroked her thick fur. I wanted to upchuck my soul, but it wouldn't let me.

Instead, I took Ranger out on the lake in my kayak. We paddled out into the main channel until I was tired, and then we paddled back. There was very little boat traffic that day, so Ranger jumped into the water when he got hot and swam alongside. Eventually, I heaved him back into the boat and we continued down to the end of the cove. There were some red flowers growing on the bank among the tall grasses and reeds—I reached out and picked one.

We kept moving, past the beaver lodge, past the dead poplar tree that had fallen into the lake last spring, and stopped under a sprawling sycamore that the March winds had blown over onto its side. Half of its roots had been lifted out of the soil, but the other half seemed to be keeping it alive. We sat in the shade for a long time watching the waterfall at the back of the cove in silence. Memories of Drew as a child came flooding back. Mental pictures of him in the paddleboat with Cassie, chasing frogs with Ranger, fishing off the dock in the summer, scampering around the property in nothing but a pair of shorts that I think he wore for a week at a time.

When it got too warm, I sprinkled a handful of Drew's ashes into the water and floated the red flower on top of them. They floated away through the cove, mingling with a flurry of feathers where the ducks swim and the geese come in to roost. Ranger and I sat there and watched them go.

This sort of grief had a life of its own. Sometimes on anniversaries, sometimes out of the blue, it would come down like an avalanche and bury me under its weight. Memories that were just too hard to deal with worked the same way. On Drew's first birthday after his death, I found myself without words, without joy, without hope. Usually I could write it out of my soul but not that day. The only thing to do was to shelter myself in the reeds of the creek, paddle my kayak with Ranger, touch the water, and drift.

Nineteen

Back to the Mountains

On the first day of August, my good friend Cindy and I went out to Colorado. She flew from Raleigh, North Carolina, and I flew out of Roanoke, which is the airport closest to where I live at Smith Mountain Lake.

Cindy and I were flying across the country that day because the Moonrise Mountain Lodge and Resort, where Drew had worked for the last four years, was dedicating a memorial in his honor and I had been invited to be there.

Karen was busy with kids at the end of summer. Baseball was over but football was about to begin, and everyone needed new clothes for school. Michael's job had him embroiled in a major move from New York to San Francisco, so he couldn't be there.

So that left me, and the dog who wasn't going to Colorado. The airline people seem to think he's too big to sit by me, and I think he'd be frightened in the hold in a cage. So Ranger stayed with Jim while I was away. Miss Kitty had no interest in anything that involved getting into her cat bag, which she made abundantly clear during her last trip to the vet. So Jim planned to come over and visit with her while I was gone. Then Cindy asked if I would like some company.

"I would love it," I emailed her back.

And that's how, one brilliantly sunlit morning, I found myself riding the shuttle bus between Denver and Moonrise Mountain, some two hours away from the city I'd landed in at midmorning.

Cindy and I had spoken on the phone the night before, and she was sure we were going to get a sign from Drew that he was here with us. "I just *know* it. What if I'm psychic too?"

"I'm sure you are," I told her.

Happy with the assurance, she re-named herself "Psychic 2."

༄

Drew was in the shuttle bus. It's funny how I could feel the full *being* of him when he popped in. I could feel his warmth, his breath, the feel of his skin, his hair, the sound of him—his presence. It was all around me, filling the bus.

I'm riding with you, Mom. Massive sculptures of red rocky peaks and deep canyons echoed his thoughts … Bouncing them back into my soul. *I'm here … I'm here … I'm herrre …*

"That's nice, darling," I answered. "I know you are. But would you give me something...solid? Something to show me you're here, that leaves absolutely no doubt?"

I think I heard him laugh.

When I stepped out at the Moonrise Mountain Lodge, Drew's friends were there to greet me. It brought back so many memories as I hugged them all and went up to my room with Ashley. They had given Cindy and me a suite with two bedrooms, each with its own bath, high beds, and a fireplace for the cool summer nights. On the hallway desk was a bottle of wine and flowers from Drew's friends. There was a bowl of chocolates on the desk. I felt tears come to my eyes. "Oh Ashley, thank you," I said. "It's so beautiful!"

"Only the best for Drew's Mom," Ashley said, smiling and almost in tears herself.

It was a bittersweet time. The resort, built in the style of a massive lodge, was tucked into the Precambrian rock formation of the range. Its giant beams and peaked roofs seemed to reach out and draw me in toward the warmth of its heart, where even in August the long burned-out fires of winter left their memories glimmering in the grates of its massive walk-in fireplace.

There were reminders of Drew everywhere I went. He was in the lobby, at the front desk of the club floor, in the hallways—just as he had been in life when I came to visit him.

I could hear his voice. "Hi Mom!" I remember his cheeks flushed with pleasure as he met my car at the front entrance. "How was your trip?"

This morning I walked across the stone floors of the lobby, down amber-lit hallways without him, but accompanied by people who had known and loved him. My heart was full and very empty at the same time.

Cindy arrived a couple of hours after me. She stood teary-eyed on the threshold of our suite, and as she walked in and made her way to the windows that looked out onto the mountains, she began to cry.

And kept crying. I offered her a piece of chocolate and took a piece for myself. What else was there to do?

But she teared-up again when we walked out onto the balcony. "I don't know what's wrong with you!" she blurted. "Or me! Look at you—you're not crying... why aren't you crying? I'm drowning!"

"I don't know." It was spooky how calm I felt. "I guess you'll just have to be the official mourner." I ate another chocolate, feeling weirdly inadequate in some way.

She laughed and snorted and gave me a soggy smile.

Looking out at the mountains, I felt strangely at peace. And later, going down to the spa it was as though I was a droplet, floating in some sublime aerosol, wafting down the corridors in the base of the hotel and into the grotto-like room full of the scented ambience of soap and flowers.

It's a wacky thing, this grief. The tears don't just happen. They can catch you at the oddest times—but when you're armed and ready for them, they don't come. This removed feeling was something I had encountered only once before. It was in the few days following Drew's death when we returned to the lodge on Moonrise Mountain to say goodbye to his friends. We held an in-house memorial at the hotel one evening, and during that event, I felt completely disassociated from what was really happening. The general manager spoke for us and Michael who wanted to follow him, but found he was just too shaken up. So I stepped in and began to speak. I spoke to a gathering of over a hundred people without notes. My nerves were steady and I felt strangely peaceful as I talked about Drew. It was as though I had to stay strong for this time. I was the grown-up and I must be strong. Of course, that was just an illusion. But no one expects strength and poise. It shocked me, too, but it appeared to serve me in those few hours. It's a very strange thing. I was sure this was what was happening now.

I remembered the first time I ever came down here. Drew was showing me around his hotel, and it was the first time I met Tory the spa manager and Drew's friend. It was Tory who found Drew that afternoon and got him into hospital. Who could have imagined what was coming next…

Later as the sun began to set, we stood on the flagstone pool deck staring up at the mountains, relaxing in the flower-filled breeze that drifted off the raised poppy and petunia beds that surrounded the patio.

Cindy's eyes brimmed with tears. Again.

I felt in awe of the high peaks and ridges all around us. "*I will look to the mountains, from whence cometh my strength…*" I murmured.

"What?" Cindy's eyes opened wide.

Yes, no wonder she looked surprised. Unaccustomed as I am to spouting from the Bible, no one was more surprised than me. "…from the mountains cometh my strength."

"I thought that's what you said!"

Darn! I ought to be in tears. But it wasn't happening. Instead I was wafting around quoting Saint James. It was too damn weird!

That first evening in the mountains, we went downstairs for a drink in the hotel pub and to visit with the bartender, Drew's friend who had been in Denver with us last November. He bought us dinner and we talked about Drew.

Afterward, we took our glasses of wine out onto the flagstone patio, found a couple of vacant Adirondack chairs and settled down in front of the blazing fire pit. Low rock walls and beds of lupine and daisies hugged the outside walls of the massive lodge, and floodlit aspens shimmered near the swimming pool, awash in pale blue light.

We were on our way to a rendezvous with Drew. But neither Psychic 1 nor Psychic 2 picked up on it.

There were twenty or thirty guests doing what we were doing, just sitting, relaxing by the fire or watching kids. Parents stood close to the edge of the pit threading marshmallows on long sticks for them to roast.

Drew used to tell me about this place. He came down often in the evenings to roast marshmallows with the children. Sometimes after work he would volunteer to babysit for a family staying on the club floor.

Sitting here watching the flames and listening to the children playing under the outside lights felt very right. I was feeling mellow. Cindy was relaxing in the next chair, staring at the flames in the fire pit, watching the children.

And then there was a Plop! And heavy panting coming from the chair beside me.

"Whew!" I heard as I looked into the hot and sweaty face of a little boy. His cheeks were flushed, his light brown hair stuck to his temples.

Cindy leaned forward to see who had joined us. "Well, hi!" I said, as he flung himself backwards and rubbed the back of his hand across his sticky, pink mouth.

"Hi!" He glanced over at me, and then squirmed his way to the chair arm nearest to me. "I'm hot! I've been running."

"I can see that," I said.

He launched into a flood of conversation, cupping his chin in one hand. I couldn't tell you what we talked about, but I listened, fascinated with this child—no more than about five—so at ease with a strange person. He's just like Drew, I thought. I stared into a pair of big brown eyes, at the little body, the legs and arms that were streaked with dirt, and the sweaty and floppy golden-brown hair. Black dirt powdered the side of one cheek and grubby fingers left smudges on his forehead.

"Talkative little guy," Cindy remarked.

"What's your name?" I asked. But before he could answer, a harried-looking young woman came wheeling around the corner of one of the rock planters and stood there with one hand on her hip. "Andrew! *I've been looking everywhere for you!*"

"Oh my God!" Cindy hissed. "Andrew!"

"Yeah—he looked just like him. Just like my Andrew when he was little."

"I think it's a sign," said my psychic friend. Her eyes were fixed on the child being admonished by his parent for running off and not telling her where he was going.

"Definitely a sign," Cindy repeated as our young friend Andrew was carted off to bed.

"That was extraordinary," I said. "He looked so much like Drew at that age. It startled me." There was a distinct chill in the high mountain air and I rubbed my arms. "I think I'll go upstairs, it's getting cool."

"Me too," she said. "Let's go."

The warmth from the lodge was inviting. As we made our way upstairs, we walked through heavy oak doors into our two-bedroom suite on the seventh floor of the hotel. It was as spacious and luxurious as only the staff at Moonrise Mountain Lodge can do it. Low fires glimmered from the gas logs in the fireplaces and snow-white comforters had been turned down on high wooden beds.

A bottle of wine was cooling in a silver ice bucket beside a tray of cheese and crackers. They had been sent up to the room with a small silver tray that held the general manager's card and a "welcome back" message.

The last time I was here there was a vase full of western Protea from Drew. The Protea, or sugar bush, is the national flower of the country I was born in, South Africa. Drew had found them in the hotel gift shop that morning. There were always flowers from Drew when I got to his hotel. This time the hotel staff, his friends, had sent me flowers.

Soft music played from the bedside radios. It floated into my mind on gossamer sails. That song... I opened a kitchen cabinet looking for a glass. I felt so calm, so at peace here.

Cindy had disappeared into her room on the other side of the lounge. "Do you like the music?" she called, "I can change it..."

"No!" I stopped halfway to my bedroom and listened. "Listen to that song! Leave it on..." I walked quickly into her room. "Oh my God... Listen to that!"

"*I Will Always Love you!*" Cindy said. "Get the chocolate."

"It's Whitney's song!" I said.

Cindy's eyes shone bright in the low firelight, threatening to overflow again as the melody whispered the sweet lyric of loss, and she announced, "It's another sign!"

❦

I woke up before Cindy the next morning and sat up in bed with the pillows piled around me watching the sunrise. I could see the Gore Range Mountains to the east—high and snow-capped, glinting pink and pale yellow in the dawn. Bright rays streaked the still-dark rock face, light streamers in the early dawn. It was going to be a beautiful day and I wanted to savor every minute of it, so I got out of bed and tiptoed into the lounge. There was no sound coming from Cindy's bedroom.

Pulling on jeans and a sweater, I let myself out of the suite and headed to the lounge to find a cup of coffee.

The concierge on duty was the only other person up and about this early. I remembered her from another stay here when Drew had been training the concierges on this floor.

It was quiet up here. I took the cup of coffee she made for me and walked out through the glass doors onto the balcony. I stood there, cup in hand, watching the sunlight seeping over the far ridge, spiking the clouds with crystal rays, bathing the valley in light.

"How many times did you arrive early for work and stand here, my love?" I asked her silently. "How often were you here at daybreak to see the sun crest the high range … to watch the first silver rays awaken the slopes and the valley below the lodge? What a glorious place to begin your day."

I stood there lost in the sparkle of early morning, sipping my coffee, and as I watched the golden rim of the sun appear over the tops of the mountains, a white dove flew out of the shadows and perched on one of the peaked roofs of the lodge directly below the balcony on which I stood. My eyes filled with tears and I began to cry. *Finally*, I cried. I cried for me and for Drew that he will never see another sunrise from here. I cried for the times we spent together in this hotel and I cried for all the glorious days he'll miss in these Rocky Mountains. Mostly, I cried for the life we wouldn't be sharing anymore. The dove was still there when I left the lounge and when Cindy and I came back later for a late breakfast. Ashley, the club floor manager and Drew's friend, told me it had flown away minutes after I left that morning.

"Let me show you where it was perched," I said to Cindy. We walked out onto the balcony with our plates and set them down on the small glass tabletop.

"It was ..." I scanned the roof tops for only a minute and then, "Oh my God! There it is! Oh Cindy, look! It's back." A lone white dove with its head turned toward us was perched in the same place I had seen it early that morning.

"Definitely a sign!" Cindy declared.

"If you don't believe in coincidences," I said.

Twenty

They Come in Threes

After breakfast, we drove into the small town of Edwards and found a flower shop and nursery. There were racks of seed packets, and we chose a variety of wildflower seeds to scatter on the mountain slope where we planned to leave some of Drew's ashes.

We asked the person who owned the shop about picking roadside flowers for a bouquet we could leave behind. She told us that Colorado has a law against picking wildflowers, but wanted to help, so she went out into her own meadow and came back with a bunch of wild daisies, flocks, asters, and poppies for us to take to the site.

We got lost on the way back to the hotel, which wasn't much of a surprise. From the valley, you can see the hotel and the road winding up to it, but when we got onto that winding road we couldn't tell where we were. All we could see were mountains and more mountains, and valleys and one winding road.

"We must have taken a fork in the road somewhere," I said.

"The wrong fork," said Cindy.

We continued driving upward hoping to get high enough to be able to look down and get our bearings. Eventually, we found ourselves at a big resort in the village of Eagle Roost that we'd never seen before. And more mountain ranges. Then, as we were about to turn back and start all over from the bottom of the mountain, we saw a sign on the side of the dirt road that said, "Riding Stables," and because Cindy wanted to see the horses, we kept going.

We were way off the beaten path. There was nothing out here but one gravel road, dusty roadsides, meadows full of summer flowers, and range upon range of Rocky Mountains. Then about a quarter of the way up the slope we turned a corner and came across a young boy sprawled on the road. He was about ten years old and it looked as though he had fallen off his bike. We stopped the car and got out.

"Hey, what happened to you? Did you skid on the gravel?" Cindy asked before bending down to look at a bloody gash on his leg.

His face was tear-streaked, his elbow was grazed, and his hand appeared to be bleeding.

"I was riding with a friend who got ahead of me and I skidded 'round this curve and fell ... I yelled at him to stop but he was too far down the hill."

We called his folks, gave them the bad news, and then got the boy down the mountain. But the bike, which we had pulled over onto the side of the road, had to be picked up by the rental shop, so we made a stop there and picked up a young man who worked there, and back up the mountain we went.

He was about twenty-five and spent the ride leaning over the front seat chattering all the way up the mountain. He was suntanned and healthy from the Colorado summer, full of vitality, and was determined to tell us all about the valley in the ten minutes or so it took to retrieve the bike.

We dropped him off and he stuck his head back through the window. "Thank you, guys! It would have been a long hike up here. Appreciate it!" He picked up the bike and waved to us.

"Hey! Wait!" I said, "What's your name?"

"Andy!" He smiled and wheeled off down the gravel road.

"Yup!" was all Cindy said.

"There'll be three of them. Just wait …" I told her. "They come in threes."

"Hmmmm."

～⌒

That afternoon we went up the mountain right behind the resort. I had left home with a small bag filled with Drew's ashes and we were heading to an aspen grove Drew's friends had found at the top of the mountain—a good place to scatter them. So, with the guys he spent most of his off-duty time with and two dog friends of Drew's, we set off up the mountain in an SUV. I carried the ashes in a borrowed crystal wine glass, which was carried inside a borrowed silver ice bucket from the suite. The wildflower seeds were in another glass.

Cindy carried the flowers, fighting tears all the way up. I was floating as usual in some weird ethereal cloud that had somehow penetrated the sadness of the day and neutralized it. All I could feel was the warmth of this summer day, the smell of warm grass and fresh flowers, and the weight of the ice bucket and Drew's ashes in my lap. It occurred to me that Drew would thoroughly approve of this mode of transportation.

How many times had he carried one of these silver buckets to a guest's room? I caught my breath and stared out of the window, silent grief cutting through my heart. But still, I didn't cry.

As we reached the top of the mountain, dark clouds were gathering across the valley, hanging low on the far range. They moved slowly, billowing ominously, and we cast anxious eyes to the sky as they got closer, sprawling above the valley looking like giant, crouching bears.

The wind blew, rippling the alpine flowers that covered the mountain, scattering the ashes and seeds that we spread over the red brown soil. Thunder rumbled and a flash of lightning seared the hillside, crackling as it struck the ground.

The words of peace from Saint Francis, the Hopi prayer, and our music fell softly on the flowers and ashes at our feet, mingling with our tears and memories of the times Drew had skied this mountain. Drew's young friends wept openly.

Cindy was quiet until it was her turn to read a prayer. As I listened to her, tears started to prickle behind my eyes and then spilled over as the words of the ancient prayer fell like raindrops on the soil.

"*Do not stand at my grave and weep,*" she spoke quietly.

"*I am not here, I do not sleep.*
I am a thousand winds that blow
I am the diamond glint on snow . . ."

The boys' heads were bowed and the dogs were still. The wind ruffled the meadow flowers.

"My time has come,
I am at rest.
I am the sunset in the west ... "

The lovely words of the Hopi prayer fell softly on the red mountain earth, branding my heart forever.

Cindy lifted her eyes when she had finished, and we stood with our arms around one another.

But we did not stand at the grave and weep too long. We were silent for a while with our own thoughts, waiting for the drenching rain that never fell. The bright white bark of the shimmering aspens was stark in contrast to the now indigo-colored clouds. Thunder rumbled, flexing its muscles, sending out forks of lightning that pierced the ground. But the rain never fell, and we left the mountain in brilliant sunshine.

⚬⚬⚬

There was a reception for us that evening on the patio. The hotel staff had gathered on the flagstones for the dedication of a memorial bench for Drew. It was not just any bench. This one was hand hewn from Pole Pines that had fallen on the slopes of the mountains. They were big, round logs of polished wood. Bright and sturdy. There was a small brass plaque embedded in the back rest with Drew's name and dates engraved on it, and another larger plaque was cemented onto a rock beside the bench citing the qualities of an outstanding employee.

The dedication was followed by an annual banquet singling out more outstanding employees, at which many of Drew's friends were honored that night. Drew was awarded the highest award for excellence that the resort gives. I thought I would die with pride. "Well done Drew!" I whispered as I watched the summer moon rise high above the mountain.

❧

We left the next morning. I went up to the club floor to say goodbye to all the friends who worked up there with Drew, but when I got off the elevator, I was told that everyone was downstairs waiting to say goodbye to us.

I went back to the elevator and was joined by a man and a little boy with brown eyes and tangled hair. The two talked quietly to each other and when the elevator stopped, they moved past me and got out. The little boy ran ahead and the man called to him to slow down. I held the door open for a minute, and then I called after them, "Sorry—I heard you call him—what did you say his name was?"

The man, holding the child by one hand, looked back over his shoulder. "Andrew. But we call him Drew."

I closed my eyes. That was one heck of a sign. Three Andrew's. One for each day we were there. Wow.

We said goodbye to everyone—all of us in tears—and left the hotel, headed for the village. I patted the bumpy side of my purse that held the remaining chocolates

So maybe Cindy and I are going nuts. We decided to go to the Eagle River, which was where Drew used to fish as well as the location of his very first apartment. On the drive over, high in that blue Colorado sky, was an arc of white cloud formations that looked exactly like doves flying on invisible air currents, lifting and swaying across the sky. There was no mistaking them for anything else. This was no random cloud formation. With their fan tails and distinctive beaks, they were unmistakably white doves.

"I know, I know," Cindy exclaimed. "The dove on the roof top, these cloud doves—there'll be one more sighting! I'm getting this stuff, Psychic 1."

"Yup. They come in threes," I said, unnecessarily.

We pulled into the apartment complex and walked down to the river. It was running strongly, tumbling over boulders, coursing through black rock gullies and rapids, foaming white, and bouncing spray high in the air. Wild flowers and sagebrush lined its banks, tall cotton woods and aspens waved in the light breeze.

I picked a boulder on the edge of the river, round, black, and smooth from the rushing torrent, sat down on it, and scattered a handful of Drew's ashes into the current.

Then, picking my way over the rocky shoreline as we left the river, the toe of my shoe touched a perfectly heart-shaped stone. I picked it up. It was one more souvenir from Drew.

On the way out of town, we stopped at Drew's favorite Friday night karaoke spot, O'Malley's, and toasted him over a lunchtime beer—and got teary again.

There was a young man dismantling microphones on the small stage, and as he turned away from us we saw an arc of five white doves on the back of his T-shirt.

"That's three sets of white doves!" Cindy whispered. "I have to get a picture."

༄

We left the valley after lunch and motored over to a place high in the mountains called Grand Lake. The reason we were headed for Grand Lake is that Cindy's daughter Spencer was appearing in Gilbert and Sullivan's *Pirates of Penzance* that was playing in this small resort town. Her performance as Mabel brought the audience to its feet. She poured life into the role, her vibrant soprano filling the theater, her humor sparkled and her soul was center stage. The applause was deafening, the "encores" kept coming ,and the young cast was flushed and thrilled with their success.

During the interval, I looked down at the program in my lap, and at the end of Spencer's bio she had written, "For Drew."

My heart swelled with emotion as my eyes filled with tears and heaving sobs shook my shoulders.

At the end of the show, I hugged the leading lady and she whispered, "*Drew was center stage!* All night! You should have seen him! He was hamming it up and loving it! He was dressed as the Pirate King—I have never seen anything so—*dashing!*" Her eyes glinted. "And you won't believe the number of peacocks that followed me all the way from North Carolina!"

"Don't forget the zebra wall hanging—over the bed!" Cindy interjected.

These two …

༄

My flight left Denver at noon the next day, so I was up early packing and getting ready to meet the limo that would drive me to Denver. Cindy was staying for another week to be with Spencer. The birds were starting to wake up outside my window, and through the open blinds I could see the mountains, still dark and silhouetted against the rising sun.

It was time to go.

My spirit always has to be tugged home from the mountains. It's a place where thoughts and dreams and memories can soar. There is nothing pressing down, nothing holding back, only clear blue and white skies, so high they may touch eternity and as such, there are no boundaries here.

But here on earth, my shuttle was waiting. It was time to go.

Ginny and Drew in Colorado.

Twenty-One

The Last Time
I Saw Drew

*I*t was a rainy morning in late August. Lying here at six with the French doors open listening to the rain falling on the deck, I could smell wet earth and watch the mist shrouding the lake, lifting and falling on the movement of a light breeze.

Wrens and cardinals, golden finches, and chickadees were tucked into the thicket of blue spruce growing at the corner of the house. They were calling to each other ... asking when the rain would end, no doubt. A pair of mourning doves huddled together among the leaves of the giant hickory tree cooing softly. There was rain in my heart that day. I, too, wondered when it would end.

The end of August was a difficult time. The last week of August was the last time I saw Drew.

He called me late one night and said "Surprise! I'm coming home for a few days next week!"

"Great!" I said "Where are you flying into?" In our part of the world, we have a choice of three airports: Greensboro or Raleigh in North Carolina or Roanoke, Virginia.

"Well that's the problem. I'm coming into Washington, D.C."

"Oh ... do you want me to pick you up?"

"I would like you to," said Drew.

"Okay. What time?" It was a much longer drive, but not impossible.

"Well that's the thing—I don't land until 11:30 at night ...," Drew said.

"Yeah, that's a bit of a problem ..." I didn't want to be driving around D. C. late at night by myself. I'd never considered myself a huge wimp or anything, but that scared me.

"Mom—you there?"

"Yup, I'm thinking. How about this? When you land at 11:30, get a hotel room at the airport for the night. Then get up and catch the train down to Fredericksburg in the morning. I'll spend the night in Richmond with Karen and run up and pick you up at the station."

He said it was a plan.

When I saw him next day, he was dragging an old black suitcase of mine with no trolley wheels, a big smile on his face.

"Drew!" I hugged him. It felt so good to see him again. I missed this youngest son of mine and would have given anything for him to live closer to home. "You need a new suitcase."

The plan was to drive to Karen's in King William before heading home. He was anxious to get to the lake. "Will we be at Karen's long?" he asked. I told him no, we were just stopping in to say hi and grab a quick bite to eat.

Karen wanted us to stay, but I knew he had plans to see his friends at the lake and spend as much time playing on the water as he could.

He fell asleep in the car on the way home.

That evening he and I had dinner with Jim at his place. I think Drew was unsure about another man in my life, but he handled it with grace and was relieved when Sara arrived to pick him up and take him into the world of lake parties and old friends.

❦

As it turned out, Drew had one more plan to spring on me that weekend. He wanted to go back to college. "I've just gone as far as I can hands on in this business. I have to have a degree if I'm going to move up."

Was I hearing things? This was the kid whose father and I had delivered to the front door of the junior college, not once, but twice only to have him come home later in the day saying, "It's not for me." We had finally believed him. Now he was saying it was time to go back to school, and he wanted to come home and do that in Roanoke. *That's* why he brought the big old black suitcase home. It probably had all his clothes in it because he was planning to stay. Then I supposed the plan was to drive back to Colorado and move his stuff.

With some trepidation, I encouraged him to go up to the college and find out what he had to do. But when he went up to register, he found out that registration had just closed.

He thought he would do his first semester online, but when he shared his ideas with Michael and Karen, we all urged him to go back to Colorado and come back and register in the spring.

He had a great job in Colorado and was excelling in his chosen field. And although I could see how having a degree might help him move up, I wanted to know that he was going to stick with it this time. We agreed he'd try it in spring.

I drove Drew back to Richmond when it was time for him to go and we sang his songs and mine all the way there. He was telling me about his karaoke nights and how much fun he had singing on Friday evenings at O'Malley's.

On the evening of August 26 we hugged and said goodbye at the station, never dreaming it was the last time we would be together.

Yes, a year later, August 26 was a very difficult day. There was no way to escape it. After that day, I would never again be able to say, "This time last year, Drew was still here."

Over and over again I retraced the way we spent that last day we had together. From the last breakfast we shared to the last moment before he ran for the train. Could I have stopped him going and maybe changed the course of his life? Could I have stopped the wheel of his life from taking the fatal turn that it did? I could have stopped him at any time. But can anybody change another person's life path? I don't believe so. If Drew was meant to take another path, the direction he would have taken would have been completely different. For one thing, he might have come home two days earlier and made the college registration deadline, but all the markers, the arrows on his path, seemed to point the other way.

Still, when he died in November, doubt almost crushed me. I was assailed by thoughts of "I'm the mommy! I should have kept him safe." What if he'd stayed? Would he still be alive? What if he'd been at home when this happened? Would I have realized something was wrong? Would I have tried to wake him the next morning, instead of letting him sleep?

Probably not, my mind says. Drew always slept in on the weekends. I would have let him sleep. His bedroom is downstairs. Mine is above his. Would I have heard anything?

Probably not, my mind says. The roommates said Drew hadn't moved in his sleep the night his system crashed. He had fallen asleep on the couch and when Tory found him he was in the same position they had seen him in the night before when they all went to bed.

But then the mother thing comes back with all the angst and guilt that can accompany it. It's always been my job to keep my child alive. I wasn't there when he needed me.

But sometimes, you can't keep anyone alive. Not even when you're there. The "what-ifs" are rotten. Trash them.

❧

Soon it was September. The leaves were just beginning to turn and the lake was empty of tourists. Yellow school buses were running again and the rusty sedum and sky blue cariopteris were in bloom.

I had gone to bed at about ten o'clock and had just picked up a book to read when Drew burst into my room. It was just the way he used to when he came in from being out all evening. I could feel the big mass of warm energy that I know by now is his. In my minds' eye I could see his hand on the doorknob, his face damp with exertion, flushed and excited.

He sat down beside me on the bed.

Who's that kid? I got. Drew had a feeling of frustration around him. Somehow, I knew he was talking about Matt, Pat's son. We hadn't mentioned Matt in our talks for some time.

Yeah, that's it! Matt!

I hadn't spoken or even fully formed the thought.

He's so cool! Cooler than I thought when I first met him at the lake—over here he's teaching me a lot about water skiing. I'm showing him some snowboarding tricks—and wakeboarding tricks!

I smiled and said, "That's nice, darling. What else do you do?" He gave me the image of a 1950's diner sparkling with chrome and red vinyl table cloths.

I can sing karaoke here—there are lots of cool karaoke places here. Huge stages! I've learned to play the guitar. So many people here—so friendly, teaching me things . . . and you should hear my voice! Man! It's sweet—better than it ever was.

We were quiet.

Dad comes to listen. He wants me to teach him to sing . . .

We both laughed at that. Walt sounded like an off-key frog when he sang.

Nan (my mother) comes too. She likes Dad . . . likes listening to me. Papa's too busy! But he's learning to play the guitar. I'm teaching him.

"Be happy Drew." I could feel my eyes warming with tears again.

You be happy, I heard. But I wasn't sure if that would ever happen. *You can be happy, Mom.* Again he had picked up my thought, faster than I could think it … Then he had to go. I could feel his energy pulling back, leaving.

I love you.

"I love you, too." It was the way we always ended our phone calls before and after Drew moved away from home. We spoke to each other three days before he went to sleep for the last time, never to wake up in this life again. Those were the last words we said to each other.

❧

I told Pat the Earth Angel about my talk with Drew the next time we met for lunch.

The Angel Lunches were going strong. We met at noon in an old red barn in the mountains. It was attached to an old plantation house that was built high on a cliff overlooking the river that tumbled and cascaded over rocks far below before tumbling into the lake. The restaurant had a fireplace in the dining room in winter and it was comfortable, casual, and charming.

We sometimes referred to ourselves as "The Club That Nobody Wants To Belong To." But, like it or not, we were members, and as such, a special bond formed. We talked about our lives and about our kids, and Lenny our waiter kept the wine coming. When we laughed he smiled from wherever he happened to be in the dining room. After the third glass of wine, we could be heard laughing from a fair distance away. The wine did nothing for our muddled memories, but for a few hours a month it didn't matter. Some days we cried, and when we cried

Lenny got teary eyed, too. He never minded that we stayed long after the last lunch guests had gone home. I think he may be an Earth Angel, too.

If there's one thing we Club Members know, it's this. It's comforting to talk about our children. We don't see them as "gone." We haven't written them off in any way. We want to talk about them and we don't want people to be uncomfortable with that. These lunches with other parents who have lost children let us do that.

There's an unseen umbilical cord between us and our kids that doesn't snap with death. And that keeps these children close. We love to talk about them because when we do, they live. We can hear them, we can see them. We can relive their successes and their goof-ups and the big bear hugs from our grown-up boys and the slippery, glossy kisses from our daughters.

∿

In October 2009, I went to northwest Arkansas. It was autumn in the Ozark Mountains and the trees were in full, brilliant fall foliage. The colors were radiant reds, oranges, and luminescent yellows clinging to blackened twigs.

The first evening there, I stood underneath an ancient oak on the campus of the University of Arkansas in the shadow of Old Main, where I saw myself glowing in the brilliance of reflected sunlight firing gold through the leaves.

This is where Walt went to college. Michael was born in this town. My mother died here. My sister lives here and all her grand children were born in Fayetteville. A lot of my memories live here.

Standing on the old land grant campus, flickers of long-ago movie reels from the '70s and '80s played across my mind. I could hear the twang and beat of Nitty Gritty Dirt Band strumming loudly from the stadium, and watched people clad in filmy skirts and shawls, blue jeans and sandals scurrying between classes, long hair fluttering in the wind on both men and women.

This was where four-year-old Drew was given his first puppy, a rambunctious blond Lab named Cassie. In my mind, I could see them tumble and wrestle on the lawn—so perfect the bond, so intact their joy in one another. They were one in the truest sense.

There was a lot of my family here.

I spent my birthday on October 10 with my niece Kellie Anne and her family and my sister. Karen and Michael called me that day. This was the first birthday since Drew was born that I wouldn't get a hug or a kiss or a call from him. I watched the Razorbacks play football against Auburn. The Hogs won! I might have cried if they had lost. This was a bad weepy time.

When the game was over, a big crowd was spread out on the grassy banks behind the stadium waiting for traffic to clear enough to make the ride home less stressful. Kids threw footballs to each other, and a few people broke out picnic baskets to share while they waited. The air was filled with excitement over the big win, young men high-fived each other, little girls twirled in their bright red skirts and jeans, scarlet ribbons flying in the mid-October breeze.

I caught a glimpse of Drew among them tossing a red and white football in the crowd.

To Dance with You on
an Autumn Evening

*I*t was late November back here on the East Coast and the leaves had fallen off the trees. All were barren but the stubborn white oaks that wouldn't fall in step, hanging on to their papery brown leaves until the spring, extending the raking season, and making us crazy.

As I wandered through the woods, listening to the soles of my shoes biting into the dead leaves, snapping twigs, it occurred to me that I wouldn't make a great hunter. How on earth did they creep through the trees in their moccasins without ever crunching a leaf? I sounded like a buffalo plowing through them. But then, becoming a great hunter wasn't an ambition of mine, so I let it go. There was peace here. My mind wasn't racing, my chest wasn't clenched, I could think clearly. The damp air was rich with the scent of old leaves and bark. There was peace here.

The sun was descending slowly into the southwestern sky, and a light breeze tugged at the remaining leaves still clinging to their boughs. I carried an armful of fall foliage for my vases. This late in the year, the leaves were starting to curl at the edges and black dots speckled the deep reds and yellows. Soon there would be no color in the forests, except for the cedars and southern pine.

Would I cut boughs of pine for the mantle this year, as I did every Christmas? I didn't know.

Emerging from the evening gloom of the forest, clutching my branches, I noticed that there were tiny spiders clinging to the dying leaves. I shook them over the grass at the edge of the woods and carried the branches to the fire pit patio, laying them down on a concrete bench to let the straggling spiders move off at their leisure.

Settling myself on one of the big rocks that were piled in a circle to make the rim of the fire pit, I turned slightly to face the lake.

The water was calm this evening. I counted nine mallards paddling around the grasses in search of whatever it is wild ducks have for dinner. A mud patch bloomed near the shore, belying the presence of a large snapping turtle that had lived in that spot since Drew was a little boy. It had grown from a saucer-sized turtle to one big snapping dude. Twenty-two years later, he was about eighteen inches in diameter. Right now he was churning up a mess of twigs and dirt as I watched. Or maybe 'he' was really a 'she' and this was some sort of a nest building thing going on.

As I watched, a red-tailed hawk flew low over the water, disappearing into the woods behind me.

We're all connected you know. The ducks, the old turtle... the spiders on the leaves... even those flowers in the rock bed... we don't recognize that on earth, but here—it all comes clear.

My heart leapt. Old habit made me look around for Drew. Then I focused in on my son's energy and the giant presence of his being.

He was sitting in one of the wrought iron chairs opposite me leaning back, turned away from the water. His left leg was bent, his right ankle resting on its knee. His arms were relaxed, hands holding the calf of the right leg. His hair was longer than I had seen it for several years. His face had a pensive look.

"Hey, Drew."

Earth can be so... cloudy... it's like looking through dirty glass. People on earth hardly ever see things as they really are. You know it's hard to be down there, you just don't realize how hard... Over here you find out that everything's connected. Me and you, them—heaven and earth. You just know it. I'm one with everything...

"Like a giant mass—a big ball of... stuff?"

No. All separate, but together in mind and spirit.

I was remembering the bond between Drew and his old Lab, Cassie.

There's great understanding here. It's so weird! Not like earth where none of us seem to understand each other... Here we all communicate with one another, mostly through thought. Sometimes voice, but not often. There's no need for it. We read each other's energy.

My heart started to beat in anticipation as he spoke. "Where's 'here' Drew? Where is the place you're in?"

Very close to you—to earth—just another dimension ... another layer ...

"Like another planet?" I asked.

Sort of—but huge. Much bigger than earth. You can't imagine ...
Then he switched the thought.

Remember the big lion? I can talk to him and understand him and all animals ... and plants. Flowers and trees ... and I feel them talk back. It all happens with thought and energy.

On earth we're always wanting to forgive each other or ourselves, but here there's no need for forgiveness ... we understand why we do things and there's no judgment. We accept everyone totally. There's so much love. You can feel it all around you.

I wish I had better words to show you what I mean. Today, I sat beside a group of flowers and one of them leaned toward me and brushed my hand. I felt something really sweet and gentle. Love has different colors and textures ... different sounds ...

"Oh Drew ..."

And Mom ... you should see these trees! They're so alive! They give off huge energy. I feel 'invited' by them to sit beside them. To lean on them, and when I do I feel myself absorbing their strength. It's almost like a ... transfusion of life. But better. It's light and bright and full ... it lets me see so clearly. Lets me be anything I want to be ... as strong as a bear!

He threw back his head and I heard him laugh. I watched as he ran both hands over his head the way he used to do when he was explaining something.

I love it! Have you any idea how strong that is? To be as strong as a bear ... and I discovered that when I'm with a bear I can think like a bear—I can BE him if I want to ... tried it out in a stream today catching fish! Man that was cool!

"Did you catch any fish?"

YEEEAH! Just dipped my hand in the water and snapped them up!

This would fit so well into Drew's heaven. Old pictures of him sitting on the dock at the lake for hours, dangling a piece of string on the end of a bamboo pole, and casting with bacon scraps, reeled across my mind.

I smiled.

Yeah! Dad likes being around the trees. He used up a lot of energy while he was on earth. I think he rested for a long time when he first got back here. I've learned how hard it was for him to live there.

Guess what—sometimes he likes to walk around in the house at the lake and check things out. See all the woodworking he did while he was there.

I treasured those pieces.

Can you feel him?

I nodded. "And sometimes I can smell his cigarette smoke."

Remember the fire in the chimney? He was there then.

"Oh Drew! I saw a shadow go across the hallway and I heard his footsteps! I knew it was him. Please tell him I know it's him."

He had to go and see that everything was okay. He watches over you.

I felt my heart swell. I knew that. So many times I'd felt him here—usually when I was upset or stressed or on the verge of a freak-out. That usually happens when something like a toilet runs over or a pipe leaks or an electric circuit blows and I don't know how to fix it.

He still does a lot of crafting with wood. Sometimes the trees drop wood for him to work with. You should see the things he makes—smooth, golden, soft—they keep the life force of the tree it seems. Dad says that he can feel the wood moving in his hands ... can feel life in it even when you think it's dried up ... it's teaching him, he says. He likes making balls. He holds a piece of wood in his hand, stroking it until it becomes round and smooth and begins to shine. No words to explain ... He's got a whole box full of them.

Drew laughed and uncrossed his leg. He used his hands to shape the balls he was telling me about.

They're all sizes ... some are that clear golden color ... almost like apple juice but clearer and brighter ... those are my favorite. Others are shiny deep browns and reds ... He's found all kinds of trees I've never heard of, like Takamaka! Dragon's blood!

"Those are the trees he saw for the first time in the Seychelles, the islands where we got married. He built two deep-sea fishing boats with that tropical wood ... it's like teak I think ... Dad and an old man called Grandcaz." He used to go down to the old man's boat yard every day after work and work with him on the boats. "And the wood called 'Dragon's blood' got that name because of the crimson sap that trickled down its bark when it was cut." The memories swept my mind like a sandy breeze. The people of the Seychelles, once a French colony, used the French name, Sang Dragon.

*He talks about Grandcaz when I sit with him while he's pol-
ishing his wood. He's even got some golden-green balls...I can't
even describe the color. It's alive.*

Living color. The moviemakers used that phrase. I bet they
have no clue what living color really is.

*And he found a piece of driftwood on the beach—you knew he
had a cottage on the beach, didn't you?*

It was more a statement than a question. Not long after
Walt died, while I was meditating—or was it a dream...I
couldn't recall...he showed me a snapshot of his heaven and it
included a tropical beach, a small house, and the biggest deep
sea fishing boat I'd ever seen—sparkling white, complete with
outriggers and mahogany decking.

*Anyway, he took this piece of driftwood, and all he did was
smooth it out along its natural lines...it's a long piece, swirly and
graceful...and you should see the colors that came up when he
buffed and polished it! Deep blues, grays, and blacks with streaks
of bone white...there's a glow or something that seems to come
from inside it.*

"I'm speechless..." I bent down and picked up a petunia
blossom that had fallen off its stem and twirled it between my
fingers. "Tell me about the flowers, Drew."

*Oh boy. The only way I can describe them is that...they are
the "princesses" here! They are indescribable! Their colors...alive,
translucent, glowing...like nothing you've ever seen on earth...all
different kinds of stems and petals...some smooth and luminescent, others lacy and...light and "giggly!" All shapes. Some are tu-
bular—they are the singing flowers.*

*If you sit with them, they fill you with...joy. Fun. They're
fun! Always happy. They like preening. No mirrors needed to*

admire themselves in—they see themselves in each other. I felt Drew's face split into a big smile. *They love who they are! I like to watch them showing off—they sway, they laugh. They fill every space with ... a feeling of happiness! They'll sing to you if you want them to, or if you want to just lie down in the grass, they'll just fan you and leave you alone. But I can feel them there. Full of peaceful thoughts and dreams. It's the closest thing to dreaming up here— it's when I can feel you most ... especially when you're thinking of me. I've been with you a lot while you're writing ... when you're happy ... I'm there ...*

"I know that. I can feel you."

When you're sad I'm with you and the flowers ... Thank you for the flowers beside my picture ...

He looks at me through those light brown eyes. In their light, I see more understanding than I have ever known.

And then I go and find the music. All I have to do is think it—reach out and it's with me. It teaches me to feel ... on so many levels ... very deeply, or lighter than air ... It generates light ... silver and rose colored light ... and deep reds ... sunlight! No words ... the greens and blues of the ocean are swept up and swirl in the being of music.

It dances. Not enough words ... Music is alive. It's alive with light and feeling ... and movement. It carries you—and Mom, when you dance with it, it lifts you off your feet! You float! You swing, you twirl—you fly!

The passion in my son stirred my senses and filled me with a fleeting happiness that was not of this earth.

You should see the rapsters! All those guys who sang rap when I was a kid? Man, can they move ... it's like watching magic!

Music folds me into its mood ... I feel it trembling, I feel it breathe; I feel its punch when it storms those earth notes. It rocks! I become one with it. When it moves, I do; when it rises, I rise with it; when it falls, I fall with it ... and sway and swoop and soar and dive ... I am music ... It's my favorite teacher.

"And you're mine ..."

Gotta go! Can you hear those chimes? I think there's someone I'm supposed to meet arriving ...

I was struck by a sense of urgency. He was distracted now, he was fading, but I could see him smile. "Who is it?" I started to ask. But he was gone. His warmth lingered and suddenly I found myself thinking of those flowers in heaven.

Ahhh! To dance with him—and the music that is his ... Drew and the music stayed with me as I gave the crimson branches one final shake dislodging the last reluctant spider, and headed toward the house in the gathering dark.

I wondered who was arriving ...

⁂

That night I heard from Walt's family. They told me that Drew's grandfather, Berry Brock, who'd been bedridden for the last year, was not expected to last the night. They told us that Drew's death was too much for him. It sounded to them as though the old man had just given up and was waiting to die. Which isn't a bad thing to do when you're ninety-four years old.

His daughters told me he had been speaking to Drew and Walt for weeks before he died. Just rambling, they said. When Karen took her children to visit him for the last time, he mistook Brock for Drew and began to cry. Brock has the same dark-brown curly hair and good looks that Drew had, and his voice matches Drew's.

I prayed for Berry Brock that night; prayed that my old father-in-law of four decades would go peacefully. As I did so, I saw Drew standing on the edge of my world and his. The atmosphere around him was alive—electric with anticipation. It prickled with sparking energy, and I could feel his excitement that his grandfather was coming. It made me smile. It was as though he couldn't wait for him to get there so he could show him around.

I fell asleep feeling his happiness, and when Walt's sister called early the next morning to tell me that their father had died, I realized that he died in the same week of November that Drew did the year before. I felt joy for him knowing that he would be with Drew.

It was seven o'clock in the morning, and if I hadn't known better, I would have sworn there was someone smoking a cigarette in the house.

An Anniversary—
and the Holidays

*T*he day was November 28, 2009, and I was in San
Francisco with Michael and Mary Katherine and the
kids. It was exactly one year ago that we lost Drew on that
snowy day in Denver.

My heart was both empty and full at the same time. How
could that be? Maybe I'd finally gone mad. I wondered about
that for a minute. And I wondered if it showed. Perhaps it
wouldn't be so noticeable in the Bay Area where we were yesterday, or on the Monterey Peninsula, our next destination.

The icy-cold emptiness in my soul needed no explanation,
but another part of me was filled with California sunshine and
the laughter of my young grandchildren: bright and adventurous

279

James, who at ten was like his dad; Caroline, a redheaded pixie with enough magic to charm trolls off their bridges; and baby Tucker with his auburn curls, who appeared to have taken a dislike to this grandmother. He was wondering if I was the new babysitter, Mary Katherine said. I chose to believe her.

Besides the emptiness and the California sunshine, the love and caring I felt coming from Michael and his young family had warmed every crease and crevice of this difficult week.

I'd been there nearly six days and they had filled every minute of the week with a new place to go or a new experience, a new beach, or just about anything that would keep our minds off that time last year. Michael had taken a lot of time off work.

On Thursday, we all pitched in and made Thanksgiving dinner, sidestepping Lego creatures of indeterminate species, Tucker's fire trucks, and the Pixie's baby dolls—and the memories of Drew in Denver.

But half-way through the martini Michael made me, the sidestepping got trickier. By dinnertime, we are able to let in the memory of young Drew in Dubai, cruising knee-high among the adults, clutching a meatball in one hand and a handful of potato chips in the other. Then other Thanksgiving Day memories slipped in. Five-year-old Michael, standing beside his dad, watching him carve the turkey, picking off piece after piece of crispy skin until the bird was naked and pale and ugly. He ate the whole darn turkey skin, and Walt let him.

The duality of our human nature is fascinating to watch. There is so much more room in our hearts than we ever imagined. At that moment, that Thanksgiving Day, in Mary Katherine and Michael's kitchen with flowers and candles and greasy fingers, we were having fun. It was warm and alive in there—the best it could be that year.

Ever since we lost Drew, pondering this duality of human nature has been a part of my existence. No matter how dark it gets, it seems like something or someone will come along and turn on the lights. Conversely, no matter how happy I get, something sinister or small can flip the switch and the lights go out. I wonder how I can change moods so quickly. Am I that shallow?

And then I've been noticing that there is a duality in most things. It must be what they call the "contrast" that has to exist for our learning while we're on this earth. The yin and the yang. You can't appreciate one without the other.

Constant euphoria would, I suppose, be exhausting after a while. Not to mention how much it would irritate everyone you know. Good way to clear the room in a hurry. Ditto drenching sadness. I think we can all take some of each, but none of us can take one of them for any length of time. It's that "balance" thing again.

❧

The road to Monterrey the next morning was curvy, hugging the tops of high cliffs, towering over the rough Pacific surf. High rollers crashed mightily on the shiny water-swept sand below the curve of their crest, and spray was flung high into the air as wave after wave pounded rocky outcrops that dripped black and glossy in the sun.

I wondered who gave this angry ocean its name. There was the duality thing again. Perhaps this ocean, too, had a sweeter side. It must be somewhere around the shores of an island like

Fiji or Tahiti... That was part of this craziness too. How could anything be this two-sided?

All along the road to Monterrey (sounded like the old Bing Crosby and Bob Hope movies: *The Road to Naples, The Road to Monterey*), there were places with names I'd heard all my life: San Jose, Half Moon Bay, and Santa Cruz.

Speaking of Bing and Bob, as I looked out over the strawberry fields, the high cliffs, this scenery reminded me of so many other old movies that painted their stories against this backdrop. Most of those I could remember starred Doris Day with a number of different, impossibly handsome leading men like Cary Grant, Rock Hudson, and Gregory Peck.

Dreamy. The things that picture books and movies are made of.

Looking out of the car window, I found that I could put myself inside that story book, that movie. It carried me to another place. Imagine. There I was in the starring role, racing down Highway One.

Me and Cary Grant. Me with my scarlet scarf flying out behind me as we tore along the cliffs in our white 1950s convertible. The images rolled on. We were laughing, tossing our heads back—my too-blond tresses sparkled with sunlight—his too-white teeth glinted handsomely in the brightness of the day... Hollywood love was all around.

But in keeping with the duality of things, you *knew* this story had another side.

You just knew that Alfred Hitchcock was directing this thing, and he was lurking around somewhere waiting to screw things up. But so far, we'd kept him at bay.

In real life, we were all tearing along in a giant SUV loaded down with coolers and sippy-cups, diaper bags, Lego people and baby dolls, and a stroller.

I was riding shotgun so that Mary Katherine could concentrate on dousing brush fires in the back seats. It was a beautiful California morning and life was actually good. How could that be? It was the day Drew died last year.

And here came Hitchcock. He was making his traditional cameo appearance in my movie as he did in all of his. I suddenly found myself in a dark alley in the middle of all this sunshine. The lights began to dip.

Then I had the feeling that there was someone else riding with us. I reached behind my headrest, because it felt to me as though Drew was leaning forward between the driver's seat and mine.

"Is that you, Drew?" I asked him silently.

I felt his spirit touch mine and I heard him laughing, saw him pointing to the sights along the way—Mexican restaurants, beach hotels, and fields full of artichokes. He was enjoying the ride and the lights were coming back on.

I basked in the silence and allowed myself to just BE with this lovely day and that part of Drew I was getting to know well.

Michael and Ginny in Monterrey.

In Monterrey, we strolled down one of two piers that run out on either side of the yacht basin, dodging the waiters along the wharf who were hell-bent on force-feeding us their clam chowders. They came at us in waves with their white aprons flapping in the wind, carrying trays of little white bowls of soup, booming at us to try one.

The yachts in the harbor were glistening white with blue and green or black trim. Their sails were furled and the strong hemp ropes that moored them to the pier were dripping with salty water. The sea was calm and blue here, and the piers were packed with sightseers that morning.

We found ourselves involved in an intricate quick step as we sidestepped children and waiters and veered clear of tourists laden down with heavy duty baskets full of souvenirs.

Somebody made the decision to get off the pier before we lost one of the kids in this crowd, and we headed for a small pub at the top end of the opposite pier. There was space to breathe here. The souvenir shops and restaurants on the other pier had kept the crowds captive and sipping free soup while they shopped, which is something you could do if you weren't trying to keep up with three kids. Although there must have been a hundred kids over there doing quite well, completely unattended and unhampered by any adult supervision. Running wild perhaps, but their unconcerned parents probably wouldn't lose any of them to the walrus-infested waters, lapping at the piling. That's always the way it is.

With nine-year-old James in our party it was a certainty that we might lose one.

So here we were, sitting outside the main pub restaurant under a broad awning with kids firmly tucked in between us. It was still not a given that one of them might escape the patio, so we were a little over-the-top overprotective. We were absolutely not going to lose a kid off the end of a pier or any other way. It was not an option this year.

The outside area was sheltered—out of the wind and sunny. Within minutes of the meal arriving, the seagulls discovered us and thirty-five of them were soon perched on the surrounding trellis, convinced that they knew where their next meal was coming from. They were so big, I thought they might be feeding them on steroids.

This thought made me picture two-year-old Tuck being swung aloft by a hungry gull with all of us yelling, *"Bring him back! Dammit!"* But I didn't think it would be prudent to voice that thought. It was a crazy time. Often since Drew died, I found myself fearing for my other children.

I went shopping after lunch while Michael and Mary Katherine took their family to the aquarium. Christmas would soon be upon us and presents had been the farthest thing from my mind this month. But there were children expecting Santa and Mimi to show up, so I went into high shopping gear and dragged myself into the outlets just down the road from the aquarium.

Two hours later I emerged—battered, bruised but unbowed by the staggering Saturday-afternoon crowds—and stashed my shopping bags in the car before walking slowly back down the sidewalk to meet my kids. There was a stiff breeze coming off the ocean and I could smell the sea spray bouncing off the rocks, salting down cars parked by the water's edge as it drifted inland across the peninsula.

The sidewalks were lined with gardens that belong to the state of California. They were filled with hardy perennials that didn't seem to mind the salt air or the heat coming of the asphalt. Succulents grew vigorously along the way, their thick green leaves showing off bunches of sea grapes. Sprays of sea oats whipped this way and that in the ever constant breezes— and then my heart stopped and did a flop.

As soon as I could breathe again I walked toward a high white wall behind which stood a deep green, spiky leaved shrub. I studied it minutely. It was the same as its sisters that grow along the Garden Route along the coast of the Eastern Cape of South Africa.

Protea! Woody stems held aloft star-like pale pink spiky blooms, their heads nodding toward the bay. Protea. The identical flowers that were in my room waiting the first time I visited

Drew's hotel in Colorado. I still kept them on my dresser beside his picture in my bedroom. They were dry and a little dusty, but they'd be there until they were no more.

"Oh Drew! Thank you!" I leaned across the whitewashed wall, not caring who saw me, and snapped a single stem off the bush in the state park. I held it to my heart and my eyes filled as I whispered. "I really needed this today. Thank you, my Angel!"

In all the years I've lived in the United States, I had never seen these flowers growing here until that day.

❧

Christmas Day came right on time. One child was born in Bethlehem thousands of years ago and another died in Denver just one year ago. "C'est La Vie" and the Gallic shrug didn't quite do it for me this year.

When Walt died and then Drew, I was warned that the holidays would be sad and depressing but I let that be; knowing that the only way through this hell is straight ahead one tiny step at a time.

As it turned out, I floated through Christmas like a spirit on a hilltop in spring. The sun came out and then disappeared again. Raindrops fell and went away, replaced by sunshine. It rained, and then it shone.

The yin and the yang of things.

The sun came out for me in the children's laughter, in the table set for Christmas dinner. Candles flickered their warmth around the room, their flames bouncing off tinsel and silverware, cut glass, and the discarded wrapping paper that littered the living room floor.

My daughter's arm rested around my shoulders. "I love you, Mom," she said softly.

"I love you more." I smiled and she smiled back.

Then came the blessing, remembering family and friends who'd passed swept a cool gust of wind across my soul.

I closed my eyes. I floated upward to find the sun, found gray clouds tossed on troubled skies, darkening and lowering their bulk around me. They rumbled across the sun, covering its light. I floated onward, feeling my soul tumble through the deepening colors of cobalt blues and gray. As I landed—hard,—I dropped my head and saw a shaft of sunshine lighting the ground beneath my feet.

A sticky smile lit up Becca's face, her small hand tucked into mine as we listened to my son-in-law Randy pray. Becca's smile opened a window and let the sun in, lighting the space we found ourselves in this Christmas Day.

Perhaps I wasn't wholly there in body, but I was in and out, here and there, and that would do. The floating part wasn't all that bad, but I had to learn how to make softer landings.

From somewhere around us, I heard Drew's voice saying, *There's a knack to this.* There is indeed. I can't wait to master it. The smells from the kitchen were good. The sight of Brock's football cleats hanging in the mudroom brought Drew close. Brock was wearing his jersey with the number 50 painted on the back. Drew's high school football number was 80.

Looking around the table, I saw my family. An earthbound family, struggling with this school of hard knocks. We had all been damaged by life. We had been thrown about in storms that no one saw coming. They had left us bruised and purple and sad, but we were a family who had come through the darkness still standing to welcome the light that filled the house this Christmas day.

We were together, and the music that I heard in Brock's gruff sixteen-year-old voice and Courtney's spirited reprimand in, "Becca, don't touch! Don't you dare open that!" told me that if indeed ALL wasn't well, at least some of it was okay, and some of it was good.

Twenty-Four

Journey Back
to the Beginning

A few weeks into the New Year, with snow mounding along the sides of the driveway and a cold wind blowing out of the north, icing the walkway and freezing the edges of the lake, I traveled southward. I made the long flight across the North and South Atlantic oceans to South Africa, the land where I was born, and the land of Drew's heart.

Then, one night when the moon was a large orange ball riding low on the horizon and stars filled the Southern Hemisphere, I scattered his ashes under the banks of white roses in the gardens of my childhood home, beneath the tall Jacaranda tree that I used to play under, which continues to grow beside a pool that Drew swam in many times.

An image of the black-maned lion lying beside Drew drifted through my mind. I saw him lift his head and yawn sleepily. His teeth were the purest, unblemished ivory. His whiskers long and straight. I could smell the long grass crushed beneath him and feel the warmth of his giant body lying close to my son. *I can talk to him…* Drew's voice carried on the cool breeze of the African night. A breeze filled with the scent of black soil, Jacaranda blooms, and crushed rose petals.

I knelt on the cool grass beside the beds, ran my hand over the pale dust that speckled the soil, and asked the ancient spirits of Africa, animal and human, of this earth and from far beyond this earth, to love my son.

⚬⚬

Six weeks after my return from South Africa, I left for the Middle East. I think I was on a mission of some sort.

Old friends, people we'd known when we lived in Dubai when the children were young, had been urging me to visit them. "Just get away from it all!" Dolly's East Indian voice echoed down the phone line across the 6,000 miles that separated our continents.

"Just tell us when!" exclaimed Hemant, Dolly's husband, who was already making plans.

They had been our next-door neighbors when we all lived in Dubai twenty-five years ago. They had two little girls who played with Drew, Indian nannies who made him cakes and cookies, and an American mom at my house, me, who toasted Kellogg's Pop Tarts, much to the delight of the little girls.

Drew was spoiled by all of them. And long after everyone had grown up and scattered—the girls to universities, Drew to Colorado, and Walt and I to Virginia—Dolly and Hemant stayed in Dubai and we remained friends throughout the years. They visited us in Houston and Virginia, and we saw them in New York when they came in to see their girls.

～

Seated inside the airplane, my fingers touched the inside of the window. The outside air was cold on this February night in 2010. It felt good to settle down into the cushioned seats of Emirates Airlines and feel the giant wide-bodied Boeing 777 rise fast over the New York skyline, eastward bound. A twelve-hour flight stretched ahead of me. But that was okay. A poet once said that to fly is "to break the bonds of earth ..." Up here, miles above the earth, the umbilical cord to my life was broken for a while. Up here there was peace. I felt at peace with myself and at peace with life. There were no strings binding me. I could fly.

Only a hundred miles out across the ocean, I began to sense the approach of the mystical east. The controlled air in the cabin carried the smell of spices from the galley. Cardamom, curry, lime, and grilled meats mingled with the mild scents of gardenia and rose. Heavy perfumes buried in the folds of long black skirts and the rich deep-throated sounds of Arabic being spoken from the seat across from mine carried me away from the west. From somewhere behind me, a woman's voice, her sing song Hindi as she quieted her infant, took me further and further east.

I kicked back and abandoned myself to the warmth of my small world, roaring through the sky. I was on a mission to bask in the sweetness of old friends and to touch the roots of Drew's birthplace. In my luggage I carried a handful of his ashes to scatter in the blue green waters of the Arabian Gulf.

❧

Drew's birthplace had been a new and developing nation in 1982, still in its infancy in the scheme of things. But everything grows up very fast these days, and Dubai was more precocious than most. It was the leader of the pack as far as I could see. Over the twenty years that I'd been gone, the small town of Dubai had grown into a very big city.

The tallest building in the world, the Burj Khalifa, towered over a thousand imposing skyscrapers that crowded the banks of the Dubai Creek, a spectacular waterway that wound through the city. The old Trade Center, a fifty-story building that was once the tallest in all seven Emirates, was now dwarfed by its younger sisters, not many of them under seventy or eighty stories high.

There were no clouds in these desert skies. Bright sunlight in January sparked off its white-walled villas with red roofs, drenching the magenta bougainvillea that draped high walls, flaunting its beauty in full-bloomed harlotry.

A stream of parties followed one on top of the other, and just when you thought everyone must be exhausted by now—the phone rang and off we went again!

I was awestruck by the changes and suffering from severe sensory overload. Shopping malls! Every new one I was shown was bigger and more spectacular than the one before. My hosts exalted in showing me everything that had happened since we'd been gone. Late-night visits to exotic restaurants seldom seen in my world, sent us haring for the gym every morning at nine. Then, showered and held together with ginger and cardamom tea, the glorious rounds of food and drinks and parties started all over again.

Dolly became my tour guide by day, and we left no door unopened, no sight unseen, and no bridge uncrossed as we barreled our way in her Land Rover through crowded streets and traffic to one destination after another.

There were occasional and fleeting glimpses of the old town. Hemant accompanied me to the old fort, the sand stone museum. There was an old hotel I recognized, and an old home crouching behind crumbling concrete walls held together, it seemed by a vigorously strong coral creeper. It was a shrub planted by me nearly thirty years ago.

This was Drew's first home.

I visited the school the children went to. I walked through the gym where Michael had played basketball, hearing the echoing slap of tennis shoes on the linoleum and the raucous cries from cheering parents as their boys clinched the Middle Eastern Conference Championship, wresting it away from schools that traveled from Egypt, Jordan, Athens, Abu Dhabi, and Lebanon. I strolled out to the football field where Karen had cheered while her younger brother played football. In one corner of the field there was a tee-ball stand. Still there, still standing.

I had watched Michael play there, and then Drew, three afternoons a week.

Lingering in the kindergarten, I felt a momentary shadow drift across the cool January sun. But then it was gone, disappearing in the garish little kid paintings tacked to the walls, the higgledy-piggledy, tiny chairs and desks, and a row of pegs on the walls with various items of clothing suspended four feet above the tiled floor.

From very long ago, I heard Drew shriek, as he saw me in the doorway, and I felt my face split into the smile that I keep only for my children.

⁓

The day before I left Dubai, Dolly and I stood on a promontory of rock jutting out into the Arabian Gulf. I held in my hands a bouquet of flowers from Dolly and Hemant's garden. Bougainvillea and petunias that grew so well in this desert place...and a small bag that contained some of Drew's ashes.

As I knelt on the rough granite rocks and threw the flowers into the sea, the Call to Prayer rose from a small minaret atop a mosque built on a corner of the beach. I hadn't even noticed it when we drove up.

The male voice of the Mullah, deep and mellow, rang out across the sands, out across the Gulf, upward to where a mass of seagulls flew. The midday prayer echoed through the village behind the mosque and around the rocks we stood on.

Allah O Akbar....

Dolly and I smiled at each other. "That was perfect!" she said softly.

"Yes," I answered, knowing that we couldn't have timed this better if we had tried. "God is great."

Allah O Akbar!

When I raised my eyes to the bluest skies and no clouds, there were no tears in them. No sorrow filled my heart. Perhaps there are times when all this is too deep for tears. That's it!

I felt Walt beside me as I let the ashes leave my hand, falling on floating blossom, speckling the light blue waters of the sea. I could feel my husband's strength, his warmth. I saw the wind ruffle his hair that was as dark and glossy as it was on that day so long ago when Drew was born. His eyes were as blue as early autumn skies and my heart lurched as it did the first time that we met.

We watched together as the white crests of the waves lapped the rocks under our feet and carried our son's remains across the waters. Our baby, who was born here in the Arabian desert beside the sea, was drifting with the current to the sound of the music from the minaret.

❧

As night engulfed the cove and the mountains darkened around the lake and my Virginia home, I climbed into bed feeling tired, happy, sad, and complete. I picked up my journal and wrote, "The book is done, Sweet Drew," and as I closed its leather cover, three petals fluttered to the comforter pulled up over my knees. Creamy, heart-shaped... still white and satin smooth.

I had almost forgotten the dogwood blossom from last spring.

Closing my eyes and settling into the comfort of the pillows, the sound of the Call to Prayer echoed across oceans. The wailing from the seaside minaret many thousands of miles away in Dubai, was clear and mellow, and within its melody I heard

Drew's baby laugh shrieking with glee as the foamy wavelets lapped around his toes. I heard the squeals of joyous excitement from Karen and Michael as they played as children in the blue waters of the Arabian Gulf. And I felt Walter's love surround me as we watched our children.

Epilogue

A year after Drew's passing from this earth, leaving me on this planet that rests for the most part in the third dimension, I no longer use the word "paranormal." The so-called paranormal has become The Norm for me. And when Drew drops in, it's like greeting a dear one who has been gone too long, and when I am invited to cross dimensions to where he is, it has all the excitement and anticipation of a long-awaited visit.

There is more out there than we can possibly learn in just one lifetime. At this point in our human evolution our brains have not been able to show us all that they can do. Perhaps one day we will learn that they can connect us with our ethereal beings, our spirits. We'll discover a new line tucked into one of those crevices of the brain that has always been there but, none of us knew the right buttons to push. No one gave us the number.

I want to be here when that happens—when someone hands us the code. But for that to happen, I suspect I'll have to agree to another lifetime hundreds of years from now. Maybe when I get over this one I will. Perhaps Drew will come back with me to finish this life that was cut so short for us. I hear we are given that choice.

But for the time being, our intellect is stumped. Being the miniscule faction that it is, it cannot begin to realize the whole. Perhaps there will come a time when we—*the ethereal we*—may become the teachers of our human intellect—as we always do. We already know there is another world out there. We already know what our brains cannot yet grasp in its entirety or our own entirety.

The other part of us, the part I call spirit, *knows* this stuff. We just have to acknowledge it. Then, and only then, we in our earthly incarnations will finally recognize who we are.

Consciousness is changing every day. In fact, the changes are galloping. Our bookstores are stocking more and more "spirit stuff," our movie screens and television stations can't get enough of it, and the History and Discovery channels are pushing the search a little further all the time.

Far better minds than mine have embraced the theories. Far more spiritual people than I have experienced more than I have in the far flung realms of spirit.

I only know what I know. And I am sure of it.

More and more I'm learning to see through Drew's eyes, and what I see now is everyone just trying to cope with this earth place any way they can. Some people can get pretty radical. But I find that in some funny way, I can be okay with that, recognizing that they too are struggling.

We're all in this mess together.

Thank you, dear reader, for walking with me on what has been the journey of a lifetime, through what I believe is the next step in the evolution of the human body, mind, and spirit. To my loving family and closest friends, thank you for the strength of your spirits who held me up when I cried, who urged me on, and keeping the image of you and Drew in mind, gave me the strength to cross the finish line.

Drew is still with me. He has been with me throughout the writing of this book and two nights ago he came again. It was late in the evening as I sat on the couch, my computer on my lap, editing the font and tidying up the manuscript. I was tired and my mind was cruising on its own, picking up the font I had been using for when Drew speaks, and changing it to something else. My fingers moved independently of any conscious thought, my mind was disengaged. I suppose you could say I was zoned out. Until suddenly—the screen flared up in front of me, jolting me back to earth and there in bold, eighty-four point script covering the page, I read,

I love you, Mom.

I know that in my half-asleep state, my fingers accidently touched the wrong command. I also know that I had no idea what page I was on at the time or what was written on it. This sentence occurs only once in the manuscript. And I don't believe in coincidences.

The End

Afterword

*I*t's late summer in 2011—almost three years since Drew left this world. It was three years this past August that he came home to the lake house for the last time. No one knew then, that his time on earth was almost over. Or that the next phase of his life was about to begin. Part of this next phase was to assure me and everyone who reads this book that he, and everyone we know living on the other side of the veil, are alive and living lives that are fuller and more vibrant than any of us in this dimension can possibly imagine.

I saw him three nights ago. It was well past too late for me to be up, but I had a book I couldn't put down and, in fact, didn't want to put it down even when Miss Kitty sat bolt upright on the end of my bed, ears perked, and all her instincts firing on Red Alert.

"Who's there, Miss Kitty?" I asked. Silence. As you know by now, she doesn't always speak when she is spoken too.

But I could see for myself that Drew was standing in the doorway, in a great hurry, breathing fast and pink in the face. He wore a safari jacket of all things, and a bush hat with its ties undone. "*Wh…*" I began to ask him what on earth he was doing all dressed up like that. But of course, he wasn't actually on earth and I suddenly got the clearest image of the African bush all around him, the scent of hot animals and tall, dry grasslands. I could see the wind fanning the red acacia leaves of the trees where he stood and flipping the laces of his hat, when he blurted, *I love the book! They love it! Go for it, Mom!*

He was beaming. He knew that the contract from the publisher had arrived and that I had spent all afternoon studying it and mulling it over in my mind.

Then he told me that he was working with wild animals. *I'm being taught how to teach them to survive in a shrinking environment… teaching them how to adapt to climate changes and dry water holes and things… they used to be able to cope with by migrating but now the migration routes are too dry and too few.* Then he waved his hat, *We're working in the bush today—hands on!*

The next time I saw him was late one evening on a flight to California just before Thanksgiving 2011 to visit Michael and Mary Katherine. We were almost there. The lights in the cabin were dim, and as I leaned back in the seat and closed my eyes I heard,

Hey, Mom. I want to tell you about that day… the day I left…

I was wide awake and fully aware of Drew's spirit very close to me.

I tried to talk to you—kept saying, "I'm here. Look at me!" You couldn't hear me—nobody could… I was standing right there… then Tory came and I just knew he would hear me—but

he didn't. You were all so sad and all I wanted to do was to tell you "I'm right here!"

The plane was quiet. Drew went on. *It was weird ... sometimes I thought I was dreaming—aware of Michael—thank you for the music ... saw Karen cry—I knew Randy was there ... aware of Brittany ... knew she hurt.*

I could hardly feel myself breathing. So many questions were being answered.

You were ... how can I describe it? Almost a part of me—your spirit—heavy. I could feel your heart ... you didn't understand. I slept. Then Dad came and I didn't know what was happening ... I saw myself asleep on the bed but I knew you left the room. Then I felt myself moving—getting further away ... I was confused about leaving me there on the bed. Saw you on the street. Saw snow—it was snowing. Then bright white light—I thought it was sun on the snow. Bright white ...

And he was gone.

❧

Everything changes. Nothing stays the same and even in my world there have been more adjustments to be made. One of the most difficult was losing my old dog Ranger. He was fourteen last summer when he developed what the vet called "laryngeal paralysis." He couldn't pant so he couldn't sweat, so he overheated, and eventually his old heart and lungs were struggling for every breath. I gave him back to heaven on a beautiful September morning after a feast of roast chicken and chocolate ice cream.

Blinded by tears, I left the vet's office remembering how Drew had walked these same steps when he'd brought his Lab,

Cassie, in for the last time. He was much braver than me. Or maybe with Walt, Drew, and now Ranger leaving—it was just too damn hard.

Then, as my hand reached for the car door handle I heard a voice. I looked over to my right and saw Drew bending down, patting his knees. *Here Boy!* I heard him call, and there was Ranger. His coat was glossy and black, his ears flopping, his tongue lolling as he raced toward his boy.

My second book—yet to be titled—is a semi-novel about reincarnation and is in its second draft. The main characters are fictional as are the modern day events, but guess what—everything else is real.

Back in Dubai, my old friend Hemant passed away, leaving Dolly to go the rest of the way without the love of her life.

Here in Virginia, we've seen hurricanes and earthquakes and tornadoes, but out west, California hasn't fallen off the edge of the continent yet, so Michael's hanging tough, too—not struggling too much with all the brilliant sunshine, blue seas, and a great new job. Karen untied the apron strings this year and let go of one of her brood—Brock is now a College Man and (yessss!) they're all loving that.

Meanwhile, a few summers ago while on a trail ride in the Ouachita Mountains of western Arkansas, Walter's sister and her husband stopped at the site on Wilhelmina Mountain where I had scattered her brother's ashes.

"Look at these pictures taken at the site," she emailed me. "They're full of orbs! And look at this!" A flourishing bush of yellow daisies filled the picture—the bouquet of wild daisies had seeded new life—and the Cherokee spirit braves were still there.

❧

It's been a sensational time—these years since Drew left us. When I look back, I remember silver mornings touched by dawn rising over the lake and starry nights high above Manhattan, watching the first pinpricks of light flare in myriad windows, waking up the city. I remember sunrises and moonrises over the Rocky Mountains and waking up with lions in the African savanna.

It's been a light-filled year with Drew beside me every step of the way.

The sadness still comes and goes, and it probably always will. Now, when it does, when the winds threaten to overwhelm me, I adjust the sails and head for the open ocean where the waves are few and far between. I ride the gentle swells, breathe in the sea air, and keep moving.

I took a major step about a year ago, and graduated from the girlie gym. Yes indeed! I put my big girl shorts on and headed for the Y—that intensely athletic place full of girl and boy jocks and their scary black machines. But I'm not fooling with those. *I do Zumba!* That fast-paced Brazilian aerobics dance thing. If you ever need a smile, a laugh, or a lift—better than sugar—better than maybe even chocolate—join a Zumba group. The music is over the top, in the moment fantastic, and it will take you to Rio or Spain or India—or gently around the block, if you prefer. I don't prefer. I love the hip-shaking, the shoulder wiggling, the tummy jiggling, and the zest and the musical flavors of *Brazilia*.

It might kill me, but if it does I'm going down doing on a wave of Salsa and Marengai laughing my booty off.

❧

"When that happens, how will I know I'm not dreaming, Drew?"

You'll walk through the light, Mom—remember that translucent blue light we saw that night in Denver? I'll be there and you'll know for sure that you're not dreaming.

GET MORE AT LLEWELLYN.COM

Visit us online to browse hundreds of our books and decks, plus sign up to receive our e-newsletters and exclusive online offers.

- • Free tarot readings • Spell-a-Day • Moon phases
- • Recipes, spells, and tips • Blogs • Encyclopedia
- • Author interviews, articles, and upcoming events

GET SOCIAL WITH LLEWELLYN

Find us on Facebook
www.Facebook.com/LlewellynBooks

Follow us on twitter™
www.Twitter.com/Llewellynbooks

GET BOOKS AT LLEWELLYN

LLEWELLYN ORDERING INFORMATION

Order online: Visit our website at www.llewellyn.com to select your books and place an order on our secure server.

Order by phone:
- • Call toll free within the U.S. at 1-877-NEW-WRLD (1-877-639-9753)
- • Call toll free within Canada at 1-866-NEW-WRLD (1-866-639-9753)
- • We accept VISA, MasterCard, and American Express

Order by mail:
Send the full price of your order (MN residents add 6.875% sales tax) in U.S. funds, plus postage and handling to: Llewellyn Worldwide, 2143 Wooddale Drive Woodbury, MN 55125-2989

POSTAGE AND HANDLING:

STANDARD: (U.S. & Canada)
(Please allow 2 business days)
$25.00 and under, add $4.00.
$25.01 and over, FREE SHIPPING.

INTERNATIONAL ORDERS (airmail only):
$16.00 for one book, plus $3.00 for each additional book.

Visit us online for more shipping options. Prices subject to change.

FREE CATALOG!

To order, call 1-877-NEW-WRLD ext. 8236 or visit our website

PATRICK MATHEWS

Author of the Bestselling *Never Say Goodbye*

FOREVER
WITH YOU

Inspiring Messages of Healing & Wisdom
from Your Loved Ones in the Afterlife

Forever With You
Inspiring Messages of Healing & Wisdom from your Loved Ones in the Afterlife
Patrick Mathews

After the phenomenal success of *Never Say Goodbye,* Patrick Mathews became one of the most recognized mediums in the country. *Forever With You* invites us back for a closer look at his fascinating life as a spirit communicator and all he's learned.

These vivid and unforgettable stories help us understand what it's like to talk to spirits, how our loved ones have— and haven't—changed since crossing over, and how they continue to impact our lives. Answering questions only a medium can, Mathews offers insight into life's biggest mysteries—what happens when we pass into spirit, heaven and hell, God and angels, reincarnation, the purpose of our physical life, and more.

978-0-7387-2766-0, 264 pp., 5³⁄₁₆ x 8   **$15.95**

PATRICK MATHEWS

NEVER SAY GOODBYE

A Mediums' Stories of
Connecting with Your Loved Ones

Never Say Goodbye
A Medium's Stories of
Connecting with Your Loved Ones
Patrick Mathews

"I'm a normal guy … I just speak to dead people."

When he was six years old, Patrick Mathews came face to face with the spirit of his dead Uncle Edward. As an adult, Mathews serves as a vessel of hope for those who wish to communicate with their loved ones in spirit.

The stories Mathews tells of his life and the people he has helped are humorous, heartwarming, and compelling. Part of his gift is in showing the living that they can still recognize and continue ongoing relationships with the departed.

Mathews takes the reader on a roller coaster of emotional stories, from the dead husband who stood by his wife's side during her wedding to a new man, to the brazen spirit who flashed her chest to get her point across. You will also learn step-by-step methods for recognizing your own communications from beyond.

978-0-7387-0353-4, 216 pp., 6 x 9 $15.95

When
Tomorrow
Speaks
❖ ❖ ❖ **T O** ❖ ❖ ❖
me

M EMOIRS
of an I RISH M EDIUM

Bridget Benson

When Tomorrow Speaks to Me
Memoirs of an Irish Medium
Bridget Benson

Tragic deaths, secret love affairs, and powerful messages from the spirit world have colored Bridget Benson's life. She grew up in the small Irish farming village of Straide, County Mayo, a county of lush meadows and peat bogs, purple heather–clad moorland, and sandy-beached lakes. Bridget lived with her eight siblings, parents, grandparents, and great aunt in a house with no electricity or running water. When her grandma died on her seventh birthday, Bridget received a message that her beloved father, who also had "the gift," would die when she was twelve years old, and that she would carry on as the family seer.

When Tomorrow Speaks to Me tells the story of Bridget Benson's remarkably spiritual life, from her childhood experiences with spirit guides, ghosts, fairies, and leprechauns to the development of her career as a successful full-time medium.

978-0-7387-2106-4, 240 pp., 5 ³⁄₁₆ x 8   **$15.95**

MICHAEL NEWTON, PH.D.

JOURNEY
OF
SOULS

CASE STUDIES OF
LIFE BETWEEN LIVES

Journey of Souls
Case Studies of Life Between Lives
MICHAEL NEWTON, PH.D.

This remarkable book uncovers—for the first time—the mystery of life in the spirit world after death on earth. Dr. Michael Newton, a hypnotherapist in private practice, has developed his own hypnosis technique to reach his subjects' hidden memories of the hereafter. The narrative is woven as a progressive travelogue around the accounts of twenty-nine people who were placed in a state of superconsciousness. While in deep hypnosis, these subjects describe what has happened to them between their former incarnations on earth. They reveal graphic details about how it feels to die, who meets us right after death, what the spirit world is really like, where we go and what we do as souls, and why we choose to come back in certain bodies.

After reading *Journey of Souls*, you will acquire a better understanding of the immortality of the human soul. Plus, you will meet day-to-day personal challenges with a greater sense of purpose as you begin to understand the reasons behind events in your own life.

978-1-5671-8485-3, 288 pp., 6 x 9 $16.95